Contract Law in Spain

Contract Law in Spain

Third Edition

Antoni Vaquer

This book was originally published as a monograph in the International Encyclopaedia of Laws/Contracts.

Founding Editor: Roger Blanpain
General Editor: Frank Hendrickx
Volume Editor: Jacques Herbots

Wolters Kluwer

Published by:
Kluwer Law International B.V.
PO Box 316
2400 AH Alphen aan den Rijn
The Netherlands
E-mail: international-sales@wolterskluwer.com
Website: lrus.wolterskluwer.com

Sold and distributed in North, Central and South America by:
Wolters Kluwer Legal & Regulatory U.S.
7201 McKinney Circle
Frederick, MD 21704
United States of America
Email: customer.service@wolterskluwer.com

Sold and distributed in all other countries by:
Air Business Subscriptions
Rockwood House
Haywards Heath
West Sussex
RH16 3DH
United Kingdom
Email: international-customerservice@wolterskluwer.com

Printed on acid-free paper

ISBN 978-90-411-9546-3

e-Book: ISBN 978-90-411-9547-0
web-PDF: ISBN 978-90-411-9548-7

Printed in the United Kingdom.

The Author

Prof. Dr Antoni Vaquer (born 16 August 1965) studied law at the University of Barcelona, Spain (1983–1988). He was awarded his PhD in 1992 at the same University with Special Honours. In 2002, he was appointed to a chair of private law at the University of Lleida, Spain, where he mainly gives lectures on Contract Law, Property and Succession Law. In addition, one of his main fields of interest is the harmonization process of private law within the European Union, to which he has contributed a number of articles and the editions of several books. He also participates in the Study Group on a European Civil Code and the Acquis-Group. Professor Vaquer is holder of the German stipendium of the Alexander von Humboldt Foundation (2001, 2004). In 1998, he was appointed substitute judge at the Court of Appeal of Lleida, where he has been active until 2015. He has been Head of the Department of Private Law at the University of Lleida, Spain and is a member of the Catalan Commission on Codification and of the Catalan *Conseil d'État.*

The Author

Table of Contents

Table of Contents

Table of Contents

List of Abbreviations

AC	*Actualidad Civil*
ADC	*Anuario de Derecho Civil*
Art.	Article
CC	Spanish Civil Code
CCA	Code of the Foral Law of Aragon
CC Cat	Civil Code of Catalonia
CCom	Commercial Code
CDCC	Compilation of the Civil Law of Catalonia
CE	Spanish Constitution
CISG	United Nations Convention on the International Sale of Goods
Comp. Nav.	Compilation of the Civil Law of Navarre
CP	Código Penal (Criminal Code)
ERPL	*European Review of Private Law*
ff	following
LCCh	*Ley* 19/1985, of 16 July, *cambiaria y del cheque* (Act on bills of exchange and cheque)
LCS	*Ley del contrato de seguro* (Act on insurance contracts)
LEC	*Ley de enjuiciamiento civil* (Act on civil procedure)
LECrim	*Ley de enjuiciamiento criminal* (Act on the criminal procedure)
LGDCU	*Ley* 26/1984, of 19 July, *general para la protección de los consumidores y usuarios* (General Act on the protection of consumers)
New LGDCU	Legislative Decree 1/2007, of 16 November, approving the adapted text of the General Act on the protection of consumers
LH	*Ley Hipotecaria* (Act on mortgages and Land Register)

LOPJ	*Ley Orgánica del Poder Judicial* (Act on the Judicial Power)
LOTC	*Ley Orgánica del Tribunal Constitucional* (Act on the Constitutional Court)
LPH	*Ley de Propiedad Horizontal* (Act on flats and horizontal property)
PECL	Principles of European Contract Law
RCDI	*Revista Crítica de Derecho Inmobiliario*
RDP	*Revista de Derecho Privado*
RJC	*Revista Jurídica de Catalunya*
RJ Navarra	*Revista Jurídica de Navarra*
RN	Reglamento Notarial (Notarial Regulation)
STS	Decision of the Supreme Court
TC	Tribunal Constitucional (Constitutional Court)
TS	Tribunal Supremo (Supreme Court)
TSJ	Tribunal Superior de Justicia (High Court of Justice)

§1. Databases

RJ, JUR	Repertorio Aranzadi de Jurisprudencia
RTC	*Repertorio del Tribunal Constitucional*

§2. Handbooks

Albaladejo, *Derecho civil*	Manuel Albaladejo, *Derecho civil*, I, Madrid, 2004; II, Barcelona, 2002.
Díez-Picazo/Gullón, *Sistema*, II	Luis Díez-Picazo, Antonio Gullón, *Sistema de derecho civil*, II, Madrid, 2015–2016.
Díez-Picazo, *Fundamentos*	Luis Díez-Picazo, *Fundamentos del derecho civil patrimonial*, Madrid, 1996.
Lacruz, *Elementos* II	José L. Lacruz et al., *Elementos de derecho civil*, II, Madrid, 2005–2007.
Van Erp & Vaquer, *Introduction*	Sjef van Erp, Antoni Vaquer (ed.), *Introduction to Spanish Patrimonial Law*, Granada, 2006.

General Introduction

Chapter 1. The General Background of the Country

§1. Geography

1. Spain is situated in the south of Europe, in the Iberian Peninsula. In 2014, Spain had a population of 46,528,966 inhabitants (1 January 2017). As it covers an area of 506,000 km^2, the population density was 92.9 inhabitants per km^2. Spain borders on the Mediterranean Sea and the Atlantic Ocean, Portugal, France and Andorra.

§2. Cultural Composition

2. Spain is a pluricultural State. Four main languages, with their own dialects, are spoken: Spanish, Catalan, Basque and Galician. Spanish is the official language of the State, while the others are the official languages in their respective Autonomous Community. Thus, Catalan is the official language in Catalonia, the Balearic Islands and Valencia, where it is known as Valencian, and it is also spoken in the eastern part of Aragon. Basque is the official language in the Basque Country and Navarre, Galician in Galicia.

On 1 January 2017, 4,424,409 foreigners were living legally in Spain (according to the last report issued by the Statistics National Institute). The majority of them came from South America. Nevertheless, the largest national community of immigrants is that of Romanians.

Population (2014)	
Andalucia	8,402,305
Aragon	1,325,385
Asturias	1,061,756
Balearic Islands	1,103,442
Basque Country	2,188,985
Canary Islands	2,104,815
Cantabria	588,656
Castille and Leon	2,494,790

Population (2014)	
Castille and La Mancha	2,078,611
Catalonia	7,518,903
Ceuta	84,963
Extremadura	1,099,632
Galicia	2,748,695
Madrid	6,454,440
Melilla	84,509
Murcia	1,466,818
Navarre	640,790
La Rioja	319,002
Valencia	5,113,815

§3. POLITICAL SYSTEM

3. The modern concept of Spain does not appear until the eighteenth century, after the defeat of the lands that made up the Crown of Aragon in the Spanish Succession War. Until then, every kingdom in the Iberian Peninsula had their own peculiar evolution of political and legal systems. The marriage of the Catholic Kings, Ferdinand of Aragon and Isabel of Castille (1464), led to a mere personal union of the two realms. Soon afterwards, Navarre was incorporated into the Crown of Castille. From there on, different kingdoms shared the same King, but each of them was formally independent.

I. The Constitutional Framework

4. The current Spanish Constitution (CE), promulgated in 1978, set up a decentralized parliamentary monarchy. The King is the head of State but does not rule. Spain is organized into seventeen Autonomous Communities and two Autonomous Cities (Ceuta and Melilla). A double series of powers are listed in Articles 148 and 149 CE. Article 149 deals with the exclusive competence of the State, while Article 148 deals with the competence that can be assumed by the autonomous regions. The so-called *historical* Autonomous Communities (Basque Country, Catalonia, Galicia and Andalusia) were supposed to have more powers than the rest, but nowadays the differences are not substantial. Nevertheless, the Basque Country and Catalonia have their own police. The Basque Country and Navarre have a different financial system from the rest of the Autonomous Communities.

5. The Constitution sets out the principle of separation between the three powers of the State. The legislative power is wielded by the Spanish Parliament

(*Cortes*). The Parliament consists of two houses, namely the Congress and the Senate. The two houses do not have the same powers and, although they share the legislative power, the Congress takes the ultimate decision; nevertheless, the Congress normally adopts the amendments on the bills introduced by the Senate.

The Congress has 350 members, who are elected by universal suffrage of men and women aged 18 years and over. The Senate has 208 members elected by universal suffrage (four in each province notwithstanding its population, three in the major islands, one in the minor islands and two in Ceuta and Melilla) and, nowadays, fifty-six members appointed by the Autonomous Communities (one for each one and one more per each million inhabitants). Moreover, every Autonomous Community has one Parliamentary Assembly. Elections take place every four years unless the Parliament is dissolved earlier.

6. The executive power is vested in the President of the Government and the Ministers. The Congress elects the President of the Government at the proposal of the King. The King (currently Philip VI) normally proposes the leader of the dominating party after the general elections. Similarly, there is a government in every Autonomous Community, whose President is elected by the regional Assembly.

7. The judicial power is exercised by judges and courts. They are only submitted to the law. Judges are civil servants appointed after passing specific exams (*oposiciones*). Besides there are magistrates (*Jueces de paz*), that decide minor cases in small villages.

II. Private Law, the State and the Autonomous Communities

8. The possibility of assuming powers on private law does not appear in Article 148 CE, but in Article 149. Thus, the regions do not need to expressly assume the competence (implicitly admitted by the Constitutional Court in the Decision 88/1993). Nevertheless, not every region can legislate on civil law. The competence is restricted to those regions where a civil law was in force before the Constitution was passed. In other words, only the regions whose civil law had been compiled are empowered to legislate on civil law.[1]

The regions' competence on civil law is not unlimited. On the one hand, the following areas of civil law are reserved 'in any case' to the State:

1. rules on the application and the efficacy of statutory provisions;
2. legal relationships related to the forms of marriage;
3. organization of public registers;
4. bases of contractual obligations; and
5. norms to solve conflict of laws.

1. However, although a Compilation of the Civil Law of Valencia had never been passed since the *Furs* were repealed after the Spanish Succession War, the Constitutional Court upheld the Valentian Act on historical leases (Decision 121/1992). *See* now Carmen López Beltrán de Heredia et al., *Curso de derecho civil valenciano* (Valencia, 2000).

The determination of the sources of law also belongs to the State, but it must fully respect the sources of the regional laws. On the other hand, Article 149.1.8 CE qualifies this competence with three substantives: conservation, modification and development of the 'foral' or 'special' civil laws. Of course, the key concepts are 'development' and 'civil law'. As for its interpretation, several positions can be found among the authors. The more restrictive approach identifies 'civil law' and compilation, so that the 'development' refers to 'the compiled institutions'. The more extensive approach considers that the only limitation to the competence of the Autonomous Communities rests on the aforementioned areas reserved 'in any case' to the State.[2] The competence on commercial and procedural law (except the particularities derived from regional private laws) belongs to the State (Article 149.1.6 CE).

9. The Constitutional Court has adopted a more cautious approach (Decisions 88/1993 and 156/1993), since it has rejected the idea of a competence only limited by the aforementioned five areas, arguing that Article 149.1.8 refers first to the exclusive competence of the State on private law, yet it goes beyond the idea that the regions can only develop the compiled institutions. In the opinion of the Court, the regions can legislate on 'linked institutions' to the ones compiled. This sort of Solomonic decision is rather unsatisfactory. It introduces a new concept: 'linked institution' which, instead of solving the problems already existing in the constitutional provision, adds further doubts to its interpretation. The best example of this is the Judgment 88/1993. The Constitutional Court had to decide whether an Aragonese Act providing that children born in or out of wedlock had equal rights was against the constitutional distribution of competence or not. For the Court, affiliation was linked to family law and succession, regardless of the fact that the Compilation of Aragon had no rules on affiliation.[3] Hence, it is hardly surprising that the

2. For an overview of the debate, Encarna Roca Trias, 'El derecho civil catalán en la Constitución de 1978', RJC (1979): 23; Jesús Delgado Echeverría, 'Los derechos civiles forales en la Constitución', RJC (1979): 648; Carlos Lasarte, *Autonomías y derecho privado en la Constitución española* (Madrid, 1980); Ferran Badosa Coll, 'L'àmbit del dret civil català', in *Materials de les II Jornades de dret català a Tossa* (Barcelona, S.d.), 25; Rodrigo Bercovitz Rodríguez-Cano, 'Las competencias de las Comunidades Autónomas en materia de derecho civil', in *Primer Congreso de derecho vasco: la actualización del derecho civil* (Oñati, 1983), 89; Luis Díez-Picazo y Ponce de León, 'Las competencias del Estado y de las Comunidades Autónomas en materia de derecho civil', in *Competencia en materia civil de las Comunidades Autónomas*, coord., Bernardo Moreno Quesada (Madrid, 1989); Antoni Vaquer Aloy, 'Los conceptos de "conservación", "modificación"y "desarrollo"del artículo 149.1.8ode la Constitución: su interpretación por el legislador catalán', *Derecho privado y Constitución* 2 (1994): 239; Mariano Yzquierdo Tolsada, 'Nuevos Estatutos de Autonomía y *legiferación* civil', *Derecho Privado y Constitución* (2007): 331. In English, the succinct overview by Miquel Martín Casals, 'Catalan Civil Law and Its Main Institutions', in *Catalonia, Spain, Europe and Latin America: Regional Legal Systems and Their Literature*, ed. Jürgen C. Gödan & Bernard D. Reams Jr, 93–94.
3. On the decisions of the Constitutional Court, Enrique Rubio Torrano, 'El artículo 149.1.8 de la Constitución y su reciente jurisprudencia constitucional', *RJ Navarra* (1993): 293; Rodrigo Bercovitz Rodríguez-Cano, 'La conservación, modificación y desarrollo por las Comunidades Autónomas de los derechos civiles, forales o especiales', *Derecho Privado y Constitución* 1 (1993): 36; Badosa Coll, 'La recent jurisprudència constitucional', *Iuris* 1 (1994): 11; Jesús Delgado Echeverría, 'Doctrina reciente del Tribunal Constitucional sobre la competencia legislativa de las Comunidades Autónomas

main representative of the doctrine of the 'linked institutions' has blamed the Constitutional Court for being 'too permissive' and 'too generous'.[4]

Twenty-five years after the CE entered into force there are still issues regarding the boundaries of the powers of the State and of the Autonomous Communities. In its Decision 40/2014, the Constitutional Court has considered that the Autonomous Communities cannot set out different requirements to become a registered unmarried couple as a means to apply for basic rights common to all Spanish citizens. By virtue of this decision, the Court annulled a State rule of the Social Security system that resorted to the regional regulations in order to determine which cohabitants could apply for a survivor's pension.

What is clear now is that legal diversity in Spain is guaranteed by the Constitution. In this respect, it is worth mentioning the recent Decision 236/2000 of the Constitutional Court. Since political autonomy is recognized by the Regions and their legislative powers, there is no discrimination if the decision of a single case differs because of the application of a regional law or the Spanish Civil Code (CC).[5]

The debate on the powers' extent on private law is again a highly topical question. The former conservative Spanish government challenged before the Constitutional Court two acts passed by the Parliament of Catalonia, namely the Act on occupation and accession and the first Act of the Catalan Civil Code. The key argument in the second case was that an Autonomous Community cannot enact a Civil Code. In August 2004, the socialist Government of the State has withdrawn from the claim before the Constitutional Court, as a result of a pact with the Government of Catalonia, and no other Catalan private law act has been challenged. Currently, the Spanish government has challenged before the Constitutional Court the regulation of shared property and of several provisions of the Book 6 on contracts of the Civil Code of Catalonia (CC Cat), mainly dealing with sales and mandate. From a political point of view, the judgment of the Constitutional Court 31/2010 on the new Statute for Catalonia (2006) has been a hot issue and somehow has resulted in the quest for a secession referendum. The Court considered contrary to the Constitution most of the new powers that Catalonia tried to attract. The position of the Catalan language in the education system has been threatened. Nevertheless, in relation to private law the judgment repeats the doctrine established in previous decisions without adding new arguments.

---

en materia de derecho civil', *Iuris* 1 (1994): 37; Miguel Coca Payeras, 'Conservación, modificación y desarrollo del derecho civil propio, en la doctrina del Tribunal Constitucional', RJC (1994): 435.

4. Rodrigo Bercovitz Rodríguez-Cano, 'La conservación', 72 and 'Competencia del Estado y de las Comunidades Autónomas en materia de legislación civil', *Iuris* 1 (1994): 94; his formulation of the theory of the 'linked institutions' in 'Las competencias' passim.

5. The plaintiff before the Constitutional Court sought the declaration that Art. 71 Comp. Nav. was against the principle of equality and non-discrimination (Art. 14 CE). According to the local provision, a father is not entitled to claim paternity of a child born out of wedlock, but he would have been entitled to do so had the Spanish Civil Code been applicable. This doctrine was confirmed in the subsequent Decision 245/2000. This involved a Catalan plaintiff who claimed that he had been discriminated against because the Art. 127 *Código civil* had not been applied to him by the High Court of Catalonia. Art. 127 establishes that every demand on affiliation must be accompanied by some evidence. However, this provision is not considered to be applicable in Catalonia due to the strong influence of the principle of free investigation of paternity and maternity (*see* Art. 98 CF).

In a clear attempt to diminish the legislative powers of the Autonomous Communities, the Spanish government passed a bill on a new Commercial Code (CCom).[6] Only the State has powers on commercial law (Article 149.1.8 Constitution). Moreover, the bill extended to a lot of civil law areas, which had been in many cases already regulated by the laws of the Autonomous Communities (e.g., prescription). The aim was the unification of contract law by means of a CCom. The dismissal of the Minister of Justice in September 2014 has led the government to shelve the bill. Another bill, this one on a reform of the civil procedure law launched on 27 February 2015, proposes a drastic reduction of the general period of prescription to five years.

A. *Criteria for Applying One of the Spanish Laws in Force*

10. The *Código civil* sets up different criteria in order to decide which of the different civil laws in force in Spain is to be applied to citizens. Concerning personal status, the application of a concrete law depends on the *vecindad civil* of the party. *Vecindad civil* is a term barely translatable into English, and one that does not match the concept of residence. An individual acquires *vecindad civil* in one territory first because of *ius sanguinis*, so that the children acquire the *vecindad* of their parents (Article 14.2). In cases where the parents have a different *vecindad*, the children acquire the *vecindad* of that parent whose affiliation has been previously established. If it is still not possible to determine the *vecindad*, it will then be the place of birth. As a final criterion, the 'common' *vecindad* is attributed, that is to say, the personal law will be the *Código civil* (Article 14.3).[7]

But a *vecindad civil* can also be acquired by means of residence. Residing for ten years in a territory where a different civil law is in force without expressing the intention to keep the previous *vecindad* leads to the automatic acquisition of a new *vecindad*, that of the place of residence. Once the intention to preserve the *vecindad* has been expressed, this does not need to be repeated. Finally, after two years of residence, the individual can opt for the *vecindad* of that place (Article 14.5 CC); as such, a new lapse of ten years is not enough to lose it.[8]

Aliens who acquire Spanish nationality must opt between one of these *vecindades*: the one corresponding to the residence, to the place of birth, the last *vecindad* of their parents or the one of the spouse (Article 15 CC).

Concerning real status, the applicable law is the *lex rei sitae* (Article 10.1 CC).

6. *See* critically María Paz García Rubio, 'Algunas consideraciones sobre las normas de obligaciones y contratos de la Propuesta de Código Mercantil', *Revista de Derecho Civil,* 2014/1: 7; Francisco Oliva Blázquez, 'El Anteproyecto de Código Mercantil en el contexto del proceso internacional de unificación del Derecho privado de los contratos', *Revista de Derecho civil,* 2014/3: 37.
7. This final criterion was held to be concordant to the Constitution by the Decision 226/1993 of the Constitutional Court.
8. *See* the judgments of the High Court of Navarre of 3 Mar. 1994 (RJ 1994/2115) and of the High Court of Catalonia of 13 May 1999 (RJ 2000/8037).

B. The Extent of the Regional Private Laws

11. Regional laws have largely developed since the Constitution came into force. The best example is Catalonia, where a Civil Code that covers all areas of law but some specific contracts and the general theory of obligations and contracts for the time being. The Catalan legislature has also regulated other forms of cohabitation (Act 19/1998, regarding cohabitation situations for mutual assistance, and the elderly in care acts 22/2000 and 11/2001) now enshrined in the CC Cat.[9] Aragon is another region that has passed a Code of Foral Law (2011); although it is not as extensive as the Catalan Civil Code, it takes the symbolic denomination of 'code'. The Balearic Islands have amended the Compilation (Act 8/1990) and regulated unmarried couples (Act 18/2001). Navarre, besides revising the Compilation, has regulated foundations (Act 10/1996) and unmarried couples (Act 6/2000, annulled by the judgment of the Constitutional Court 93/2013 in its fundamental rules).[10] The Basque Country has passed an Act of the Civil Law (2015) and an Act on Associations, which was partially annulled by the Constitutional Court, as well as an Act on Foundations (1994). Galicia has reformed the Compilation as well (Act 2/2006, of 14 June, on the Civil Law of Galicia), and has also legislated on foundations (Act 12/2006, of 1 December), on historical land leases (Act 3/1993, modified by Act 6/2005) and on family and infancy (Act 3/1997). Even the Parliament of Valencia has passed some statutes on civil matters (Act 8/1998 on foundations, Act 1/2001 on unmarried couples, Act 10/2007, of 20 March, on marriage property).[11]

III. Political Parties

12. The 2016 elections resulted in four dominant political parties in Spain, namely the conservative Popular Party (Partido Polular (PP)), the Socialist Party (Partido Socialista Obrero Español (PSOE)) and the new parties Podemos (left) and Ciudadanos (liberals). In three of the Autonomous Communities, there are also nationalist parties some of which have been quite influential in the State when none

9. Though not updated, *see* in French and English Esther Arroyo Amayuelas, 'Le pluralisme de l'ordonnancement civil en Espagne et le droit civil en vigueur en Catalogne', *RevueGénerale de droit* (1998): 411; Martín Casals, 'Catalan Civil Law and Its Main Institutions', in *Catalonia, Spain, Europe and Latin America: Regional Legal Systems and Their Literature*, ed. Jürgen C. Gödan & Bernard D. Reams Jr, ss 87; Santiago Espiau, 'Unification of the European Law of Obligations and Codification of Catalan Civil Law', in *Regional Private Laws and Codification in Europe*, ed. Hector L. MacQueen, Antoni Vaquer & Santiago Espiau, 172–198.

10. According to the Constitutional Court, the fundamental principle of free development of the personality enshrined in Art. 10 Spanish Constitution because the Navarre Act imposed a compulsory legal status to cohabitants irrespective of their intention if they have cohabited for one year or a child was born. *See* the comments by Miguel Coca Payeras, 'Competencia legislativa civil, parejas de hecho, libre desarrollo de la personalidad e ilimitada autonomía de la voluntad', *Revista de Derecho Civil*, 2014/1: 69; Miquel Martín-Casals, 'El derecho a la "convivencia anómica en pareja": ¿Un nuevo derecho fundamental?', *InDret*, 2013/3; Irantzu Beriain Flores, 'Las uniones no matrimoniales y el derecho al libre desarrollo de la personalidad (A propósito de la sentencia del Tribunal Constitucional 93/2013, de 23 de abril)', *Derecho Privado y Constitución*, 2014: 137.

11. But this Act has been challenged by the Spanish government before the Constitutional Court and annulled by the Constitutional Court (Decision 82/2016).

of the 'national' parties obtained an absolute majority (Convergència i Unió (CiU), currently PDCat, and the pro-independence Esquerra Republicana de Catalunya (ERC) in Catalonia, Euzko Alderdi Jeltzalea/Partido Nacionalista Vasco (EAJ/PNV) and the coalition Bildu in the Basque Country, and Coalición Canaria in the Canary Islands).

The General Elections of 2011	
Congress	
PP	137
PSOE	85
Unidos Podemos (including Marea and Compromis)	71
Ciudadanos	32
ERC	9
CiU (PDCat)	8
PNV	5
Bildu	2
Coalición Canaria	1
Senate	
PP	130
PSOE	43
Podemos-Compromís-Marea	16
ERC	10
PNV	5
CDC (PdCat)	2
Varia	2

IV. Social and Cultural Values

13. Spain is a free market economy. Freedom of commerce and industry is even guaranteed by the Constitution (Article 38), whilst freedom of contract is one of the pillars of the Civil Code (Article 1255). But at the same time, freedom of economic initiative is also recognized in favour of the State (Article 118.2 CE). The Constitution also tries to establish a balance between the companies' interests on the one hand, and the consumers' interests on the other, since the protection of the consumer is also established in the Constitution among the 'guiding principles of social and economic policies' (Article 58). As we shall see later, the principle of consumers' protection has altered the freedom of contract as established in the Civil Code.

Private property is another pillar of the social and economic system. Article 33 CE guarantees property and the right of inheritance. Individuals may only be deprived of their assets by means of expropriation. However, private property is subordinated to the general interest (Article 128.1 CE), and its social function is stressed by the same Article 33 CE.

As elsewhere, the crisis of the welfare State has led to privatization of social services and reduction of the State's intervention in the market. Nevertheless, the government does not renounce promoting social policies in favour of weaker persons resorting to private law.[12]

12. The Act 41/2003, of 18 November provides a good example. In order to protect disabled persons, testators are allowed to dispose of their assets in favour of their disabled children or descendants postponing the payment of the legitimacy of the other children or the descendants until the death of the former. In other words, a sort of tacit disinheritance is introduced in the law of successions in order to favour care of disabled persons.

Chapter 2. Spanish Law Belongs to the Romanistic Legal Family

14. During the Middle Ages, in most of the Spanish territories there was a broad reception of Roman law. Local laws were supplemented by Roman law, and even in Catalonia, for example, Roman law has been the supplementary law until the enactment of the Compilation of the Civil Law in 1960.

The CC promulgated in 1889 and still in force was deeply inspired by the French Civil Code. The inspiration extends to the contents and to the structure of the Civil Code. Concerning the contents, a number of articles were directly copied from the French Code. As to the structure, the CC is divided in a Preliminary Title (drafted anew in 1974) and four books (persons, goods and property, means of acquiring property and obligations and contracts). There is no book devoted to family law, which is to be found partially in Book I (the personal aspects of family law: marriage, affiliation, guardianship) and in Book IV (the economics of marriage). Nevertheless, the French influence should not be exaggerated. For instance, the Spanish Code rejects the consensual transmission of property and requires delivery, and succession law and marriage property are deeply rooted in the Castilian tradition, only to highlight some examples. Besides, it is noteworthy that Spain has traditionally considered German doctrine very highly. One of the main features of this German influence is to be found in legal studies, since the curriculum – and consequently handbooks – does (do) not follow the systematic of the Civil Code, but the pandectist approach. Several proposals on reforming the Civil Code have been launched by the Codification General Commission (2009) and the Civil Law Professors Association (2017), yet the Spanish government seems unwilling to reform the *Código.*

15. The enactment of the Civil Code was a long and cumbersome process. Already the first CE of 1812, still under the French occupation, fostered the legislative unification of Spain by means of 'single codes for the whole monarchy'. The desire of a unifying codification was repeated in every Constitution, but the successive drafts did not succeed; only the CCom was passed in 1829. Among the reasons for the delay in codifying, the opposition of the territories with local laws has to be stressed, although the need for consolidation of liberal property was not less important. Thus, as early as in 1861, the *Ley Hipotecaria* (dealing with Land Register and mortgages) was passed without any complaint from the 'foral' territories; it is interesting to note that the *Ley Hipotecaria* was inspired also in Germanic principles. The most significant draft was the one elaborated in 1851 by a commission headed by Florencio García Goyena. This draft was the basis of the current Civil Code. Its failure resulted in the abandonment of the unifying idea, since the Civil Code repeals only the Laws of Castille, and Laws other than that of Castille were upheld provisionally, 'for the time being' (Article 12.2 CC).[13] In brief, codification in Spain was reduced to codification of the Law of Castille.

13. *See* Ferran Badosa Coll, 'Quae ad ius cathalanicum pertinet', in *Regional Private Laws and Codification in Europe*, ed. Hector MacQueen, Antoni Vaquer & Santiago Espiau (Cambridge, 2003) (paperback edition 2007), 136 et seq.

16. Some of the contents of the Civil Code exceed private law. For example, the regulation of nationality is contained in Articles 17–27 CC. Moreover, the Civil Code supplements private and public law statutes (Article 4.3 CC). The provisions of the Preliminary Title dealing with the sources, effects and application of the law are applicable to the whole system of law. However, the Civil Code does not encapsulate the entirety of private law. Land Register and mortgages have already been pointed out. Consumer law is regulated in a series of statutes, as well as leases, flats or some specific torts.

17. The Civil Code is a liberal body of law. The right of property appears almost unlimited (Article 348) and becomes one of the pillars of the system. The right of property is based on land property (*see* Article 1577), since the Civil Code does not seriously consider the property over movables as a source of wealth (e.g., machinery); it has to be borne in mind that the industrial revolution only took place in some parts of Spain such as the Basque Country and Catalonia. The other pillar of the system is freedom of contract (Article 1255 CC), that presupposes an equal bargaining between the parties. It is not surprising, therefore, that the Civil Code has been repeatedly amended, especially in relation to family law. Divorce was introduced in 1981, guardianship was thoroughly reformed in 1983, the restrictions to adoption have been abrogated and the main interest is now on the protection of children put up for adoption (last amendment in 1987), marriage has been opened to homosexual couples. By contrast, the patrimonial law of the Civil Code remains essentially unaltered, yet significant modifications have been introduced by means of statutes. Consumer law is contained in a specific statute (the General Act for the Protection of Consumers of Users), amended several times in order to transpose European Directives.

Chapter 3. Primacy of Legislation

18. Article 1 CC states the sources of law and establishes their hierarchy. The first source in the hierarchy is the legal rule ('ley'), the second one is the custom and the general principles of law are the third one. The law is primarily thought of as being the body of rules enacted by the legislative power. When the Preliminary Title of the CC was passed in 1974, the concept of legal rule could be equated to statute and other enactments. Nevertheless, the Constitution of 1978 altered this concept. The Constitution is the supreme norm of the Spanish legal order, since any former statute against its principles has been automatically repealed and any posterior statute can be annulled by the Constitutional Court if it does not match the principles established by the latter. Moreover, statutes have to be interpreted according to the Constitution (Article 5.1 LOPJ). Besides, Spain being a member of the European Union, the European treaties are also part of the Spanish law (Article 93 Constitution).

The ordinary statutes include European regulations as a consequence of Spain being a member of the European Union. Since the Constitution provides the Autonomous Communities with legislative powers, the statutes passed by the Spanish Parliament and the statutes passed by the Regional Parliaments have the same force within their respective competence. In order to be properly enacted, statutes must be sanctioned by the King and published in the *Boletín Oficial del Estado* or the regional equivalent of official publication. Unless otherwise established, statutes come into force twenty days after their publication (Article 2.1 CC). Finally, international treaties also become part of the legal order once they are published in the *Boletín Oficial del Estado* (Articles 96.1 CE and 1.5 CC).

19. Custom is a binding usage born within social groups. The main characteristic is the social and repeated usage, which gives the custom the force of law. Nevertheless, to count as a custom, it cannot be against moral and public order. Moreover, custom has to be proved. Custom will only be applied in the absence of a statute. Hence, custom *secundum legem* is not a source of law. However, in Navarre custom prevails over statute (*ley* 3 Comp. Nav.), but only notorious custom does not need to be proved. Usages that are not customs are called by the legal system to complete the contractual agreements (Article 1258 CC) and to interpret contracts (Article 1287 CC).

20. When statute and custom are lacking, according to Article 1.4 CC, the general principles of law apply. However, the general principles of law have, at the same time, another function in Spanish law: they 'inform' the legal system. Therefore, they represent the social consciousness and the fundamental convictions of the community. The most important are those enshrined in the Constitution, like freedom, justice, equality, political pluralism, obedience to the law, dignity of the person, free development of the personality and so on. Other principles are to be found in the Civil Code: freedom of contract, reparation of damages caused by negligence, protection of the contractual weaker party, restitution of unjust enrichment, etc.

The Supreme Court requires the plaintiff to prove that the general principle is in force and applicable to the case as well as to quote the legal provision that contains it or the judgment that includes it.[14]

21. Whether passed by the Spanish *Cortes* or by the Regional Parliaments and legislative Assemblies, the legislation enacted has the same legal standing within the scope of the respective areas of competence of the State and the Autonomous Communities. The Constitutional Court solves the conflicts of competence. Both the President of the Government and the Regional Parliaments and Executives, as well as fifty members of the Congress or Senators (Article 32 LOTC) are entitled to challenge any Act before the Constitutional Court on the grounds of lack of competence. If the Constitutional Court decides the lack of competence, the legislation is void, unless the Court sets out a binding interpretation of the challenged Act (Article 39 LOTC).

14. *See* TS 23 Mar. 2000 (RJ 2000/2106).

Chapter 4. The Position of the Judiciary

22. Concerning private law matters, there is a hierarchical organization of the judiciary that allows at least one appellation. The first layer consists of the magistrates' courts. Magistrates can be laymen, in which case they decide minor cases (up to EUR 90 Article 47 LEC). The magistrates' judgments can be appealed to the Court of First Instance. The Judge of Court of First Instance is an ordinary judge in private law litigation (Article 45 LEC). His/her decisions in Court of First Instance are appealed to the *Audiencia Provincial* (Court of Appeal). There is one *Audiencia Provincial* in each province. Usually, if the litigation value is not higher than EUR 150,000 there is no appeal against the decision of the *Audiencia*. Otherwise, the decision can be appealed in cassation. But if contradictory case law of the *Audiencias Provinciales* exists, cassation is also permitted regardless of the litigation value (Article 477.3 LEC). If the appeal is based on regional law or on procedural breach, the Superior Court of Justice of the Autonomous Community decides the cassation (Articles 73 LOPJ and 468 et seq. LEC). If, instead, the appeal is based on general private law or on the infringement of a constitutional provision, cassation is decided by the *Tribunal Supremo*. If the decision has no further appeal but the party considers that a constitutional provision has been infringed, it can lodge *recurso de amparo* before the Constitutional Court. The *recurso de amparo* is not a new instance. The Constitutional Court cannot review the decision of, for example, the *Tribunal Supremo*, since its task is limited to the constitutional aspect of the case. Nevertheless, awkward conflicts have arisen from time to time between the Constitutional and the Supreme Courts.[15]

23. Case law is also mentioned in the provision that enumerates the sources of law (Article 1 CC). Nevertheless, according to paragraph 6 of this Article 1, case law is not a source of law, but only 'complements' the legal order. The judge is subject to (Article 117.1 CE) and applies the law (Article 5.1 LOPJ), which means that he/she does not create law. Spanish law acknowledges the separation of powers, so that only the legislature enacts the law. The Spanish system is one of rule of law, like all civil law systems. However, any lawyer has to be thoroughly familiar with case law. The judiciary is obliged to solve any unforeseen legal problem in accordance with the system of sources of law (Article 1.7 CC). Moreover, multiple layers of decisions have interpreted the legal rules. Sometimes case law has even gone further. For example, in the area of delict, the Supreme Court has turned the fault-based system of tortious liability (Article 1902 CC) into one of almost strict liability (the so-called quasi-strict liability, based on reversal of the burden of proof, risk theory, etc.),[16] or has afforded financial compensation for non-pecuniary harm. Hence, case law is not a source of law, but in fact resembles it.

---

15. *See* the chain of judgments TC 5 May 2000 (RTC 115/2000), TS 20 Jul. 2000 (RJA 6184), TC 17 Sep. 2001 (RTC 2001/186) and TS 5 Nov. 2001 (RAJ 2001/677). However, the Supreme Court (decision of 23 Jan. 2004 [RJ 2004/1]) ruled that the judges of the Constitutional Court were liable in tort as a consequence of the breach of their duty to decide every claim, and consequently each judge had to compensate the plaintiff with EUR 500.
16. For example, TS 26 Mar. 2004 (RJ 2004/1952), 3 Sep. 1996 (RJ 1996/6500), 26 Mar. 1996 (RJ 1996/2203).

There is no formal rule of stare decisis. Lower courts are not bound either by the decisions of the upper courts or even by the jurisprudence of the *Tribunal Supremo*. Nevertheless, it has to be taken into account that one of the grounds for cassation is the contradiction of the judgment to the case law of the *Tribunal Supremo* or the Superior Court in matters of regional law (Article 477.3 LEC). Therefore, even if the lower judge is not compelled to apply the doctrine established by upper courts, his/her decisions may be reversed on this ground. Overruling a decision requires:

1. that at least two judgments of the civil law division of the *Tribunal Supremo* establish the same doctrine;
2. that this doctrine was the *ratio decidendi* of the case;
3. that there is a substantial coincidence between the facts of the judgments.

However, only one judgment is enough in the case of an appeal in the interest of the law and where this changes the previous case law.[17] Own precedents do not even bind the Supreme Court. However, if it modifies its opinions, it must avoid arbitrariness and justify the reasons for withdrawing from any previous decisions.[18]

17. TS 19 May 2000 (RJA 3992), 9 Mar. 1999 (RJA 1408), 17 Nov. 1998 (RJA 8811), among many others.
18. Decisions of the TC 17 May 1993 (RTC 1993/160) and 23 Jul. 1994 (RTC 1994/192), TS 11 Dec. 1997 (RJ 1997/8973), 18 Apr. 1995 (RJ 1995/3421).

Chapter 5. Distinction Between Public Law and Private Law

24. The dividing line between public and private law is blurring because of the changes in the role of the State, especially in the last decades. 'Grey zones' multiply, since public bodies tend to use private law techniques in order to achieve specific goals, while public law displays an important influence in institutions considered as part of private law. Thus, on the one hand, the crisis of the welfare state has led to privatization of public services. On the other hand, there is a growing intervention of the administrative authorities in disparate fields such as adoption or protection of consumers – by means of administrative controls and sanctions – among many others. The constitutional framework has contributed to this process, because the State is qualified as 'social and democratic' and some private rights are guaranteed by the supreme norm, namely privacy (Article 18 CE), association (Article 22 CE), property and inheritance (Article 33 CE).[19]

25. The dichotomy public law/private law also becomes apparent in the field of contract law. Spanish law distinguishes between administrative contracts and private law contracts; the latter remain subject to the provisions of the Civil Code and other statutes, whereas the former are governed by the administrative law. The contract is administrative if at least one of the parties is a public authority and its object relates to its public goals. According to Article 7 Act *Real Decreto-legislativo* 2/2000 of 16 June, on administrative contracts, administrative law governs the preparation, the adjudication, the effects and the extinction of administrative contracts. However, public authorities may also resort to private contracts, although their preparation and adjudication of the contract is, in this case, still governed by administrative law (Article 9).

Between administrative and private contracts there are significant differences. The requisites of determination of object and price are much stricter (Article 11.2.c and 11.2.d), it is necessary that a previous budget allocation and the preparation of the contract is governed by the administrative procedural provisions. Moreover, administrative contracts are formal and have to be recorded. Final, and most important, administrative contracts are submitted to the jurisdiction of the administrative courts.

19. Thus, the Decision TC 7 Feb. 1984 (RTC 18/1984).

Chapter 6. Distinction Between Civil Law and Commercial Law

26. In Spain, commercial transactions are governed by special rules to be found in the CCom and related legislation, although such transactions fall under the jurisdiction of ordinary courts.[20] In fact, as mentioned above, the codification of commercial law was completed about sixty years before the civil codification.

The distinction between commercial and civil contracts has been much disputed. Although Article 2 CCom apparently adopts an objective criterion of distinction based on the type of transaction (the concept of 'commercial act'), the majority of the authors tend to prefer a mixed criterion of distinguishing commercial and civil contracts. Thus, one of the parties has to be a merchant, but the economic goal of the transaction has to be to obtain a benefit. For example, only if a merchant buys in order to resell, the sale is a commercial one. Nevertheless, in some contracts, it is enough if one of the parties is a merchant, namely the contract of transport.

27. Although the categorization of a contract as commercial implies differences in substantive law (delay, latent defects, lesion, limitation of actions), the importance of the distinction is diminishing, along the lines of modern codes (such as the New Dutch Civil Code) and soft law (PECL and Principles Unidroit). Consumer law, especially because of the transposition of European Directives, seems to be alien to the dichotomy. One of the main differences between commercial and civil contracts concerned its conclusion. According to the former Article 54 CCom, a contract between distant persons was concluded when acceptance was dispatched, whereas the former Article 1262 CC required knowledge – or the possibility of such knowledge – of acceptance. Now both provisions share the same wordings, introduced by Act 34/2002 of 11 July, transposing the e-Commerce Directive. The solution is the one enshrined formerly in the CC as qualified by case law and doctrine. Nevertheless, the dichotomy is not going to disappear. The mercantile section of the Spanish Commission on Codification has prepared a bill on a general part of the CCom on contracts and on prescription of commercial claims (2006).[21] Even if this initiative is never passed, it reflects how deeply rooted is in the legal mentalité the distinction between civil and commercial law.

20. Nevertheless, the new Insolvency Act has paved the way to Mercantile courts, but only in the biggest cities they have been settled separately.
21. Accessible on the internet at http://www.mjusticia.gob.es/cs/Satellite/Portal/1292427025146?blobheader=application%2Fpdf&blobheadername1=Content-Disposition&blobheadervalue1=attachment%3B+filename%3DAPL_C%C3%93DIGO_MERCANTIL__TEXTO_WEB%2C2.PDF.PDF.

Introduction to the Law of Contracts

Chapter 1. Definition of Contract

§1. Basic Principles

28. According to Article 1254 CC, a contract exists 'when one or more persons agree on obligating themselves towards one or more other persons, to give something or to render some service'. It is not surprising, therefore, that contract is one of the sources of obligations enumerated in Article 1089. Along these lines, Article 1091 CC specifies that 'the obligations arising from a contract have legal force between the parties'. Contract is therefore the agreement of at least two persons in order to create legal obligations. However, this broad concept of agreement could be valid for public law or family law, as well. In a more restricted sense, contract refers to patrimonial relations. Hence, contract can be defined as a bilateral transaction whose legal consequence is the creation, modification or extinction of a patrimonial juridical relation. 'Patrimonial' means in this context capable of economic valuation.

29. The requirements of any contract are enumerated in Article 1261 CC: the consent of the parties, a certain object and the cause of the obligation. These requirements will be further developed.[22] It must be stressed that the expression 'to give' is used in its technical sense, meaning the transfer of ownership or any real or personal right on a thing.

30. The requirement of consent highlights the role of the will. A contract presupposes the meeting of two wills and the exchange of consents. The parties are normally free to enter into a contract and free to shape the contents of the contract. Freedom of contract, enshrined in Article 1255 CC, is a cornerstone of the Spanish system of law. However, freedom of contract is by no means unlimited. The same Article 1255 CC points out the borders of freedom of contract: the law, the morals and the public order (*see also* Article 1258 CC). Freedom of contract, therefore, is limited by the mandatory law and by the moral principles encapsulated in the whole system of law.[23] Besides, as already mentioned, the object of the contract, namely the obligations of the parties, must be economically valuable. The obligations of the

22. *See* paras 121 et seq.
23. *See* TS 11 Feb. 2002 (RJ 2002/3107), 26 Apr. 2001 (2001/2037).

parties must be enforceable and capable of conversion into money (damages) in case of non-performance.

§2. Contract and the Sources of Obligations

31. As stated above, contract is one of the sources of obligations according to Article 1089 CC. This provision enumerates the following sources of obligations: the law, contracts, quasi-contracts, unlawful acts and omissions (crimes) and negligent acts and omissions (torts). In this context, sources are the facts from which obligations derive. The origin of this enumeration goes back to Roman law and, more specifically, to the *contractum-delictum* dichotomy. Subsequently, Justinian compilers added the *quasi ex contractu* and *quasi ex delicto* obligations which, through the so-called Theophilus paraphrase, gave rise to the figures of quasi-contract and quasi-delict.[24] Pothier incorporated into this fourfold scheme the law. The list of sources of obligations entered the French Civil Code, from which – via the Italian Civil Code of 1865 – it was included in the Spanish CC.

Strictly speaking, the enumeration established by Article 1089 CC sets the *law* against a heterogeneous category of transactions and juridical acts, whose sole common feature is that they give rise to obligations. In this sense, all obligations *arise* from the law, including contractual obligations, since it is the law that recognizes its binding effect. This is not, however, the aim of the reference to the *law* in the context of Article 1089 CC. The allusion to the *law* intends to group all of those facts and circumstances not mentioned in Article 1089 CC but which similarly give rise to an obligation. Thus, the obligation of alimony would be legal, because it arises from a situation of need in which a person finds oneself and from the kinship that links one person to another who has the means to defray in this situation (Articles 142 et seq. CC). Therefore, the enumeration of the sources of obligations enshrined in Article 1089 CC may be reduced to the dichotomy of voluntary-legal obligations. The former ones derive from the intention of the parties, namely by way of a contract and other legal transactions and, more specifically, from the intention of the party to whom the legal position of debtor corresponds, who is supposed to have assumed such position. The latter arise independent of such intention.

§3. Unilateral Acts as a Source of Obligations

32. There is no specific provision in the CC that admits unilateral acts as a source of obligations. Most authors and case law consider that any sort of acceptance by the creditor is required for the relationship to be contractual; yet the distinction with a unilateral contract – a contract where only one of the parties undertakes performance of an obligation – fades away. Moreover, it is pointed out that if unilateral will were admitted as a source of obligations one could acquire a right of credit without or even against its intention. There is only one undisputed

24. *See* Reinhard Zimmermann, *The Law of Obligations* (Oxford, 1996), 10 et seq.

case of obligations arising from a unilateral act: the promise of a reward. The public promise of a reward is the declaration of will addressed to the general public by which one person obliges himself/herself to perform in favour of whoever achieves a specific result or carries out an activity. The promise has to be addressed to an indeterminate number of people through the media. The promisor is obliged if someone achieves the result or carries out the activity notwithstanding the fact that the latter was unaware of the promise.[25]

§4. CONTRACT AS A JURIDICAL ACT

33. The distinguishing feature of a juridical act is that it derives from a conscious human behaviour. The juridical act is an expression of the will. The legal consequences of the juridical act are linked to the intention of its author. The act is voluntarily aimed at the production of such consequences. The juridical act is capable of a further subdivision between strict juridical acts and juridical transactions (*Rechtsgeschäft* in the pandectist terminology). The law predetermines the consequences of a strict juridical act, inasmuch as carrying out the behaviour produces the consequences irrespective of the real intention of the author. For example, when the creditor summons the debtor asking for payment of the debt, the legal consequence is *mora debitoris*,[26] although the creditor pursued fulfilment. Instead, the transaction shows the parties' power of self-regulation. The consequences of a transaction are wanted and decided by the parties within the limits of freedom of contract. Contract is the paradigm of juridical transactions.

Because the CC follows the structure of the French Civil Code and not the pandectist approach, the theory of the juridical transaction is built mainly on the basis of the provisions dealing with contracts. But, once the category is drawn up, the rules of law relating to the validity of juridical acts are applicable to contracts. Hence, the general rules relating to the personal capacity of the parties, form, vices of will or illegality apply to contracts.

25. *See* in the case law TS 10 Jun. 1977 (RJ 1977/2876). Another example is the prizes offered in quiz shows. TS 12 Jun. 1997 (RJ 1997/4771) deals with the substitution by the advertiser, a chocolate shake brand, of the offered flat at the seaside by a bungalow. The decision considers that according to Art. 1091 CC in relation to Arts 1254, 1255 and 1258 CC, once the plaintiffs had accepted to take part in the quiz, the promisor could not alter the object of its obligation. The court adds that it was not a pure gratuitous obligation, since the plaintiffs had to buy the chocolate shake. *See also* TS 7 Jun. 1999 (RJ 1999/4728).
26. *See* on *mora debitoris*, paras 238 et seq.

Chapter 2. Historical Background of the Law of Contracts

34. The conception of the contract as a source of obligations deriving from the free consent of the parties is the result of a long evolution departing from Roman law. In fact, the word contract is seldom used in Roman texts. A general theory of contract was not formulated, but different specific transactions based on a rigid formalism. Gaius set out a fourfold classification: 'aut enim re contrahitur obligatio aut verbis aut litteris aut consensu' (*Instituta* 3, 12, 3). Hence, consent was only the basis of a kind of contracts. Together with these nominate contracts, a large number of innominate contracts were regulated, although because they have no name they lack a specific *actio*. Finally, there were also *pacta*, based on consent as well, which only gave rise to a defence. Therefore, consent is considered as a common feature to all sorts of agreements and as the foundation of the consequences of one kind of contractual obligations.[27] Thanks to Glossators, Post-Glossators and Commentators, influenced by Canon law and commercial practices, consensualism gained ground.[28] Donellus and later the natural lawyers, especially Grotius, definitively shaped the consensual character of contract.

35. Spanish authors did not play a secondary role in this process. The so-called single law of the Title XVI of the *Ordenamiento de Alcalá* (1348) abandoned formalism and, consequently, consent was stressed. The original wording of the text was '. . . *que sea valedera la obligacion o el contrato que fueren fechos en cualquier manera que paresca que alguno se quiso obligar a otro, e façer contracto con el*',[29] which can be translated as follows: 'the obligation or the contract is valid regardless the way it has been made as long as it shows that one wanted to be obliged to another, or to contract with him'. Late Spanish scholastics (Francisco de Vitoria, Luis de Molina, Diego Covarruvias, Domingo de Soto) reorganized Roman law in accordance with the Aristotelic and Thomistic concept of justice and laid the foundations of the modern theory of contract. Their doctrines were taken over by Grotius and the Natural Lawyers.[30] Among the successors of Grotius, Domat and Pothier had a great influence on the drafters of the French *Code Civil*. As the Spanish draft of 1851 much mirrored the French Code, one could say that the liberal conception of contract that flows through the Civil Code corresponds to a long tradition.

In 2009, the Spanish Commission on Codification launched a proposal for the modernization of the law of obligations.[31] This proposal takes into account the European soft law and introduces into the Civil Code concepts such as nonconformity of the goods, hardship and a new regulation of sales. The same does the

27. M.C. Gete-Alonso, *Estructura y funcióndel tipo contractual* (Barcelona, 1979), 63.
28. Zimmermann, *Law of obligations*, 540 et seq.
29. Gete-Alonso, *Estructura y función*, 159 et seq.
30. *See* James Gordley, *The Philosophical Origins of Modern Contract Doctrine* (Oxford, 1991), 69 et seq.
31. Accessible on the internet at http://www.mjusticia.gob.es/cs/Satellite/es/1215198250496/Estructura_ C/1215198250781/Detalle.html.

proposal of the Private Law Professors Association.[32] For the time being, the Spanish government has taken into account none of the proposals. Nevertheless, case law considers European soft law as a means for the modernization of Spanish contract law.

32. Asociación de Profesores de Derecho civil, *Propuesta de Código Civil. Libros V y VI*, (Valencia 2016).

Chapter 3. Classification of Contracts

§1. Consensual and Real Contracts

36. Consensual contracts are concluded, and thus produce their legal consequences, by the sole consent of the parties. Sale, lease or mandate are consensual contracts. Real contracts are a category that goes back to Roman law. Besides consent, real contracts need the delivery of a thing to come into existence. Loan (either for consumption or for use, Article 1740 CC),[33] deposit (Article 1758 CC) and pledge (Article 1863 CC) are real contracts.

§2. Solemn Contracts

37. Exceptionally, the conclusion of a contract may require a formality. The formality may consist of the writing of the contract or a notarial deed. However, it is not always clear which are the consequences of the absence of the form. For example, Article 6 Act 28/1998 of 13 July, on sale on instalments,[34] requires the wording 'for the validity of the contracts submitted to the Act'. The absence of the form leads to the nullity of the contract. Article 9 Act 42/1998, of 15 December, on timesharing, also requires the writing. But, according to Article 10, 'if the contract does not contain any of the mentions or the documents to which Article 9 refers', the purchaser has a right of withdrawal.

§3. Unilateral and Bilateral (Synallagmatic) Contracts

38. Contract is always bilateral, since it requires at least two parties. The distinction between unilateral and bilateral contracts is based on the creation of obligations in one party or in both parties. Where both parties assume reciprocal obligations, the more suitable denomination is synallagmatic contracts.

The distinction has some important practical consequences. On the one hand, the parties must perform simultaneously. If one party has performed and the other does not fulfil its obligations, the latter incurs delay (*mora debitoris*)[35] (Article 1100 *in fine* CC). On the other hand, the non-performance of the synallagmatic obligation becomes a defence, so that a party may withhold performance until the other has tendered performance or has performed. It is the old *exceptio non adimpleti contractus*, which in case of defective performance turns into *exceptio non rite adimpleti contractus*. The defence is a legal one, since the parties need not incorporate it voluntarily into the contract. Besides, the aggrieved party may terminate

33. *See* TS 18 Jan. 2002 (RJ 2002/679), 2 Nov. 2002 (RJ 2002/9738) and 30 Nov. 2007 (RJ 2007/8857), some recent decisions that recognize loan as a real contract.
34. *See* paras 401-402.
35. *See* paras 238 et seq.

the contract.[36] Nevertheless, according to Article 1124 CC, the creditor may opt for claiming performance.

39. As an intermediate category, Spanish doctrine talks about bilateral contracts ex post facto, imperfect bilateral contracts or contracts giving rise to eventual obligations. In principle, the contract only creates obligations in one party, but unexpected circumstances (expenses, damages) may give rise to obligations in the other party. For example, the contract of deposit only creates obligations in the depository (restitution of property), but if this party has incurred expenses, the depositor has to compensate the expenses. The provisions on synallagmatic contracts do not apply to this intermediate category of contracts.

§4. Gratuitous and Onerous Contracts

40. In onerous contracts, one party confers an advantage on the other party in exchange of the reciprocal advantage that he/she obtains for himself/herself. In the gratuitous contract, the advantage conferred by the obliged party has no counter-performance. All the synallagmatic contracts are onerous, but not all onerous contracts are synallagmatic (e.g., the loan with interest). Examples of gratuitous contracts are mandate (Article 1711 CC) and loan for use (Article 1741 CC). The distinction relates to the notion of cause (gratuitous and onerous cause, Article 1274 CC). In the Civil Code, the relationship of equivalence between the respective prestations of the parties is subjective, whereas in Catalan law the equivalence is purely objective. Hence, if the price of the thing is less than half its market value, the contract can be rescinded (lesion, Articles 321 et seq. CDCC).[37]

41. The distinction has important practical consequences. The parties of an onerous contract assume responsibility for eviction and latent defects (*saneamiento*, in the terminology of the Civil Code). The provisions on *saneamiento* (Articles 1474 CC (sale); 1540 (exchange); 1553 (lease); 1681 (partnership)) are included now in the broader concept of *non-conformity* established in Directive 1999/44/CE, transposed through the Act 23/2003 of 10 July, on guarantees of the sale of consumer goods, and now enshrined in the General Act on the Protection of Consumers. The new Book 6 of the CC Cat has shifted to conformity for every sales contract, whether B2C or C2C. Concerning gratuitous contracts, they are under suspicion, since the lack of counter-performance implies the diminution of the creditor's assets and, therefore, the reduction of the universal patrimonial responsibility of the debtor (Article 1911 CC). The legislator protects the creditors by means of the Paulian action (Articles 1111 and 1291.3 CC) and, in Catalan law, the non-opposability of the gratuitous act (Article 531-14 CCCat).[38]

36. *See* paras 295 et seq.
37. *See* para. 137.
38. *See* para. 224.

§5. Commutative and Aleatory Contracts

42. Within the onerous contracts, a subdistinction can be drawn up between commutative and aleatory contracts. In commutative contracts, the parties know from the beginning the relationship of equivalence between the respective performances. A contract is aleatory when the extent of one party's performance depends on some uncertain events, and the other party's performance does not vary correspondingly (Article 1790 CC). A very frequent aleatory contract is the contract of insurance, regulated in Act 50/1980 of 8 October. The main consequence of the aleatory character of a contract is that its rescission on the grounds of lesion is not available (Article 321.2 CDCC).

§6. Nominate and Innominate Contracts

43. Nominate contracts are those governed by the rules of the Civil Code or other statutes. The parties may modify the legal regulation of such contracts, provided they respect the mandatory provisions. But parties are also allowed to combine elements of different contracts in order to create a new contract or even to agree on a content that differs substantially from other (nominate) contracts, within the limits of freedom of contract, especially in relation to the mandatory rules. Such innominate contracts are governed not only by the will of the parties primarily (Articles 1255 and 1258 CC), but also by the regime of similar nominate contracts by analogy, taking into account the aim of the parties. Innominate contracts appear when the legal system does not offer a proper solution for practical questions, and they are often imported from other systems (renting, franchising, etc.).

§7. Instantaneous, Long-Term and on Instalment Contracts

44. The simultaneous contract is performed in a sole act (sale). Long-term contracts presuppose that the contractual link lasts for a period of time; during this period of time, the parties fulfil their respective obligations (contract of work). Contracts are on instalment when at least one of the parties must fulfil regularly the same obligation (the payment of the rent in a lease). The most important consequence of the distinction is that the doctrine of unforeseen circumstances (hardship, clause *rebus sic stantibus*) is only applicable to long-term and on instalment contracts.[39]

39. TS 27 May 2002 (RJ 2002/4573). *See* para. 261.

Chapter 4. Contract and Tort

45. Tort law is regulated in Articles 1902 et seq. CC and in a range of statutes (product liability, nuclear damages, hunting liability, etc.). Article 1902 CC establishes a general clause of liability: everyone is responsible for the damage caused by his/her negligence. Provided that the requirements of action or omission, damage and causation are satisfied, the basis of Article 1902 is the fault principle. The rest of the rules contained in the Civil Code regulate with different criteria a variety of situations: liability for others (parents and guardians, employers, educational institutions, Articles 1903, 1904), strict liability in case of damages caused by animals (Article 1905) or noxious fumes (Article 1908.2), fault-based liability (damages caused by the ruin of a building, Article 1907). Civil liability derived from crime is governed by the Penal Code.

§1. Contract Law and Tort Law

46. The dichotomy between tort and contract is known in Spanish law, and the two fields are not always easily distinguishable. Intuitively, the purpose of tort law is the compensation of damages inflicted on another person outside any contractual relationship. But, in practice, pure contractual or tort cases are not the commonest. The doctrine and the Supreme Court have drawn up different theories in order to distinguish both fields of law, because their respective rules differ in significant aspects. Two are now the predominant theories in case law, which the Supreme Court often combines. According to the former, when the act that causes damage is at the same time a breach of contract and an infringement of the general duty not to harm another, the plaintiff can opt for actions either in contract or in tort. According to the latter, actions can be brought to court alternatively or subsidiarily in contract or in tort, being enough that the plaintiff merely presents the facts to the judge in order that the very judge decides which action is more suitable in the case *iura novit curia*.[40]

47. The differences between contractual and tort liability have been somehow attenuated by the Supreme Court's theory of 'unity of civil fault'.[41] The main differences concern the type of liability and limitation of actions.

As for the type of liability, Article 1137 CC establishes that the obligations of several debtors are separate unless otherwise provided, so that each debtor is bound to render only part of the performance and may only be required to perform that part. However, the Supreme Court has considered that this provision does not apply to obligations arising from tort. Hence, tortfeasors are always jointly liable (solidarity).[42] It has to be borne in mind that the Supreme Court is reviewing the idea of

40. TS 12 Jun. 2007 (RJ 2007/3717), 7 Nov. 2000 (RJ 2000/8678), 24 Jul. 1998 (RJ 1998/6141), 19 May 1997 (RJ 1997/3885).
41. TS 11 May 2006 (RJ 2006/3950), 24 Dec. 1999 (RJ 2000/1612), 18 Feb. 1997 (RJ 1997/1240).
42. For example, TS 8 Sep. 2007 (RJ 2007/8253), 2 Apr. 2004 (RJ 2004/1671), 27 Mar. 2004 (RJ 2004/2068).

solidarity as an exception to separate liability in the general law of obligations. Along the lines of Article 10:102 PECL, case law now says that even if solidarity has not been expressly agreed, joint liability may result from the concurrence of the following circumstances: (a) a single price in exchange for the performance; (b) a single performance despite the fact that it could be split into parts; (c) the internal relationships between the debtors/creditors are organized in the same way as if solidarity was the applicable regime; (d) the transaction has a single object – even if it is divisible – for the profit of all debtors/creditors, is contained in a single deed and constitutes a common project for all debtors/creditors.[43]

According to Article 1968.1 CC, the action in tort prescribes within one year, from the date when the victim knew of the damage, whereas the limitation period of contractual claims is fifteen years (Article 1964 CC). The fifteen-year period also applies to delictual liability derived from crime.[44]

The Supreme Court has alleviated in favour of the victim the proof of the tortfeasor's fault. In fact, burden of proof has been reversed, since once the plaintiff has proved fact or omission, damage and causation, it is the defendant who has to prove either that he/she was not negligent or the concurrence of a cause of exemption. Although the reversion of the burden of proof has not been explicitly extended to contractual liability, the Supreme Court has resorted to the principle of facility of proof in favour of the aggrieved party, so that this distinctive criterion fades.[45]

§2. Plurality of Jurisdictions

48. As it has been pointed out, tort is regulated not only in the Civil Code, but also in the statutes and in the Criminal Code (CP). Moreover, the responsibility of public bodies is regulated in the administrative legislation, and the labour courts have jurisdiction on damages derived from labour accidents. This diversity of legislation amounts to a plurality of jurisdictions, so that civil, criminal, administrative and even labour courts can decide tort cases.

According to Article 1092 CC, *civil* obligations arising from crime are governed by the Penal Code. Hence, Articles 109–122 CP still regulate compensation for the harm caused by the commission of a crime. The reason for such duplicity of regulation is merely historical: penal codification preceded civil legislation for nearly seventy years, and when the Civil Code was enacted, the legislator simply upheld the regulation in the Penal Code. Therefore, there are two different sets of norms and two jurisdictions. The bringing of the criminal action entails the bringing of the civil action in tort, unless the plaintiff reserves the action in tort in order to bring it into the civil court (Article 109 LECrim).[46] The civil court also has jurisdiction where the pronounced verdict was not guilty, since the legal qualification of the facts is not binding.

43. TS 17 Dec. 2014 (Roj: STS 5376/2014).
44. TS 31 Jan. 2004 (RJ 2004/ 444), 4 Jul. 2000 (RJ 2000/5924).
45. TS 20 Jan. 2003 (RJ 2003/50).
46. *See* the practical consequences in TS 16 Dec. 2002 (RJ 2003/199).

49. Public bodies are subjected to strict liability for the damage that 'results from the normal or abnormal operation of the public services' (Article 32 Act 40/2015, of 1 October, on Legal Regim of the Public Sector). The claim can only be brought against the administration, not against the specific civil servant who has caused the harm. The jurisdiction corresponds to the administrative courts (*see* now Article 9.4 LOPJ), although the civil law division of the Supreme Court has expressed its reluctance in many decisions, still invoking the so-called attractive force of the civil jurisdiction.[47]

50. Case law has not been uniform in relation to which courts have jurisdiction in cases of damages derived from a labour accident. The civil law division of the Supreme Court first considered that the civil jurisdiction was the competent one. Subsequently, it changed its mind and considered that it was the labour jurisdiction. However, according to recent judgments, the civil jurisdiction is the competent one when the claim is based on Articles 1902, 1903 CC and not exclusively in the non-performance of the typical obligations of the employer in relation to safety of employees.[48] The practical negative consequence of this position is the possibility of accumulation of compensations, since 'civil compensation' is not incompatible with disability allowances paid by the (public) Social Security.[49]

47. *See* a complete summary of how legislation and case law have evolved in TS 20 Feb. 2003 (RJ 2003/1179).
48. TS 31 Dec. 2003 (RJ 2004/367), which summarizes the evolution of case law, 3 Oct. 2001 (RJ 2001/7551).
49. TS 11 May 2007 (RJ 2007/3107).

Chapter 5. Contract and Quasi-Contract

51. Quasi-contracts are enumerated explicitly among the sources of obligations in Article 1089 CC, although a legal definition is not to be found until Article 1887 CC, namely the provision that begins the Title XVI (Book IV) on 'the obligations contracted without agreement'. According to this provision, quasi-contracts are those lawful and purely voluntary acts from which its author contracts an obligation to a third person and sometimes give rise to a reciprocal engagement between the interested parties. Quasi-contract is a category of historical justification, and nowadays residual, embracing a range of licit and voluntary non-contractual obligations. In fact, the obligation arises from the mere production of the facts that the law contemplates (managing another person's interests, undue payments, enrichment without cause as developed by case law).[50]

§1. *Negotiorum Gestio*

52. Article 1888 CC defines *negotiorum gestio* as the management of another's interests without any contract, namely without mandate. The legal consequence is the engagement of the manager to continue and complete the management tacit engagement that he/she undertook. The interference in another's affairs has to be spontaneous, since it would be otherwise the fulfilment of a contractual obligation.[51] *Negotiorum gestio* is now also ruled by Articles 622–30 ff CCCat.

§2. Restitution of Payments Not Due

53. The CC regulates 'undue collection', *cobro de lo indebido*, as one of the nominate quasi-contracts (Articles 1895–1901). The Code does not refer to 'undue payment', since the legislator focuses on the party contracting the obligation (the person who receives the undue payment). The obligation consists of restitution of the object delivered. The extent of the obligation of restitution depends on the *accipiens'* good or bad faith.

§3. Enrichment Without Cause

54. Unjustified enrichment in not systematically regulated in the CC. The doctrine of unjustified enrichment is in Spain a creation of nineteenth-century case law. The *Tribunal Supremo* settled, as a legal principle rooted in *Partidas* 7.34.17, the prohibition of unjust enrichment, and granted the plaintiff a *condictio sine causa*

50. *See* further Ch. 13 of Part II and Sergio Cámara Lapuente 'Quasi-contracts', in *Introduction*, ed. Van Erp & Vaquer, 195–196.

51. The law of Navarre regulates *negotiorum gestio* along with mandate (Arts 560–561 Comp. Nav.), since the category of quasi-contracts is refused. Although the systematic framework differs from the Civil Code, the legal consequences are quite similar.

generalis. However, this construction is far from convincing, because not every enrichment must be restituted, especially in a free market economy and hence, the expression 'enrichment without cause' or 'unjustified enrichment'. The *tradens* can claim restitution by means of an action of unjustified enrichment if the *accipiens* lacks a legal ground, *cause*, to retain the transferred benefit.

Chapter 6. Contract and the Law of Property

55. The CC presupposes the distinction between rights in personam and real rights in a plurality of precepts. Article 609 deals with the modes of acquisition of real rights and, as we will see later, sets out as one of them contracts followed by delivery.[52] Consequently, Article 1095 establishes that although the creditor has the right to claim the delivery of the thing with its fruits, he/she nevertheless obtains no real right on the thing until it is effectively delivered; thus, the distinction between the two types of rights becomes evident. Moreover, Article 609 CC (confirmed by Articles 1930 and 1940) lays down that only real rights may be acquired through acquisitive prescription (*usucapio*). According to Articles 605 and 606, only real rights on immovables can enter the Land Register; personal rights can be only exceptionally registered (Article 2.5 LH). Article 1280 CC requires a public deed when the object of the contract is the constitution, transmission, modification or extinction of real rights on immovables. Finally, the distinction between real and personal rights entails different periods of limitation: personal actions prescribe within fifteen years (Article 1964 CC), whereas real actions prescribe within six (movables, Article 1962) or thirty years (immovables, Article 1963 CC).

56. A real right is a power which a person exercises directly upon a thing. This power has two main features. On the one hand, the power is opposable to any other person who is not a holder of an analogous right upon the same thing (opposability *erga omnes*).[53] On the other hand, the holder has the right of pursuit and may claim his/her property from anyone. Still a third feature can be added to the former two that have already been pointed out: the priority. Priority is a consequence of the absoluteness of the real right: the holder of the real right is preferred to everybody else (*prior tempore potior ius*). But priority is also a criterion to order identical real rights that can coexist upon the same thing, for example, a plurality of mortgages upon the same immovable.

By contrast, the personal right permits the holder to claim a certain performance from a sole person, the debtor. The debtor is the only person bound to perform, although everyone has to respect the right of the creditor; the interference of any third person may lead to tortious liability.[54] Besides, there is no equivalent to the right of pursuit.

57. Much disputed has been the question of whether real rights are a *numerus clausus*. On the one hand, some authors point out that when Article 2.2 LH enumerates the rights that can be recorded in the Land Register, it ends with the expression 'and any other real right'. Other authors consider that only the law can create new real rights (timesharing could be an example, as regulated in Act 42/1998 of 15 December). The discussion is however merely theoretical. The borderline between the power to create new real rights or only to shape the existing real rights without

52. *See* paras 61 et seq.
53. TS 3 Mar. 1995 (RJ 1995/1776).
54. *See* Ángela Fernández de Arévalo, *La lesión extracontractualdel crédito* (Valencia, 1996); Máximo Juan Pérez García, *La protección aquilianadel derecho de crédito* (Madrid, 2005).

creating a new one is really difficult to outline. Therefore, the essential point is the parties' intention to create a right characterized by its opposability *erga omnes* and which main feature is the immediate power over a thing.

58. Scholars have devoted big efforts to sketch intermediate situations between real and personal rights. The only one generally admitted is the obligation *propter rem.*[55] It is an obligation imposed on the holder of a real right precisely because he/she is the holder so that whoever is the holder of the real right assumes the obligation (lien). For example, new owners assume responsibility for any existing debts the former owners may have with the association for the payment of common expenses from the previous year and the current year. The apartment or business premises will be legally encumbered to meet this obligation.[56] Hence, an obligation *propter rem* arises.

59. On the basis of their content, real rights are divided into ownership and limited real rights. Ownership is the real right *par excellence*, since it confers the holder the maximum power upon a thing. Limited real rights presuppose the existence of ownership. Limited real rights confer on its holder only a partial power upon the thing belonging to another, thus limiting the right of ownership of the latter.

Limited real rights may be classified in rights of enjoyment, rights of guarantee and rights of acquisition. Real rights of enjoyment allow the holder to use and to obtain the profits of the thing. They are usufruct, usage, habitation, servitude and emphyteusis. Real rights of guarantee are intended to guarantee the fulfilment of an obligation, so that the holder is entitled to enforce directly the charged property to be repaid. Real rights of guarantee may be constituted over movables (pledge, right of retention) or immovables (mortgage, non-shifting pledge, antichresis). Real rights of acquisition give the holder the faculty to obtain the ownership of the property charged with such rights. They are option,[57] pre-emption (*tanteo*) and redemption (*retracto*).[58]

§1. No Distinction Between Legal and Equitable Ownership

60. In Spanish law there is no distinction between legal and equitable ownership. Ownership is a unitary right. Only empytheusis entails a separation of 'direct ownership' (*dominio directo*), and 'useful ownership' (*emphyteutic holder, dominio útil*),[59] which goes back to medieval *ius commune.* Useful ownership consists in the use and collection of the profits of the piece of land. Moreover, the useful owner may sell his/her interest in the land. The direct owner is entitled to a fixed sum, ground rent, *pensión.* He/she can demand recognition of his/her direct ownership

55. TS 28 Jun. 2004 (RJ 2004/4277), 5 Feb. 2004 (RJ 2004/216), 4 Jun. 2001 (RJ 2001/6663).
56. Article 9.1.e LPH.
57. Which nevertheless can also have only a personal character depending on the parties' will.
58. *See* Esteve Bosch Capdevila, *Opción, tanteo y retracto* (Madrid-Barcelona, 2004).
59. Articles 1628 et seq. CC.

and in case of the useful owner's interest being transferred to another, 2% of the price unless otherwise agreed is payable to the direct owner.[60]

§2. TRANSFER OF OWNERSHIP

61. Article 609 CC tries to enumerate the modes of acquisition of property and other real rights.[61] Although this enumeration has arguably deserved much criticism, some ideas emerge from this basic provision. The first idea is the existence of a mode of acquisition exclusive to the right of ownership: occupation.[62] The second mentioned mode of acquisition and transfer of real rights is the law. Acquisition and transfer by operation of the law covers a variety of situations, such as legal servitudes, legal mortgages or the acquisition derived from marriage property. The third mode is donation, although still an important number of authors consider that donation is in Spanish law a contract. The fourth mode is succession. The fifth mode, to which more attention is devoted here, is contract followed by tradition. Lastly, prescription is also mentioned.

This enumeration permits the classification of modes of acquisition of property and real rights into original and derivative modes. Original modes do not require the intervention and the consent of the former owner (occupation). Instead, derivative modes imply the acquisition from the former owner.

62. Article 609 CC – as well as the aforementioned Article 1095.II CC[63] – lays down the general rule according to which property and real rights are transferred when certain contracts are followed by *traditio*. Therefore, Spanish law has adopted the system of title (contract) *plus* mode (delivery).[64] In a sale, the contract only gives rise to a right of credit against the debtor. The vendor is obliged to deliver the purchased thing. When the vendor delivers the thing on the basis of the contract, the purchaser acquires the ownership of the thing. Hence, the Spanish system of transferring real rights is a causal one. The two requirements for transfer of property are consent and cause. Cause is provided by the contract. Consent refers not only to the contract but also to the delivery of the thing. Nevertheless, title plus mode is inappropriate when the right transferred has no possessory content,[65] for example, a negative servitude. In that case, a contract suffices to transfer the right,

60. The division of ownership has been abolished in Catalan law (*see* Act 6/1990 of 16 March).
61. *See* Tomás Rubio Garrido, 'Acquisition of Property', in *Introduction*, ed. Van Erp & Vaquer, 269 et seq.
62. Occupation may be defined as the material appropriation of a movable asset without owner.
63. *See also* para. 55.
64. TS 11 Feb. 2003 (RJ 2003/1004), 1 Dec. 1999 (RJ 1999/8529). The modalities of tradition are regulated in Arts 1462–1464 CC. Real tradition implies the transfer of the power upon a thing handing it over if it is movable or occupying it if it is immovable. Symbolic tradition takes place with the delivery of a symbol that represents the thing (e.g., the keys in the acquisition of an apartment). Consensual tradition admits two modalities: *traditio brevi manu* (the purchaser was already possessing the thing: the purchaser is the lessee) and *constitutum possessorium* (the seller keeps the possession of the thing: he/she becomes lessee of the thing sold). Finally, tradition may be instrumental: a public deed implies delivery of the thing unless otherwise provided.
65. TS 10 Jun. 1997 (RJ 1997/5464).

since delivery cannot take place. The same system applies in the civil law of Catalonia according to Article 531-1 and 531-3 CCCat.

63. The description of the Spanish system of passing of property would be incomplete without mentioning Article 1901 CC. According to the last passage of this provision, the *accipiens* assumes no obligation of restitution of the delivered thing to the *solvens* when he/she can prove that delivery took place because of liberality or *another fair cause*. If no obligation of restitution arises, the *accipiens* becomes the owner, although he/she was not engaged to pay (there was no contract). Thus, Article 1901 CC completes Article 609 CC, since the latter only envisages one of the causes of the delivery, namely the contract, and the former adds two more causes. First, *causa donandi* (the desire of liberality of the *solvens*). Second, *any other fair cause*, an expression that entails *causa solvendi* (e.g., restitution after a void contract) and *causa credendi*.

64. Registration of the transfer in the Land Register is not a part of the process of acquisition or transfer of real rights. Transfer of rights is completed when delivery follows the contract. The legal consequences attached to registration are the presumption of possession in favour of the registered proprietor (Article 38 LH) and the protection against non-registered incompatible rights, which cannot be set up against the registered proprietor (Article 32 LH). Nevertheless, registration does not validate void titles (Article 33 LH). Therefore, the protection given by the Land Register requires a valid title. Registration is purely voluntary, except for the constitution of mortgages.[66]

Nevertheless, Article 34 LH protects whoever has relied on the publicity of the register. The registered acquisition (only) by onerous title made by a third person in good faith from another person that, according to the register, could legally transfer the property is incontestable. Good faith means here that the purchaser was unaware of the inaccuracy of the Land Register, and relates to ownership and power of disposition of the person who transfers the right. The acquirer must register his/her own acquisition in order to be protected.

Exceptionally, registration can decide who the purchaser is when a plurality of persons has the title but transfer has not been completed. Article 1473 CC establishes that, in the case of the sale of the same immovable to two or more persons, the proprietor is the first purchaser that registers the acquisition.

In relation to movables, Article 464 CC sets out the ancient rule *possession vaut titre* (in Catalonia, Article 521-8 CCCat). Good faith is also required, and the provision does not apply to lost things and to those things that the owner has been deprived of.

---

66. Registration of the contract of timesharing (the public deed) is also compulsory, according to Art. 4.3 Act 42/1998 of 15 November, on timesharing. *See* on the Spanish Land Register Pedro del Pozo Carrascosa 'Land Register', in *Introduction*, ed. Van Erp & Vaquer, 329 et seq.

Chapter 7. Contract and Trust

65. Spain neither includes the trust in its domestic law nor has adhered to the Hague Trust Convention. Anglo-American trust is alien to Spanish law, although in recent times some authors have pleaded for its admission and regulation.[67] Nevertheless, it is possible to find trust-like devices which fulfil similar functions to some kinds of Anglo-American trusts.[68] Some of those trust-like devices have legal support and have generalized banking practices, namely investment funds.[69] Others belong to succession law, and have played a relevant role in some regional laws, like the fideicommissary substitution *fideicommissum*.[70] But, in the framework of contract, *fiducia* deserves special attention.

66. Case law has accepted *fiducia* as a sufficient cause in order to safeguard the validity of contracts. The gist of fiduciary transactions is that the owner transfers ownership to the fiduciary, who undertakes to use the ownership in only a particular way and subsequently to retransfer it back to the original owner or to transfer it to a third party.[71] The uses of the ownership may be in favour of the owner or in favour of the fiduciary. The former cases are gathered under the label *fiducia cum amico*, the latter ones under the label *fiducia cum creditore*.

The main feature of *fiducia cum amico* is the formal transfer of ownership to the fiduciary, who undertakes to possess the property in favour of the real owner. The aim of the owner is not necessarily unlawful.[72] The fiduciary is only the apparent proprietor and is not entitled to withhold the property. A fiduciary transaction is valid if it does not imply a circumvention of the law, and even in this latter case it is valid *inter partes*.[73] Case law also requires a convincing evidence of the fiduciary cause to uphold the claim.[74]

Fiducia cum creditore occurs when the debtor formally transfers ownership to the creditor in order to merely guarantee the performance of the undertaken obligation

67. Act 41/2003 of 18 November, regulates for the first time the *protected patrimony of disabled persons*. Although at first sight, one is reminded of trust (the term beneficiary, e.g., is used), it is not a trust-like device, since the owner of the patrimony is the same disabled person (as well as one of the persons that can constitute it). It is a separate patrimony subject to specific rules, in particular related to tax law, but not trust.
68. Sergio Cámara Lapuente, 'Trusts in Spanish Law', in *Lafiducie face au trustdans les rapportsd'affaires – Trust v.Fiducie in a Business Context*, ed. M. Cantin Cumyn (Bruxelles, 1999), 199 et seq., and the Spanish notes in M. Graziadei, U. Mattei & L. Smith (ed.), *Commercial Trusts in European Private Law* (Cambridge, 2005), by C. González Beilfuss & S. Cámara Lapuente.
69. *See* Act 35/2003, of 4 November, on collective investment entities, Royal Decree 362/2007, of 16 March, which modifies, Royal Decree 1309/2005, of 4 November.
70. The so-called heirs of confidence are regulated in Catalan law (Arts 424-11 et seq. Civil Code). The heirs of confidence undertake to allocate the estate according to the confidential instructions given by the testator.
71. TS 28 Nov. 2002 (RJ 2002/10283), quoting previous decisions.
72. For example, in TS 16 Jul. 2001 (RJ 2001/5226), the political party EAJ/PNV claimed restitution of an immovable transferred to a real estate agency in order to avoid its confiscation by the fascist government during the Spanish Civil War.
73. TS 28 Mar. 2012 (Roj: STS 1926/2012).
74. *See*, in addition to the judgment quoted in the previous footnote, TS 7 Jun. 2000 (RJ 2002/4875), 7 May 2007 (RJ 2007/3559).

(normally to pay the money back). The creditor only becomes an apparent proprietor of the transferred assets; consequently he/she is not entitled to withhold the property when the real owner asks for restitution.[75] Moreover, the so-called prohibition of *lex comissoria* applies to fiduciary transactions.[76]

The fiduciary may abuse his/her powers as apparent proprietor. Third parties will only be protected if they acquire property by virtue of an onerous contract and act in good faith (i.e., without knowledge of the fiduciary agreement). This is the risk that the real owner assumes when entering into a fiduciary transaction.

75. TS 26 Jul. 2004 (RJ 2004/6633), 1 Feb. 2002 (RJ 2002/1586), 17 Jul. 2001 (RJ 2001/6860).
76. TS 26 Apr. 2001 (RJ 2001/2037).

Chapter 8. Good Faith and Fair Dealing

67. The principle of good faith has steadily increased its practical importance since its incorporation into the Preliminary Title of the Civil Code in 1974 (Article 7.1; also Article 111-7 CC Cat). This provision establishes that rights must be exercised in accordance with the requirements of good faith. The legislator uses a general clause, which has permitted the case law to develop the principle in a similar way to – and sometimes also inspired in – German jurisprudence on the basis of §242 BGB. The principle of good faith governs the whole legal system and can be applied *ex officium* by the courts. In this context, good faith is taken in its objective sense, meaning a behavioural norm imposed on the contractual parties. It must be borne in mind that the Civil Code also refers to good faith in a subjective sense (i.e., a psychological state of mind). For example, the ignorance of the formal defects of the celebration of marriage does not amount to nullity if one of the spouses expressed consent in good faith (Articles 53 and 78 CC).

68. The principle of good faith fulfils a threefold function. It complements the legal system imposing ancillary duties and behavioural norms on the parties. A good example is to be found in Article 1258 CC, according to which contracts oblige also to all their consequences conforming with good faith. A second function consists in the limitation of subjective rights. Moreover, the principle of good faith has a corrective function, since it gives rise to the judicial formulation of certain behavioural standards. Therefore, it is possible to typify certain manifestations of the principle of good faith.

69. *Venire contra factum proprium* is one of the concretions of the principle of good faith earlier admitted by the Supreme Court and now codified in Article 111-8 of the Catalan Civil Code. A party must refrain from any incoherent behaviour in prejudice of the reliance of the other party on the maintenance of the previous behaviour. Such own facts have to be unequivocal, in the sense of having created, modified, settled down or construed a situation that concerns its author. The posterior behaviour has to contradict the party's previous behaviour and frustrate the other party's expectation.[77] For example, if one party carries out preliminary acts to prepare performance and afterwards pretends the contract was not concluded.[78]

70. The German doctrine of *Verwirkung* – disloyal delay in the exercise of rights, in Spanish wording – has been imported into Spanish case law and doctrine. The first decision of the Supreme Court applying the *Verwirkung's* doctrine was handed down on 21 May 1982,[79] and the first one that verbatim used the German term on 24 June 1996. The four factors necessary to *Verwirkung* that can be deduced from doctrine and jurisprudence are: the lapse of a significant period of time, the

77. TS 14 Dec. 2007 (RJ 2008/330), 31 Mar. 2003 (RJ 2003/1892), 30 Dec. 2002 (RJ 2003/334) quoting many previous judgments.
78. TS 31 Jan. 2003 (RJ 2003/1450).
79. RJ 1982/2588. Since then *Verwrkung* has been constantly applied; *see*, for example, TS 19 Sep 2013 (Roj: STS 4673/2013), 12 Dec. 2011 (Roj: STS 8594/2011).

plaintiff's passivity in using his/her own right or action, the reasonable assumption that the claim will not be prosecuted, and the damage caused by this delayed claim. It should be borne in mind that the circumstances of each case must be considered in relation to the four factors together.[80]

71. Article 7 CC in its second paragraph bans the abuse of rights. The abuse of rights is a creation of the Supreme Court incorporated in the Preliminary Title in 1974. The requirements for the abuse of rights in case law are the exercise of a right in an apparently legal manner, the damage to an interest without specific protection, and the immorality of such damage.[81] Lately case law seems to be more restrictive, and refers to caprice, the intention to damage or the abnormality of the right's exercise as features of the doctrine of abuse of rights.[82]

80. *See* below para. 343.
81. TS 14 Feb. 1944 (RJ 1944/293), quoted by more recent ones like TS 25 Sep. 1996 (RJ 1996/6641) or 20 Feb. 1997 (RJ 1997/1244).
82. TS 24 May 2007 (RJ 2007/3438), 6 Feb. 2003 (RJ 2003/1153), 10 Dec. 2002 (RJ 2003/121).

Chapter 9. Style of Drafting

72. The CC is more a practical body of law than a dogmatic one. It is written in plain Spanish, because it was drafted by practitioners and not by professors. In fact, the drafters were aware of their scientific limitations and preferred to copy the provisions of other codes (other than the French Civil Code, it is especially remarkable the use made of the Belgian draft by Laurent). The Code is far from the technical precision of its German counterpart. It is not difficult to find contradictions between legal provisions, because of their different source of inspiration (Articles 623 and 629 on donation, Articles 759 and 799 on the institution of heir upon condition). This simplicity, however, allowed the Civil Code to survive without relevant amendments until 1981. From 1981 onwards, reforms of the Civil Code have followed one another, at the beginning for the sake of adaptation to the new constitutional framework (the democratic Constitution of 1978) and then to modernize some institutions and regulate new ones. New provisions have not reached the literary quality of the old ones: they are more prolix and detailed, and they have not managed to remove expressions more suitable to the nineteenth century. Thus, the 'servant' is still alive, and the 'master' is believed when he/she states the salary of the 'servant' (Article 1584 CC); the son has to return to the mass (collation) the sum paid by his 'father' to avoid the military service, even though the military service is nowadays not compulsory (Article 1043 CC).

Chapter 10. Sources of the Law of Contracts

§1. Areas of Spanish Private Law, Main Codes and Enactments

73. Spanish law can be divided for academic purposes into public and private law. The borderline between these two main areas of the law is not easy to draw, especially if one takes into account, on the one hand, the process of intervention of the administrative bodies in the market economy, and on the other hand, the recent process of privatization as a consequence of the crisis of the welfare state. It is even discussed whether certain areas belong to private or to public law, for example, labour law. The outline that follows mentions the codes and principal enactments and enumerates a basic bibliography. However, it has to be borne in mind that the Constitution also has an important influence on contracts.[83]

74. Positive private law includes the following:

1. The Civil Code and related statutes. Among these statutes, the following are worth mentioning:
   a. The *Ley Hipotecaria*,[84] that is, the Act on Land Register and mortgages. It is a fundamental long Act (329 Articles) with its own developing regulation (*Reglamento Hipotecario*). The Act was passed in 1946 and has since been amended several times.
   b. The Urban Lease Act (Act 29/1994 of 24 November, *de arrendamientos urbanos*) and the Horizontal Property Act (Act 49/1960 of 21 July).[85] Both texts, however, have been amended several times.
   c. The Sale on Instalments Act (Act 28/1998 of 13 July).[86]
2. Commercial law:[87]
   a. The CCom.
   b. The Insurance Contract Act (Act 50/1980 of 8 October).

---

83. Some authors have even debated the applicability of the German doctrine of *Drittwirkung* in Spanish law. *See* Jesús Alfaro Águila-Real, 'Autonomía y derechos fundamentales', ADC (1993): 57; Ingo von Münch, Josep Ferrer i Riba & Pablo Salvador Coderch, *Asociaciones, derechos fundamentales y autonomía privada* (Madrid, 1997).

84. Ramón M. Roca Sastre, Luis Roca-Sastre Muncunill & J. Bernà i Xirgo, *Derecho hipotecario*, 9th edn (Barcelona, 2008); José M. García, *Derecho inmobiliario registral o hipotecario* (Madrid, 1988–1999); Francisco Gómez Gálligo & Pedro del Pozo Carrascosa, *Lecciones de derecho hipotecario*, 2nd edn (Madrid-Barcelona, 2006); Pedro del Pozo Carrascosa, 'Land Register', in *Introduction*, ed. Van Erp & Vaquer, 329 et seq.

85. Rodrigo Bercovitz (ed.), *Comentarios a la Ley de arrendamientos urbanos*, 4th edn (Cizur Menor, 2005); Fernando Pantaleón (ed.), *Comentario a la Ley de arrendamientos urbanos* (Madrid, 1995); Vicente Guilarte Gutiérrez (dir.), *La nueva ley de arrendamientos urbanos* (Valladolid, 1994); Manuel Cuadrado Iglesias (ed.), *Comentarios a la ley de reforma de la propiedad horizontal* (Madrid, 2000); José María Miquel (dir.), *Comentarios a la Ley de propiedad horizontal* (Madrid, 2011).

86. Fernando García Solé, *Comentarios a la ley de venta a plazos de bienes muebles* (Madrid, 1999); Francisco Blasco Gascó, *Las ventas a plazos de bienes muebles* (Valencia, 2000).

87. Rodrigo Uría, *Derecho mercantil* (Madrid-Barcelona, 2001); Franscisco Vicent Chuliá, *Introducción al derecho mercantil*, 22nd edn (Valencia, 2009); Guillermo Jiménez Sánchez (ed.), *Derecho mercantil* (Madrid, 2010).

   c. The legislation on mercantile legal persons (Royal Legislative Decree 1/2010, of 10 July, on *sociedades de capital,* modified by Act 31/2014, of 3 December).
   d. The legislation on bill of exchange and cheque (Act 19/1985 of 16 July).
   e. The Insolvency Act (Act 22/2003 of 9 July), amended ultimately by Royal Decree-*Ley* 11/2014, of 5 September.
   f. Patent and copyright law (Act 11/1986 of 20 March, on patents; Act 17/2001 of 7 December, on trademarks; Royal Legislative Decree 1/1996 of 12 April, on intellectual property, last amendment by Act 21/2014, of 4 November).
3. Consumer law, which covers general legislation, namely the General Act on the protection of consumers (Royal Legislative Decree 1/2007 of 16 November[88] amended by Act 3/2014, of 27 March), as well as statutes, such as the Act on consumer credit (Act 16/2011, of 24 June).
4. Civil procedure (Act 1/2000 of 7 January),[89] thoroughly amended by Organic Act 1/2009, of 3 November, and Act 13/2009, of 3 November and with other minor reforms.
5. International private law.[90]
6. European private law.[91]

§2. Finding the Law

I. Legislation

75. Legislation (acts, legislative decrees, royal decrees, ministerial orders) and international treaties are published in an official daily publication, the *Boletín Oficial del Estado*. They are cited as follows: Act 1/2000 of 7 January (number of the Act/year, date when the law was passed). Codes and statutes are drafted in articles (referred to as Article). The legislation enacted by the Autonomous Communities is also published in the respective official publication as well as in the *BOE*.

---

88. Rodrigo Bercovitz (dir.), *Comentario al Texto Refundido de la Ley General para la Defensa de los Consumidores y Usuarios* (Cizur Menor, 2009); Sergio Cámara Lapuente (dir.), *Comentarios a las normas de protección de consumidores* (Madrid, 2011); Manuel Rebollo Puig & Manuel Izquierdo Carrasco (dir.), *La defensa de los consumidores y usuarios* (Madrid, 2011).
89. Valentín Cortés Domínguez, Vicente Gimeno Sendra & Víctor Moreno Catena, *Derecho procesal civil*, 4th edn (Valencia, 2010); Juan Montero Aroca et al., *Derecho jurisdiccional* (Valencia, 2007); Miguel-Angel Fernández Ballesteros, José M. Rifá Soler & José F. Valls Gombau, *Comentarios a la nueva ley de enjuiciamiento civil* (Barcelona, 2000–2001).
90. José Carlos Fernández Rozas & Sixto Sánchez Lorenzo, *Derecho internacional privado*, 5th edn (Madrid, 2009); Alfonso Calvo Caravaca & Javier Carrascosa González, *Derecho internacional privado*, 10th edn (Granada, 2011); M.D. Díaz-Ambrona, *Derecho civil comunitario*, 2nd edn (Madrid, 2004).
91. Sergio Cámara Lapuente (ed.), *Derecho privado europeo* (Madrid, 2003); Santiago Espiau & Antoni Vaquer Aloy (eds), *Bases de un derecho contractual europro/Bases of a European Contract Law* (Valencia, 2004); Antoni Vaquer (ed.), *European Private Law beyond the CFR* (Groningen, 2008).

76. Many publishers offer collections of legislation containing the main codes or covering an area of the law. There are also four computerized databases: *Westlaw Aranzadi*, *El Derecho*, *La Ley-Actualidad Civil* and *Tirant on line*. The CC has been translated into English[92] and German.[93] Another translation supported by the Spanish Ministry of Justice is available on the internet. Catalan legislation on private law is available too.

II. Case Law

77. There are also three computerized databases available: *Westlaw Aranzadi*, *El Derecho* and *La Ley-Actualidad Civil*. The three offer a wide selection of decisions, *Westlaw Aranzadi* (References: RJ, AC, JUR, depending on the court), being perhaps, the most comprehensive.[94] There is also an official edition of the decisions of the Supreme Court, although it is published with some delay (*Jurisprudencia del Tribunal Supremo*, which continues the *Colección Legislativa de España*). Case law of the Supreme Court is also available on the internet: http://www.poderjudicial.es/tribunalsupremo (Reference: Roj).

Case law is also summarized in some of the reviews devoted to private law *Anuario de Derecho Civil* (ADC), *Actualidad Civil* (AC), *Revista Crítica de Derecho Inmobiliario* (RCDI). *Cuadernos Civitas de Jurisprudencia Civil* (CCJC) is a periodical exclusively devoted to the comments on relevant decisions. The *Revista de Derecho Patrimonial* comments case law dealing with patrimonial law.

78. Cases are cited giving the name of the court and the date of the decision; normally the reference to the relevant periodical or database is attached. Names of parties are not used to identify court decisions; in fact in most publications and databases, the names of the parties are deleted or substituted in order to protect privacy.

III. Books and Encyclopaedias

79. There are two encyclopaedias: *Enciclopedia Juridica Seix* (different dates of publication) and *Enciclopedia Jurídica Básica Civitas* (Madrid, 1995).

Books are cited as follows: Antoni Vaquer, *El ofrecimiento de pago en el Código civil*, Madrid, 1997, page number. Periodicals are cited by year, abbreviated title (*see* the List of Abbreviations) and page number, for example, (2002) *ADC* 35. This means page 35 of the *ADC* for 2002.

---

92. Clifford Stevens Walton, *The Civil Law in Spain and Spanish-America: Including Cuba, Puerto Rico, and Philippine Islands, and the Spanish Civil Code in Force, Annotated and With References to the Civil Codes of Mexico* (Washington D.C., 1900; reprint, 2003).

93. Witold Peuster, *Dasspanische Zivilgesetzbuch.Codigo Civil* (Frankurt am Main, 2002); Wolfgang Sohst, *Dasspanische Einkommensteuergesetz mit Durchführungsverordnung.Zweisprachige Ausgabe dervollständigen Gesetzestexte* (Berlin, 2003).

94. Citation of case law will refer in this book, unless otherwise provided, to *Aranzadi* (Westlaw) databases (RJ Supreme Courts and High Courts of Justice; JUR: Courts of Appeal) and the *Poder Judicial* website.

Part I. General Principles of the Law of Contract

Chapter 1. Formation

§1. Agreement and Quid Pro Quo (Reciprocity)

I. Offer and Acceptance

80. Any agreement into which the parties have freely entered is a binding contract. According to Spanish legislation and under the principles of freedom of form (Article 1278 CC) and freedom of will (Article 1255 CC), the contract exists from the very moment when the parties reach an agreement (Articles 1254 and 1258 CC) with regard to the object and the cause (Article 1261 CC).[95] An offer is not a contract; the contract is concluded solely when the offer is accepted.

A. *The Offer*

81. An offer is a proposal that one party submits to the other, intending the latter either to accept it or to make a counter-offer. Therefore, the offer is binding upon receipt, and it must be sufficiently precise and complete so that assent to the offer concludes the contract.[96] Hence, it must include the object, the quantity and the price or, at least, subsequent determination without a new agreement must be possible. It must contain the offeror's intention to become bound; otherwise, rather than an offer, we would be dealing with an invitation to enter into negotiations.[97]

An offer does not always need to be addressed to one or more specific persons: it may also be made to the general public.[98] The offer made to the public is a unilateral act that is binding upon its author solely from the time when acceptance has been dispatched. Nonetheless, this offer must contain all the requirements of the contract to be concluded.

95. *See* TS 14 2 Nov. 2009 (RJ 2009\7276), February 2008 (RJ 2008/1213), 14 Nov. 2003 (RJ 2003/8313).
96. *See* TS 31 May 2006 (RJ 2006/3503), 17 Nov. 2003 (RJ 2003/8322).
97. TS 20 Jan. 2009 (RJ 2009\1278).
98. For example, Art. 9.1 Act 7/1996, on retail trade.

82. The offer is not subject to any formal requirement, as a general rule.[99] However, Article 111 new LGDCU on contracts concluded away from business premises and Article 152 new LGDCU on package travel requires the offer to be made in writing, in duplicate and to be accompanied by a document enabling the consumer to exercise the right to revoke his/her acceptance. According to Article 61 new LGDCU, and taking into account the principle of good faith (Article 7.1 CC),[100] all publicity made by the offeror becomes part of the contract.

83. The offeror must keep his/her offer open for the period indicated in the offer, although Spanish authors consider that this fact does not necessarily imply that the offer is irrevocable. If there is no period indicated, the offer must be kept for such period as necessary, according to good faith, to enable the offeree to consider it. If a period of irrevocability has been expressly established, the offer is not revocable until this period of time has elapsed. Otherwise, pre-contractual liability is incurred. With the passing of time, the offer will lapse.

The offer also lapses when the offeree rejects it and when the offeror revokes it. An offer may be withdrawn if the withdrawal reaches the offeree before he/she has accepted. In case of an offer made to the general public, withdrawal requires the same publicity. The offer lapses in the case of death or incapacity of the offeror or of the offeree, unless the offer was irrevocable or made by business people in the company's normal trading,[101] in which case it binds the offeror's heirs.

B. Damage in the Case of Revocation of an Offer

84. Revocation of an offer before the period of irrevocability has elapsed and any form of revocation contrary to good faith turns into liability. This is a sort of pre-contractual liability, which is dealt with later on.[102]

C. The Acceptance

85. A contract comes into being with the acceptance of an offer. It is also a declaration of consent binding upon receipt (Article 1262 CC), which means that it may be revoked before it reaches the offeror. It must include the intention to be bound,[103] and it must be dispatched while the offer is still in force. As a general rule, acceptance needs no formal requirements either, but it needs to be conclusive and definitive.[104] Silence itself does not imply a declaration of consent and, therefore,

99. For example, TS 2 Nov. 2009 (RJ 2009\7276) qualifies as a definitive offer an email.
100. *See*, for example, TS 23 May 2003 (RJ 2003/5215), construction of three tennis courts in a housing estate.
101. TS 23 Mar. 1988 (RJ 1988/2422).
102. *See* below paras 112 and 113.
103. TS 15 Jun. 1994 (RJ 1994/4923) speaks of 'acceptance "*cumanimo contrahendo*"'.
104. TS 24 Jul. 2006 (2006\5592).

does not amount to acceptance. Nevertheless, some circumstances accompanying the silence may indicate the existence of acceptance.[105]

The acceptance must tally with the offer, without addition, limitations or other essential modifications to it (*mirror image rule*); in the event of discrepancy, the contract will not be concluded, but rather there will be a counter-offer.[106] However, case law has tended to favour the conclusion of contractual agreements, despite the existence of discrepancies, based on the so-called principle of *favor negotii*, provided there is agreement as to the essential terms.[107] Therefore, a contract may be concluded even if some complementary aspects need further completion on the basis of usages, commercial practices or good faith, according to the Supreme Court in the decision of 1 July 2010.[108]

D. Contracts by Correspondence

86. The conclusion of a contract *inter absentes* creates some specific problems, in particular as to the place and time of its completion. Article 1262 CC establishes that the contract comes into being as soon as the offeror knows of the acceptance or he/she cannot ignore it without breach of the principle of good faith. The contract is then presumed to have been concluded in the place where the offer was made. Article 1262 CC adds that if the contract is concluded by means of automatic devices, completion occurs with acceptance. It has to be borne in mind that in the distant sale, the consumer may withdraw *ad nutum* from the contract within a week after the delivery (Article 44 Act on retail trade).

II. Intention to Create Legal Relations

87. An agreement is not binding as a contract if made without any serious intention to create legal relationships. The burden of proof on the lack of such intention is on the party who asserts that no legal effect is intended. However, frequently the effectiveness of certain agreements is disputed, and whether the parties had the intention to be legally bound or not is a question of construction. Nevertheless, case law seems quite reluctant to accept convincing proof of the existence of gentlemen's agreements or letters of intention.[109]

III. Consideration

88. The English concept of consideration is alien to Spanish law. On the concept of cause, *see* below paragraphs 139 et seq.

105. TS 13 Nov. 2013 (Roj: STS 5471/2013), 4 Dec. 2007 (RJ 2007/8663), 20 Jun. 2003 (RJ 2003/4248), 21 Mar. 2003 (RJ 2003/2762).
106. TS 20 Apr. 2001 (RJ 2001/5282), 26 Jun. 1997 (RJ 1997/5395).
107. TS 30 Sep. 1995 (RJ 1995/8352).
108. RJ 2010\5696.
109. Case law requires the letters to be concrete, clear and unequivocal in relation to the obligatory content. *See* TS 14 Oct. 2014 (Roj: STS 4433/2014), 18 Mar. 2009 (Roj: STS 1257/2009).

89. A *natural obligation* is a moral obligation to which legal consequences are attached. The obligation results from a conscience duty on the part of the person obligated toward the person to whom he/she is obligated. The concept of natural obligation is not to be found in the CC. Nevertheless, case law refers to it, usually in cases of concubines or relatives of unmarried partners.[110] The party may not claim performance of the natural obligation, but he/she cannot be claimed for restitution of the money paid.

§2. Formal and Evidential Requirements

I. Formal Requirements

A. Contracts under Seal

90. 'Contracts under seal', where a person undertakes an obligation by expressing his/her intentions on paper or parchment, attaching his/her seal and delivering it 'as his/her deed', are unknown in Spanish law.

B. Solemn Contracts

91. It was seen earlier that the conclusion of a contract may exceptionally require a formality.[111] We speak then of solemn contracts, as opposed to consensual contracts. The form is necessary for validity. The formal requirement usually consists of a notarial act. Nevertheless, form may serve other purposes. For example, form sometimes makes the contract opposable to third parties. In other cases, form is only evidential.

The liberal tendency towards contractual informality is reflected in Article 1278 CC, according to which 'contracts are obligatory irrespective of the form in which they have been concluded'. This provision shows two aspects of the principle of freedom of form. On the one hand, freedom to enter into obligations, since the legal effects of contracts do not depend on its form. On the other hand, freedom of the contractual form, because form is not a general requirement for the validity of contracts, unlike consent, object and *cause* (Article 1261 CC). Exceptionally, some contracts are solemn, because form becomes part of the transaction structure. The violation of formal requirements makes the contract void. Such contracts are emphytheusis (Article 1628 CC), the contract of partnership when the partners contribute immovables or real rights (Article 1667 CC) and mortgages (Articles 1875 CC, 145 LH). Donation of immovable property also requires a public deed (Article

110. In the old case TS 17 Oct. 1932, a man seduced a young maid and some children were born out of this; the relationship broke, and the man promised to maintain her; the Supreme Court decided in favour of the woman. In the decision of the Court of Appeal of Segovia handed down on 31 Dec. 2002 (JUR 2003/37876), a man claimed the education expenses of his former partner's brother, stating that it was a loan, but the Court considered it the payment of a natural obligation.

111. *See also* para. 80.

633 CC).[112] The formal requirements are due to the real consequences of those contracts, that is, the acquisition or the transmission of property or a limited real right. It goes without saying that the parties may impose upon themselves formal requirements in accordance with the principle of freedom of contract (Article 1255 CC).

By contrast, informality is not a general principle outside the general law of contracts. Most of the declarations and transactions of family and succession law are formal. Thus, marriage agreements (Article 1327 CC; in Catalan law, Articles 231-19 et seq. CCCat), declarations in the process of adoption (Article 177 CC; in Catalan law, Articles 235-40, 235-41 CCCat) or wills (Articles 667 et seq., 687 et seq. CC; in Catalan law, Articles 421-1 et seq. CCCat) are formal.[113] Also statutes dealing with consumer law frequently lay down formal requirements.[114]

92. It is also necessary to distinguish between form and document. The document is a means of representing the transaction and, therefore, a consequence of form. The document incorporates the idea of materiality. Hence, once the formal requirements are complied with, the transaction is valid irrespective of the subsistence of the document. If the document disappears, the problem then is only evidential: how to prove the conclusion of the contract.[115]

1. Different Kinds of Formal Requirements

93. There are two main kinds of form: *forma ad substantiam* or *ad solemnitatem* and *forma ad probationem*. Form *ad substantiam* is a requirement for the validity of the transaction, while form *ad probationem* implies that the transaction can only be proved by means of the established form. Article 1280 CC enumerates some transactions that 'must be recorded in a public deed'. One could think that the law lays down a series of solemn contracts. Nevertheless, Article 1279 sets out that 'whenever the law requires a public deed in order to make effective the obligations arising from a contract, the parties may compel reciprocally to comply with the form once consent and the other requirements for its validity are completed'. We face a

112. It has to be only sketched that the legal character of donation is disputed in Spanish law. Traditionally, donation has been considered as a contract, and in fact Arts 623 and 629 (even though they contradict themselves) use the contractual terms 'conclusion' and 'acceptance'. Nevertheless, donation is regulated in Book 3 ('the modes of acquisition of property'), not in Book 4 along with obligations and contracts. Moreover, Art. 619 defines donation as an 'act of liberality whereby one person disposes gratuitously of an asset'. Finally, Art. 609 CC states that 'property and limited real rights are acquired and transferred by means of the law, *donation*, succession and *certain contracts plus traditio*'. In the Civil Code of Catalonia (Arts 531-7 et seq.) donation is regulated as a mode of acquisition of ownership. Concerning the specific formal problems of donation *see* below para. 95.

113. If form is the means by which the will is expressed outwardly, 'formality' denotes the circumstances that are linked to the conclusion of a transaction, such as the intervention of witnesses (e.g., Art. 697 CC). If the parties do not comply with the formalities, the transaction is void.

114. For example, Art. 4.3 Act 42/1998 of 15 December, on timesharing (public deed); Art. 6 Act 28/1998 of 13 July, on sale on instalments (writing); Art. 111 new LGDCU in relation to contracts concluded away from business premises (writing); Art. 154 new LGDCU in relation to travel package (writing).

115. On the classification of documents, *see* below para. 99.

form which violation does not lead to nullity of the contract, since all the requirements for validity are fulfilled. The law does not state that the form serves evidential purposes either.

The Act that established the Bases of the Civil Code (*Ley de Bases* of 11 May 1888) highlights the principle of contractual informality (Base 20) even when a public deed is required to the aims expressed in Base 19. According to the latter, 'obligations must be in writing in order to claim performance before the court'. This wording is quite similar to Article 1279 CC: 'to make effective the obligations arising from a contract'. Thus, we can talk about form *ad exercitium*: form is required to demand performance of obligations, to make them effective. The transactions enumerated in Article 1280.2, 3, 4 and (most of) 5 may affect third parties; Article 1280.1 is coherent with the legislation of the Land Register, since only public deeds can be recorded; Article 1280.6 and the rest of 1280.5 imply judicial proceedings. In other words, form makes the transaction opposable to third parties. The contract is valid since its conclusion, but is only effective against third parties (the possibility of 'detriment' of third parties) once it is recorded in a public deed. Article 1865 CC is a concretion of this form *ad exercitium*.[116]

94. The parties may reproduce the transaction, that is, conclude a new transaction under a different form. They may also recognize a former transaction, that is, confirm or facilitate the proof of it. A problem may arise if there is any discrepancy between the former and the latter. According to Article 1224 CC, the latter document does not prove anything against the former transaction, unless the parties express the explicit intention to modify it.[117]

2. Donation and Form

95. Donation of movables may be either verbal or in writing; in the latter case acceptance of the donation must also be in writing (Article 632 CC). By contrast, donation of immovables requires notarization, that is, a public deed with individual expression of the donated assets and of their burdens (Article 633 CC). Acceptance of the donation must be expressed in the same or in another public deed. The problem arises when the formal requirement is not complied with. Because taxation on donations is higher than on sales, it is common to disguise a gift under the appearance of a sale (the price is simply not paid). Simulation makes the sale void, but the parties may be willing to claim validity of the donation. The Supreme Court considers that the donation is also void, because the acceptance and the cause are not appropriate for a donation (the party accepts a sale, not a donation), especially when some sort of *animus fraudandi* is present. Exceptionally, the so-called *donaciones remuneratorias* (Article 622 CC), that is, gifts in gratitude for the merits or services

116. Pledge is not effective against third parties if the date is not certain by means of a public instrument.

117. *See* Juana Marco Molina, *El reconocimiento documental y la novación modificativadel contrato* (Madrid-Barcelona, 1998).

carried out by the donee, are valid.[118] For a while, Spanish case law seemed to be more flexible and appeared to favour the validity of donations,[119] but latest decisions have returned to the stricter approach.[120] Similarly, the Superior Court of Catalonia (in cases of Catalan law) that sustained a slightly different opinion, since it considered the donation valid if the formal requirements of the donation have been complied with in the contract of sale, has aligned with the Supreme Court.[121,122]

3. Functions of the Notary

96. A notary is a public servant conferred with the authority to attest contracts and other non-judicial acts (Article 1 *Ley del Notariado*). In practice, the function of the notary is twofold. On the one hand, the notary is an important legal adviser to individuals and families, although notaries do not possess the monopoly for the drawing of ordinary contracts. On the other hand, the notary certifies the facts and transactions that take place before him/her, and consequently draws legal instruments. Individuals may freely choose the notary they prefer. The notary only exercises its functions in its district. The districts are created by the government, which also decides the number of notaries in each district. The government appoints the notaries after a State examination.

Instruments that may be prepared by a notary include wills; antenuptial agreements; constitution, modification and extinction of legal persons; loans; protests; and, in general, all instruments concerning the transfer of real property that must be recorded. Even though the power to draw some of these instruments is not exclusive (e.g., wills may be holographic), notarial documents give stronger legal security to them. The original document prepared by the notary is kept permanently in its office for twenty-five years. Afterwards the instruments (*protocolo*) are kept in the district archives, also in charge of notaries. When the instruments become centenary, they are housed in the Historical Provincial Archive. Certified copies of notarial documents may be issued to interested parties.

Notaries depend hierarchically from the Ministry of Justice and the *Dirección General de Registros y del Notariado*. Membership in the professional organization (*Colegio de Notarios*) is compulsory. There are sixteen *Colegios* in Spain: Albacete, Palma de Majorca, Catalonia (Barcelona), Bilbao, Burgos, Cáceres, A Coruña, Granada, Las Palmas de Gran Canaria, Oviedo, Pamplona, Seville, Valencia, Valladolid and Zaragoza. The fees of the notaries are specified in an official fee schedule (*arancel*).

---

118. TS 13 Feb. 2003 (RJ 2003/1046), 2 Apr. 2001 (RJ 2001/6643). *See also* para. 146.
119. TS 27 Jun. 2005 (RJ 2005/9688).
120. TS 20 Jun. 2007 (RJ 2007/5574).
121. TSJ Catalonia 19 May 2008 (Roj: STSJ CAT 14505/2008).
122. TSJ Catalonia 6 Feb. 1995 (RJ 1995/4463), 28 Oct. 2004 (RJ 2004/7462).

II. Evidential Requirements

A. *The Law of Evidence*

97. The draftsmen of the CC followed the French pattern and included in the Civil Code 'material' rules on proof, that is, the rules on the admissibility and assessment of the means of proof, while mere 'procedural' rules were regulated in the Civil Procedural Act. The LEC, enacted in 2000, embodies now all provisions concerning proof but the assessment of documents. Those provisions are common to all kinds of declarative procedures.

B. *Documentary Evidence*

98. As mentioned above, the requirement that a transaction be in writing may be either of an evidentiary or of a substantive nature. If it is an evidentiary requirement only, its disregard does not render the act void, but merely difficult or even impossible to prove. One could think that Article 1280 *in fine* is one of form *ad probationem*. According to it, all contracts whose prestations exceed the amount of ESB 1,500 (EUR 9) must be in writing. Nevertheless, the provision lacks any practical consequence and has not been applied by case law.

C. *Probative Effect of Notarial and Other Authentic Instruments*

99. Both the CC and the LEC draw a distinction between public and private documents. Private documents are defined by exclusion, that is, they are the documents that are not public; public documents are listed in Article 317 LEC. According to Article 1216 CC, public documents are those authorized by a notary or a public officer in conformity with the solemnities legally required for instance, notarial deeds, certifications drawn up by land registers, judicial resolutions drawn up by the clerk of the court, etc. Public documents form conclusive evidence of the facts recorded, of the date of the document and of the parties (Article 319 LEC).

The conclusive probative effect of authentic instruments can be attacked in two ways: on the one hand, a criminal complaint alleging forgery may be filed with the criminal court. The decision in the criminal proceeding is conclusive in the subsequent civil proceeding where the public document should be effective. On the other hand, the other party may deny the authentic character of the document. The party that has brought the document into the court has then the burden to ask for the comparison of it with the original one kept by the notary of the public officer. If the document is not authentic, it becomes ineffective. But, if it is authentic, the costs of the comparison are borne by the other party. In addition, the court may fine the party that has attacked the document.

D. *Probative Effect of Private Documents*

100. The probative effect of private documents depends on its authentic character, which is not exclusive of public documents. A private document is authentic if it is recognized by both parties or after comparison of handwriting and signature. If that is the case and the document is genuine, it becomes conclusive. Otherwise, the court is free to determine the probative effect of the document, taking into account any form of counterproof brought into the court (Article 1228 CC). Signature is not a formal requirement of private documents to be introduced into the proceedings. Private documents include letters and commercial books of account (Article 327 LEC). If the document is written in a non-official language (other than Spanish or another official language in the Autonomous Communities, such as Catalan, Basque or Galician), the party must provide a translation (Article 144 LEC).

E. *Probative Effect of the Date of a Private Document*

101. Article 1227 CC provides that, insofar as third persons are concerned, the date of the private documents is ineffective, unless:

1. the instrument has been registered;
2. the signer of the instrument has died; or
3. the document is delivered to a public officer owing to the exercise of his/her functions.

Third persons within the scope of the provision are all persons other than the persons who signed the instrument and their successors in interest, such as heirs.

F. *Probative Effect of Copies*

102. Copies of public documents made in accordance with the legal requirements, usually by a notary, have the same effect as public documents (the so-called first copy), according to Articles 221 et seq. RN. Photocopies of private documents lack conclusive probative effect, but they can be taken into account by the courts in relation to other documents and evidence.[123]

G. *Introduction of Documents*

103. Plaintiff and defendant are burdened to provide every document that constitutes the basis of their respective allegations at the commencement of the litigation (Article 265 LEC). The subsequent introduction of documents and other proofs

123. TS 18 Dec. 2007 (RJ 2007/8938), 18 Oct. 2007 (RJ 2007/7106), 6 Apr. 2001 (RJ 2001/6646), 19 Jan. 2000 (RJ 2000/110).

is very limited. If the document is not at the disposal of the party, it is enough to indicate the archive or the register where the document can be found, unless the party could obtain a copy. However, parties and third persons are under the duty to display any relevant document related to the litigation when one party asks for it to the court (Articles 328 et seq. LEC). However, the adverse party may allege the right to privacy. Then the judge decides without right to appeal his/her decision. Public bodies may only allege the need for keeping the document secret.

H. Evidence by Testimony

104. Evidence by testimony is admissible. Testimony must always be a third person, not one of the litigation parties. No special capacity is requested to be a testimony, and even minors under 14 are able to declare; only persons of unsound mind are excluded (Article 361 LEC). But if the witness may not be impartial, the other party may exclude this evidence (the so-called *tacha de testigos*, regulated in Article 377 LEC). Plaintiff and defendant can interrogate the witnesses, and the court may ask for clarifications and further details. The testimony refers to relevant facts, but the court is not bound by his/her assertions, since it assesses freely the result of the interrogation jointly with the rest of the evidence.

I. Presumptions and Inferences

105. Presumptions are conclusions about unknown facts drawn from known facts. In this sense, a presumption is not a real means of proof, but a method of proof. Presumptions may be split up in the basic fact, the presumed fact and the logical link between them. The basic fact must be completely proved (Article 385.1 LEC).

The Civil Procedure Act distinguishes between legal and judicial presumptions. Legal presumptions are the ones prescribed by law. They can be rebuttable *iuris tantum* or irrebuttable *iuris et de iure*. As aforementioned, the interested party must prove the basic fact even when the presumption is irrebuttable. In fact, irrebuttable presumptions are substantive rules (e.g., Article 643 CC).[124] The party may rebut the rebuttable presumption if he/she proves that the basic fact does not exist or that there is no logical link between the basic fact and the presumed fact (Article 385.2 LEC). When the presumption is a judicial one, the court infers an unknown fact from a proved fact according to logical rules. According to case law, the court may only resort to presumptions when direct proofs are lacking.[125] Resorting to presumptions is facultative for courts, since courts cannot be compelled to use them.[126]

124. According to this provision, donations are always presumed to be done to the detriment of creditors if the donor has not kept enough assets to pay former debts. As a consequence, the creditor can resort to the Paulian action (*see* below paras 222 et seq.).
125. TS 21 Apr. 2003 (RJ 2003/3719), 14 Oct. 1998 (RJ 1998/8730).
126. TS 26 May 2008 (RJ 2008\3172).

J. Admissions

106. Another means of proof is the examination of plaintiff and defendant. Voluntary statements during the litigation, in particular in the writings, are not a means of proof, but the object of proof, as they are the basis of the respective claims. The new Civil Procedure Act tries to modify the proof of admission, and in fact its name has been replaced by 'interrogatory of the parties'. Nonetheless, according to Article 316.1 LEC, the court shall consider as true the facts admitted by the party who took part in them and whose certainty is detrimental to him/her. But if the facts are not detrimental to him/her, the court freely assesses the statements made by the party and in this sense, the new legislation moves away from the old proof of admission. An admission may not be partially accepted against the party who made it, that is, neither the court nor the parties are allowed to believe only those parts of the declaration that do not favour the defendant or the plaintiff and disbelieve the portions that favour him/her.[127] The examination's object is always facts, never rights (Article 302.1 LEC). Moreover, the facts must be personal to the interrogated party. If the party does not appear before the court to carry out the interrogation or his/her answers are evasive, the court may consider the facts as certain (Articles 304, 307 LEC). The examination is the first proof to be performed; the court decides if questions put to the party are admissible, but it can only ask for clarifications or additions to the answers given (Article 306.1 LEC).

K. Expert's Report

107. The expert, *perito*, provides technical, scientific or artistic knowledge in order for the court to assess the facts under litigation. The parties may bring into the court the expert's report,[128] but the genuine expert's evidence is still the one carried out by an expert appointed by the court. Nevertheless, the expert's report is not conclusive; on the contrary, the court may assess the result of the report jointly with the rest of the evidence (Article 348 LEC). The parties may refuse the experts on the ground of partiality (Articles 124, 343.1 LEC). The court and the parties may ask the expert for clarifications (Article 347 LEC). The calligraphic report is expressly regulated in Articles 349–351 LEC. The expert must use indubitable documents, which are listed in Article 350 LEC (public deeds, identity cards with signature, documents with an admitted signature, etc.).

127. TS 17 Jun. 2008 (RJ 2008/4251), 13 Sep. 2003 (RJ 2003/846), 17 May 2002 (RJ 2002/5343), still governed by Art. 1233 CC (repealed). According to the second judgment, an admission must be 'clear, precise and conclusive'.

128. In fact, the parties are burdened to bring with their initial writings the reports that they consider necessary to support their claims, but they are also allowed to ask the court to appoint a judicial expert (Art. 336 LEC).

L. *Judicial Examination*

108. Judicial examination is the only direct proof regulated in the Civil Procedure Act. The court may resort to this proof when the result of the other proofs has not completely clarified the facts (Article 353 LEC). If possible, it has to be carried out in the seat of the court, but frequently this will be impossible (e.g., the inspection of a plot of land where a servitude is under dispute). The court has broad powers to direct the proof.

III. Burden of Proof

109. As the rules on proof embodied in the Civil Code have been substituted by the Civil Procedure Act, Article 1214 CC has been repealed.[129] Nevertheless, the general principle remains unaltered. The plaintiff must prove all the elements of his/her claim for relief, and the defendant must prove all affirmative defences (Article 217.2 and 3 LEC). In an action on contract, the plaintiff has the burden of proving the existence of the contract and its breach. Concerning breach of contract, case law is ambiguous in relation to the burden of proof of fault. In tort liability, case law has shifted the burden of proof to the defendant, so that the plaintiff does not need to prove the defendant's fault, but the latter has to prove his/her diligence in order to avoid damages. Some judgments have asserted the transfer of the burden of proof to the defendant,[130] but the opposite statement is to be found in cases of professional liability.[131] In any case, the principle of facility of proof must also be taken into account (Article 217.6 LEC), in other words, the court must assess the procedural behaviour of plaintiff and defendant.[132]

A. *Exceptions to the Repartition of Burden of Proof*

110. Apart from the practical consequences of the principle of facility of proof, in the sense that it implies somehow shifting the burden of proof to the other party, the legislator may establish legal presumptions. Presumptions are rebuttable *iuris tantum* when they only shift the burden of proof.[133] Presumptions are irrebuttable *iuris et de iure* when they make any further proof unnecessary.[134]

129. According to it, the proof of the obligation encumbers the one who claims its performance, and that of the extinction who resorts to that defence.

130. TS 15 Mar. 2002 (RJ 2002/2843).

131. TS 21 Jun. 2007 (RJ 2007/3783), 20 Dec. 2002 (RJ 2003/333). Both were claims against lawyers, and that concerns the so-called *obligations demoyens*, on which *below*, para. 111. *See* TS 5 Dec. 2007 (RJ 2007/8905), 19 Oct. 2007 (RJ 2007/7308) on medical liability.

132. TS 22 Sep. 2007 (RJ 2007/8651), 18 Feb. 2003 (RJ 2003/2114), 20 Jan. 2003 (RJ 2003/350).

133. For example, Arts 1183, 1189, 1191 or 1562 CC.

134. For example, Art. 1297 CC sets forth the irrebuttable presumption of fraud to the creditor when the debtor disposes gratuitously of his/her assets (*see* TS 22 Apr. 2003, RJ 2003/2527).

B. Duty of Best Efforts and Duty to Achieve a Specific Result

111. A categorization of obligations now generally accepted by case law though lacking specific regulation in the Civil Code distinguishes between *obligación de medios* and *obligación de resultado.* Both are expressions of the obligation to do something. In the first one, the debtor is bound to carry out an activity taking the measures which a reasonable man would take to achieve the purpose of the contract. The obligation is performed when the debtor carries out the promised activity showing due diligence. In the second one, the debtor promises to achieve a specific result. Fulfilment depends on the achievement of the result.

A usual example of an obligation of best efforts is that of the doctor[135] who is bound to take reasonable steps to cure his/her patient, but who is not liable if, in spite of such steps, no cure is achieved. The doctor escapes liability if he/she shows that he/she has performed this obligation diligently. Diligence has to be assessed according to the state of the science (*lex artis* ad hoc). However, obligations to achieve a result arise, for instance, from the contract of hire of work, specifically from the building contract. Nevertheless, the borderline between both types of obligation is far from precise. One can think of cosmetic surgery or sterilization. The consequences are not irrelevant, since case law has shifted the burden of proof in the absence of fault to the tortfeasor in order to escape liability. Recent case law considers the operations of aesthetics or sterilization near to the duty to achieve a specific result, yet the proof of negligence still remains with the patient.[136] But, as proving medical negligence can be quite difficult for the patient, case law has looked for mechanisms to alleviate the burden of proof. The first mechanism is the imposition on the doctor of strict duties of information; for example, in relation to sterilization, the doctor must inform of the possibility of a spontaneous recanalization and the necessity of undergoing periodical spermiograms.[137] The second mechanism is the doctrine of the disproportionate result: when an abnormal, unexpected and severe damage is caused to the patient, the burden of proof shifts to the doctor, who then has to prove his/her complete lack of negligence (e.g., force majeure).[138]

§3. Liability and Negotiations

I. Pre-contractual Liability

112. Pre-contractual dealings are the conversations or negotiations held by the interested parties before entering into the contract and performed with the aim of specifying its terms. They end with the definitive offer. This pre-contractual stage is

135. Another one is that of the lawyer, who is not bound to win the case. *See* TS 23 Mar. 2007 (RJ 2007/1542), 30 Dec. 2002 (RJ 2003/333), 23 May 2001 (RJ 2001/3372).
136. TS 22 Nov. 2007 (RJ 2007/8651), 11 May 2001 (RJ 2001/6197).
137. TS 23 May 2007 (RJ 2007/4667), 11 May 2001 (RJ 2001/6197), 27 Apr. 2001 (RJ 2001/6891), 2 Nov. 2001 (RJ 2000/9206). Nevertheless, the doctor is not burdened to inform on all possible collateral effects of the operation; it is enough if he/she informs the patient of the seriousness of the disease and of the treatment as well as of the ordinary risks (TS 10 Apr. 2003 [RJ 2003/3702]).
138. TS 19 Oct. 2007 (RJ 2007/7308), 15 Sep. 2003 (RJ 2003/6418), 31 Mar. 2003 (RJ 2003/646).

governed by the principle of good faith (Article 7.1 CC). Therefore, the parties are under duties of disclosing information and behave loyally in order to conclude the contract. However, pre-contractual dealings do not involve the obligation to enter into the contract. But, if a breach takes place unjustifiably in the negotiations, the damages caused to the injured party must be compensated (*culpa in contrahendo*). However, the pre-contractual stage may be useful to interpret the contract once it is concluded.

Recent case law insists on the fundamental role of pre-contractual information. In swap contracts, for example, the Supreme Court[139] has stated that the bank has to warn about the risks of speculative operations. The duty of good faith entails the duty to provide the other party with the essential information on the main characters of the transaction, including the risks of the financial product at stake.

II. Breakdown of Negotiations

113. Pre-contractual liability for want of express regulation in the CC finds legislative accommodation in Article 1902 CC (the general clause of tort liability).[140] Besides, there cannot be contractual liability without contract. The requirements for liability based on *culpa in contrahendo* may be systematized as follows:

- actual negotiations between the parties;
- negotiations must generate a reliance situation in which each party can reasonably expect the cooperation of the other party to conclude the contract;
- an unjustified breakdown of negotiations contrary to the reliance generated to the other party;
- damage suffered by the aggrieved party;
- a chain of causation between reliance and damage.

The compensation is determined by the so-called negative contractual interest, which comprises redress of the expenses actually incurred, but not loss of profit (*lucrum cessans*).[141]

It is also possible to speak of *dolo in contrahendo*. This refers to the duty of the party who possesses relevant information to inform the other party (e.g., as to the urbanistic situation of a plot of land). Mere silence of one of the parties does not imply deceit, unless it is contrary to good faith. Case law requires some sort of *animus decipiendi*; this expression, although certainly difficult to specify, embodies the knowledge of the real situation and the intention to take advantage of its non-disclosure. In addition, there must be causation between non-disclosure of the

139. TS 20 Jan. 2014 (Roj: STS 354/2014).
140. TS 30 Jan. 2008 (RJ 2008/340), 31 Oct. 2001 (RJ 2001/9639), 16 Dec. 1999 (RJ 1999/8978), 16 May 1988 (RJ 1988/4308).
141. TS 16 Dec. 1999 (RJA 8978), 25 Jun. 2014 (Roj: STS 3845/2014).

information and the conclusion of the contract, that is, the aggrieved party would not have entered the contract had he/she known the real situation of the object.[142]

III. Pre-contract

114. Pre-contractual dealings should not be confused with pre-contracts. A pre-contract contains all necessary elements for the contract to come into being, and these are determined from the start between the parties. Case law focuses at that point the distinction with negotiations: in a pre-contract, all the elements of the definitive contract have to be determined, otherwise the parties are under negotiations.[143] Thus, it is a complete contract project that depends solely on the demand for it to be executed. Once the pre-contract is drawn up, a binding link between the parties comes into being, and they are subject to the general contractual rules of the Civil Code.[144] From then on, one or both parties may demand execution of the contract. At this point, it is ruled by the regulations of the Civil Code in respect of the specific contract agreed by the parties. If the projected contract has all its legal requirements determined, it can be specifically performed in spite of the unwillingness of the reluctant party. In addition, the court may substitute the declaration of will of the reluctant party (Article 708 LEC). Damages for breach of pre-contract include *lucrum cessans.*[145]

142. TS 5 May 2009 (2009\2907, piece of land unsuitable for building a petrol station), 11 Dec. 2006 (RJ 2006/9893), 27 Mar. 1989 (RJ 1989/2201, land qualified as green space), 1 Oct. 1986 (RJ 1986/5229).
143. TS 25 Jun. 2014 (Roj: STS 3845/2014).
144. TS 8 Feb. 2010 (RJ 2010\395), 17 Jun. 2008 (RJ 2008\4251).
145. TS 20 May 2014 (Roj: STS 2086/2014).

Chapter 2. Conditions of Substantive Validity

§1. Capacity of the Parties

115. From a legal point of view, every human being is a person. To be a person means to be capable of holding rights (juridical capacity or civil personality). Personality begins with birth[146] and is the same for every person irrespective of age, sex or intellectual condition. Additionally, the law also recognizes civil personality to juridical persons constituted according to the legal requirements.

The juridical capacity has to be distinguished from the capacity to enter into legal transactions. The latter is not uniform, since it presupposes the ability to take decisions and to be aware of the legal significance of such decisions. The capacity to enter into legal transactions would thus depend on the aptitude of each person to govern itself (the so-called natural capacity). Nevertheless, as that solution would imply investigating the ability of every person in relation to every legal act, the law standardizes natural capacity, by way of presuming it at a certain age. Full capacity is reached at the age of 18 (full age).[147] Any full aged person who has not been declared incapable thereof by law or judicial decision may contract.

I. Minors

116. A minor is a person of either sex who has not reached the age of 18. However, although full capacity is only achieved with majority, minors do not lack entirely the capacity to enter into legal transactions. However, some minors are assimilated to full age in terms of capacity. These are emancipated minors, whose capacity is only restricted in relation to alienation and encumbrance of immovables and especially valuable assets.[148] However, the legislator tends to take into account the natural capacity of minors at least on decisions that affect their person, so that at least they have to be heard.[149] In addition, minors having attained the age of 12 must consent to their adoption.[150] Minors of 14 years are capable of marriage[151] and of testation.[152] Minors of 16 years are allowed to administrate their assets.[153] Nevertheless, in spite of the literal wording of Article 1263 CC[154] and because of the general and increasing acceptance of the criterion of the natural capacity, it has to be concluded that minors may contract for reasonable necessaries according to

146. Notwithstanding Art. 30 CC, which has to be interpreted in the sense of the text.
147. *See* Art. 322 CC, in relation to Arts 12 CE and 315 CC. *See also* Art. 211-4 CCCat. In Aragon any married person is deemed to be of full age (Art. 4.1.b CCA).
148. Article 323 CC. Marriage causes emancipation; besides, parents and courts may grant it (Arts 316 et seq. CC).
149. Articles 154.III CC; 235-43.c, 236-19 CCCat, among others.
150. Article 177.1 CC, Art. 235-40 CF.
151. Article 46.1 in relation to Art. 48.2 CC.
152. Article 663.1 CC, Art. 421.4 CCCat. The will must be a notarial one, however.
153. Article 164.3 CC, Art. 236-25.c CCCat. Those provisions are consequent with the ability to enter into a labour contract when the minor attains the age of 16.
154. Minors not emancipated and judicially declared insane persons cannot consent.

broadly accepted social opinion. This has been now expressly acknowledged by Articles 211-5 CCCat and 7.1 CCA.

When it is proved that a minor, because of mental disturbance, might remain incapable in personal conduct and in administering property, such a minor may be placed under the status of prolonged minority.[155]

II. Aliens

117. As the subject matter of the conditions of aliens is regarded as part of private international law, it will suffice to say that in principle aliens enjoy the same rights as nationals from a private law point of view. Only specific provisions limit the capacity to enter into legal transactions. For example, Article 9.4 LAR states that no alien without residence permit is allowed to enter into agricultural leases. However, and exclusively for administrative control, foreign investments must be declared to the Treasury.[156]

III. Married Women

118. Married women were formerly subject to a far-reaching limitation of capacity. Mainly, a married woman could not enter into a contract without her husband's consent, being that the husband has the legal agent of the wife. Such incapacity has been completely repealed, even before the CE of 1978, which states that men and women have the same rights. Marriage law and marriage property law were completely reformed. The last discrimination in force was the loss of the personal (regional) law in favour of that of the husband when the spouses were not subject to the same regional law on matters of marriage property (Article 9.2 CC). This provision was only repealed in 1990; moreover, the judgment of the Constitutional Court 39/2002 of 14 February, has declared it unconstitutional, as against the principle of equality of men and women.[157]

Marriage implies that special provisions apply to the spouses. Irrespective of who is the owner, neither spouse may, without the other's consent, dispose of the rights on the familiar dwelling and its assets of ordinary use (Article 1320 CC, Article 231-9 CCCat).[158] However, any contract for the upkeep of the household, or the

155. Article 171 CC, Arts 236-33–233-36 CCCat.

156. Article 4 Royal Decree 664/1999 of 23 April, on foreign investments.

157. *See* Albert Lamarca Marquès, 'Règim econòmic dels matrimonis catalans celebrats entre el 29 December 1978 i el 6 November 1990: Inconstitucionalitat de l'art. 9.2 CC en la redacció anterior a la llei 11/1990, de 15 d'octubre (Comentari a la STC 39/2002 de 14 February 2002)', RJC (2002): 737. The decision of the Constitutional Court does not establish which law would be applicable to spouses married between December 1978 (when the Spanish Constitution came into force) and 1990. Lacking any agreement between the spouses and a common residence before they married, the most feasible solution is the application of the law of the place where they married.

158. *See* Santiago Espiau, *El régimen jurídico de la vivienda familiar en el ordenamiento jurídico civil español* (Barcelona, 1992), and 'La disposición de la vivienda familiar y de los bienes de uso ordinario en el Derecho civil catalán (notas en torno al Art. 9 CF)', *La Notaria*, April 2001, 17; M.D. Cervilla Garzón, 'El derecho a usar la vivienda en las recientes reformas del derecho de familia',

upbringing of the children will bind the spouses jointly and severally, provided that the expenditure is not disproportionate, taking into account the family's standard of life (Article 1319 CC, Article 231-8 CCCat).

IV. Insanity

119. Any valid contract presupposes the so-called natural capacity. Contracts entered into by lunatic or imbecile persons may be avoided, since they lack such capacity. Nevertheless, such persons can be judicially declared as incompetent,[159] and then no other evidence of incapacity is required. Once the person has been judicially declared as incompetent, he/she is deprived of the capacity to enter into transactions and provided with a guardian, who becomes his/her legal representative. Even transactions entered into during lucid intervals by such persons are void. Nevertheless, because of the particular mental situation, the court may not completely deprive the person of the capacity to enter into legal transactions and appoint a curator, who only complements the capacity, instead of a guardian. This is also the case of prodigals. A prodigal is a person who, owing to the disorder of his/her mind or of his/her morals dissipates his/her fortune by excessive and foolish expenditure but only if this causes detriment to the persons who are entitled to claim alimony from him/her.[160] The curator must approve the acts of prodigals and other persons with limited capacity according to the judgment. If approval is not given, the transaction may be avoided.

V. Moral Persons

120. Moral persons have legal personality and capacity to enter into transactions once they have been constituted according to legal requirements (Article 38 CC). Therefore, corporate bodies, foundations, associations, etc. possess the capacity to acquire, to own, to sue and be sued and to incur liability. However, the capacity to enter into certain transactions may be limited. For example, the usufruct in favour of moral persons cannot be constituted for more than thirty years (Article 515 CC). Foundations have a limited capacity to dispose of their assets, since they need the approval of the administration (protectorate), according to Article 21 Act 50/2002 of 26 December, on Foundations.

---

in *La reforma del matrimonio*, coord. Julio V. Gavidia Sánchez (Madrid, 2007). For Catalan law, Santiago Espiau, 'La disposición de la vivienda familiar en el Libro Segundo del Código Civil de Cataluña', in *El nuevo derecho de la persona y de la familia*, ed. R. Barrada, M. Garrido & S. Nasarre (coord.) (Barcelona, 2011), 409 et seq.

159. Article 200 CC. The procedure is regulated in Arts 756 et seq. LEC.

160. Articles 286.2, 297 CC, 223-1-c and 223-4.3 CCCat, 757.5 LEC. *See* TS 23 Dec. 1997 (RJ 1997/8902), 20 Oct. 2014 (Roj: STS 4075/2014).

§2. DEFECTS OF CONSENT

121. Since legal transactions are an expression of the autonomy of will and are aimed at production of legal consequences *ex voluntate*, they need not only an internal will, but also an external declaration of that will. The internal will and the declared will must match each other. It may happen that the declared will matches the internal will, but nevertheless the latter is defective, because the party was affected by one of the vices of consent. Article 1165 CC states accordingly that the consent given by error, extorted by violence or threat or obtained by deceit is void.

Vices of consent may affect the act of declaration, so that the consent is not expressed freely. But vices may also appear in the process of formation of consent. Consent has then been formed erroneously due to an inaccurate conception of reality, either spontaneously or caused by a third party. Violence and threat are included in the first category, whilst error and deceit belong to the second one. The nullity of the contract is always established in favour of the aggrieved party. The three vices have in common that they must have induced the party to enter into the agreement and they must also share the consequence, the nullity (*rectius*, voidability) of the contract.

I. Mistake

122. Mistake as a vice of consent must be distinguished from error in communication (*error obstativo*). Mistake in communication results from an unconscious discrepancy between consent and declaration. Therefore, it encapsulates a case of dissent and, consequently, its consequence should be nullity due to the lack of any agreement.[161] However, in many cases the consequence is only avoidance of the contract,[162] whether because Article 1266 CC does not admit distinctions to be made or because of the protection deserved by the party acting in good faith. I shall focus on mistake vice.

123. According to Article 1266 CC, error is a cause of nullity of a contract only when it affects the very substance of the thing, which is its object, or the principal conditions that moves the party to enter into the agreement. An error as to the person whom it was the intention to contract with becomes only a cause of nullity in *intuitu personae* contracts.[163]

Mistake affects the formation of the consent. The intention is based on an inaccurate belief, because of ignorance or false conception of the factual or legal reality. Hence, mistake may be classified in *error facti* and *error iuris* (legal mistake).

161. TS 22 Dec. 1999 (RJ 1999/9369).

162. However, TS 10 Apr. 2001 (RJ 2001/2127) refers to nullity, as well as TS 19 Dec. 2003 (RJ 2003/9053).

163. Contracts in which the identity of the other party was the principal reason for the agreement (Art. 1266.II CC).

Article 6.1.2 CC cautiously regulates the latter, since this provision establishes that *error iuris* will only produce the effects determined by the law.[164]

To nullify the contract three requirements have to be met: the mistake must be essential, causal and excusable.[165]

A. *Mistake as to the Substance*

124. The mistake must, according to Article 1266 CC, relate to the 'substance of the thing which is the object of the contract or the conditions which principally move the party to enter the contract'. The wording of the Civil Code is thus broad, since it includes not only the substance of the object but also its principal conditions (for example, whether a plot of land is available for building). Case law interprets this requisite in a subjective way, that is, the conditions that motivated the contracting parties to enter into the agreement.[166] The purpose pursued by the parties has to be taken into account in order to decide whether the mistake relates to the substance. Mistakes affecting the substance may appear in any contract.[167]

Case law adds a requirement: the error must be excusable in order to nullify the contract.[168] An error is inexcusable when a reasonable behaviour of the party would have avoided it. Hence, the error is due to the negligence of that party and, despite the vice of consent, the contract is not avoidable.

B. *Mistake as to the Person*

125. Mistake as to the person is a ground of avoidance only in contracts where the identity of the contracting party is a dominant consideration *intuitu personae*, such as hire of work. It can refer to the qualities of the other party, but the mistake as to the identity of the person is always an error in communication.[169]

C. *Mistake in* Corpore *and as to the Transaction*

126. Error in *corpore* is an error as to the identity of the object of the contract. It is also a dissent and prevents the formation of the contract, hence it is an error in

164. *See* TS 27 May 1982 (RJ 1982/2604). Compromise settlements (*see* Part II, Ch. 7, para. 452) are not avoidable on the basis of legal mistake according to Art. 1817 and case law (TS 20 Dec. 2000 (RJ 2001/352)).
165. TS 7 Jul. 2014 (Roj: STS 2660/2014).
166. TS 23 Sep. 1997 (RJ 1997/7181; comment by José Ramón de Verda y Beamonte in *Revista de Derecho Patrimonial*, 1998, 1, 276), 12 Nov. 1996 (RJ 1996/7919).
167. For example, the agreement to divide the estate (TS 10 Feb. 2000 [RJ 2000/2424]), lease (TS 14 Feb. 1994 [RJ 1994/1469]), etc.
168. TS 30 Mar. 2011 (RJ 2011\3133, the parties would not have incurred in mistake should they have audited the company) 13 Feb. 2007 (RJ 2007/716), 24 Jan. 2003 (RJ 2003/1995), 20 Dec. 2000 (RJ 2001/352), 8 Nov. 2000 (RJ 200/9592).
169. Albaladejo, *Derecho civil*, 638.

communication. The same is applicable to error as to the transaction; for instance, one of the parties wants to sell an asset and the other believes it is a loan, or the contracting party is induced to believe that is acquiring in full property and not in timesharing.[170] There is no *consensus in idem*, and consequently the parties do not enter into a contract.

D. Mistake Which Will Not Make the Contract Voidable

127. There are mistakes which do not make the contract voidable:

1. Mistake as to the subjective motives to enter into the contract. This error may exceptionally lead to nullification of the contract, when the motives have been raised to the cause.[171]
2. Mistake as to non-substantial qualities.
3. Mistake as to the person in contracts which are not *intuitu personae*.
4. Mistake as to the value of the thing. The principles of liberal economy governing the Civil Code ousted this error from its provisions. *Laesio ultradimidium*, however, only survives in Catalan law and, based on different principles, Navarre law.[172]
5. Mistake as to calculation (mathematical mistake) only allows its correction (Article 1266.3 CC).

E. Consequences

128. Mistake entitles the mistaken party to avoid the contract. The contract is not void (absolute nullity), but avoidable. The mistaken party must avoid the contract within four years (Article 1301 CC).[173] The mistaken party must prove the error and its substantiality. The error must be objective and unquestionable.[174] Restitution is ordered.[175]

II. Fraud (Deceit)

129. Fraud is considered threefold in the Civil Code. In succession law, fraud means the deprivation of the freedom of will (Articles 673, 674). In the law of obligations, fraud represents the intention not to perform the obligation (Articles 1101,

170. Court of Appeal of the Balearic Islands 1 Feb. 2011 (AC 2011\340).
171. *See* para. 147.
172. *See* below paras 137 et seq.
173. This period is one of lapse of rights, according to most authors. *See* below para. 147.
174. Therefore, TS 28 May 2003 (RJ 2003/7157) rejects the claim of the purchaser of a painting attributed by the time of the purchase to the famous artist Murillo but afterwards questioned by another art expert. According to the Supreme Court, the case is one of disputes among experts and not of the discovery of the truth.
175. TS 12 Nov. 2010 (RJ 2010\7587).

1102). In contract law, fraud is the behaviour of one party against the principle of good faith and entails a vice of consent. According to Article 1269, deceit exists when the words or artifices used by one party are such that otherwise the other party would not have entered into the contract. Deceit causes a mistake that induces the other party to contract. This mistake is not spontaneous, but caused intentionally by the trickery of the other party. Fraudulent conduct includes non-disclosure of relevant information and giving incorrect information. The existence of a previous reliance relationship, for example a sentimental relationship, may be taken into account by courts in order to determine the existence of fraud.[176] On the contrary, the exaggerated praise of one's own wares (*dolus bonus*) and impossible offers (gold watches of famous brands sold in bazaars at ridiculous prices) do not allow avoiding the contract on the basis of fraud. Along the same lines, the party who is aware of the conditions of the object cannot avoid the contract on the basis of fraud.[177]

130. Furthermore fraud must be a determining factor for entering into the contract ('serious' is the expression used by Article 1270.1 CC). Incidental fraud, that is, the conduct of the other party that did not lead to the conclusion of the contract but only to enter into it in less advantageous conditions is irrelevant as a vice of consent. The party has then no right to avoid the contract, but can only claim for damages (Article 1270.2 CC).

131. Article 1269 CC sets forth that the other party must cause the fraudulent representation that induces the conclusion of the contract. Therefore, fraud stemming from a third person does not entitle a party to avoid the contract, unless the other party has taken profit of it. Moreover, if the conduct is fraudulent both parties, *compensatio doli* occurs, and both parties are considered as acting in good faith.

132. Fraud entitles the deceived party to avoid the contract. The contract is not void (absolute nullity), but avoidable. The cause of the avoidance is the intention to deceive (*animus decipendi*), not the causation of damages. Fraud cannot be presumed. The deceived party must avoid the contract within four years (Article 1301 CC). Negative interest is claimable, according to the Supreme Court.[178]

III. Violence (Duress) and Threats

A. *Violence*

133. Violence is defined in the Civil Code as an 'irresistible force' (Article 1267.1). It implies an absolute constraint, physical or moral, which excludes the will

176. TS 16 Feb. 2010 (RJ 2010\1783), quoting Art. 4:109 PECL.
177. TS 15 Jul. 2003 (RJ 2003/5839) considers valid the sale of a plot of land because the purchaser was a neighbour farmer who knew that the land could flood. *See*, for the requirements established by case law, TS 11 Jun. 2003 (RJ 2003/5347), 12 Jun. 2003 (RJ 2003/5631). TS 10 Mar. 2008 (RJ 2008/1553) accepts the existence of deceit where the seller requires the payment of more money than agreed in order to fully execute the contract of sale.
178. Decision of 5 Mar. 2010 (RJ 2010\2390).

of the party. In that sense, there is a lack of consent, and the transaction should be deemed as non-existent. Nevertheless, Article 1301.2 CC submits the claim of the coerced party to the limitation period of four years typical of avoidance. As 'irresistible' force is the key concept, the age, sex and condition of the person must be taken into account. The violence may be that of a third person.

B. Threats

134. A party may avoid a contract when it has been led to conclude it by the imminent and serious threat of a harm to his/her person or assets or to the person or assets of the spouse, ascendants or descendants. This party has only two alternatives: either suffering the harm or concluding the contract (Article 1267.2 CC). There must be a link of causation between the intimidation and the declaration of consent. In addition, the threat must be unlawful and serious. Unlawfulness appears where the threat is used as a means to obtain the conclusion of a contract.[179] Pursuant to seriousness, the age, sex and condition of the person has to be taken into account. However, the wrongful harm must depend on the threatening person. Hence, the fear of displeasing people to whom the party owes obedience and respect does not suffice to avoid the contract (Article 1267.4 CC). The contract is avoidable within the limitation period of four years.

IV. Laesio

A. The Civil Code

135. Following the French pattern and reflecting the liberal ideology of the nineteenth century, Article 1293 CC states that no contract shall be set aside on the ground of lesion except the ones regulated in Article 1291.1, 2. The first exception is thus any sale concluded by guardians when the price is less than three-fourths of the real value of the asset. The second exception is the contract concluded in the name of absentees under the same requirement (lesion of one-fourth). Both remedies go back to the Roman *restitutio in integrum minorum*. Besides, partition among heirs is also rescindable in the case of lesion of one-fourth (Article 1074 CC).

136. As the regulation is completely different in Catalonia and in Navarre, it is important to highlight that the applicable law is the *lex rei sitae* and not the personal law of the parties (Article 16.1 CC in relation to Article 10.5.2 CC).[180]

179. *See* TS 8 Nov. 2007 (RJ 2008/247), 4 Oct. 2002 (RJ 2002/9797).
180. High Court of Justice of Catalonia 1 Jun. 1993 (RJ 1993/6324), 7 Oct. 1991 (RJ 1992/3909).

B. Catalan Law

137. In Catalan law, the onerous cause requires besides the exchange of prestations, an economic equivalence between those prestations.[181] This equivalence has been settled in one-half of the fair price of the thing sold. Lesion arises when the equivalence between the prestations does not reach one-half of the fair price (*laesio ultra dimidium*). The aggrieved party may then rescind the contract on the ground of lesion (Article 321 CDCC). Therefore, rescission has an objective foundation and does not require any vice of consent.[182] Nevertheless, the field of application is limited to contracts aimed at the transfer of immovable assets (sale, exchange, *datio in solutum*). Moreover, some contracts are expressly excluded from the remedy, such as sales at public auctions, aleatory contracts and compromise settlements. Commercial contracts are excluded as well.[183]

Fair price is legally defined as the sale value of the thing when the contract was concluded in relation to similar things sold in the same place (Article 323.2 CDCC).[184] Subsequent increase in the price of the thing does not allow bringing an action against the purchaser. The defendant may avoid the rescission if he/she pays a supplement of the price, including legal interests (Article 325 CDCC).

The claim for rescission lapses after four years (Article 322 CDCC). The limitation period runs from the conclusion of the contract, irrespective of the date when transfer of property was completed.[185] Only the vendor can claim for rescission on the grounds of lesion.

C. Navarre Law

138. According to *ley* 499 Comp. Nav., both contracting parties are entitled to rescind an onerous contract, if they concluded it as a result of an urgent need or from their inexperience and suffered a lesion. Such lesion is more than half the value of the respective prestation at the time of the contract. When the lesion exceeds two-thirds of the value *laesio enormissima*, the legal regime is slightly different. Nevertheless, the person who is acting for purposes relating to his/her trade, business or profession is not entitled to bring the remedy.

The remedy is a personal right that can be brought by the parties and their heirs. The claim prescribes within ten years. However, in the case of *laesio enormissima*,

---

181. María Eulalia Amat Llari, 'Compravenda Civil, Compravenda mercantil i rescissió per lesió "ultra dimidium"', RJC (2008): 705; Juan Manuel Abril Campoy, *La rescisióndel contrato por lesión* (Valencia, 2003).
182. High Court of Catalonia 23 Jan. 2012 (Roj: STSJ CAT 9/2012), 7 Jan. 2011 (RJ 2011\1418), 26 Jul. 2010 (RJ 2010\5266), 18 Sep. 2006 (RJ 2006/8118), 25 May 2000 (RJ 2000/7442), 20 Nov. 1995 (RJ 1995/9977), 22 Dec. 1993 (RJ 1993/10201).
183. High Court of Catalonia 10 Oct. 2013 (Roj: STSJ CAT 11580/2013).
184. Nevertheless, the initial interpretation of the provision (comparison with other contracts in the same place was compulsory, according to the judgment of the High Court of Catalonia handed down on 26 Feb. 1990) has been tempered (comparison is only one of the criteria and even is dispensable; *see* decisions of 20 Oct. 1992 [RJ 1994/9034], 21 Dec. 1992 [RJ 1993/2244], 19 Jun. 1997 [RJ 1998/7759]).
185. High Court of Catalonia 9 Feb. 1995 (RJ 1995/6771).

the claim prescribes within thirty years (*ley* 33 Comp. Nav.). The defendant may avoid the rescission if he/she pays a supplement of the price, including legal interests (*ley* 506 Comp. Nav.).

§3. Other Conditions of Validity

I. Existing and Lawful Cause

139. The expression 'cause' is found several times in the Civil Code.[186] The heading of section 3, Chapter II, Title II of Book V is 'on the cause of contracts'. One of the requirements for the validity of contracts established in Article 1261 CC is 'the cause of the obligation'. Article 1262 CC requires from the parties not only the consent about the object but also about the cause of the contract. Article 1901 CC refers to 'any other fair cause'. Finally, in the field of succession law, Article 767 CC speaks of a 'false cause'. One preliminary conclusion is the possibility to distinguish between two different meanings of the word 'cause'. On the one hand, cause in an objective sense, that is, the cause of the obligation, the cause of the contract and the cause of the tradition. In a very broad sense, cause may be defined as the legal foundation of the consequences of a transaction, and is required in every obligation entered into voluntarily and in every voluntary transfer of assets. On the other hand, cause in a subjective sense means the subjective reasons that move the party to enter into the transaction. In principle, such reasons are irrelevant.

140. Depending on the cause, transactions may be classified as: causal, and abstract. Causal transactions are those that require a cause, a legal ground that justifies the production of legal consequences. Abstract transactions do not need a cause. The Civil Code does not permit abstract transactions. Article 1901 requires a cause for every transfer of assets, whilst Article 1261 considers the cause a requirement for the validity of contracts, and Article 1262 mentions the 'causal agreement'. In addition, Article 1275 CC states that contracts without cause or with an unlawful cause produce no consequences. Abstract transactions are only admissible in the sense of contracts without an autonomous cause, that is, contracts based on a previous contract which is, for example, modified or guaranteed (such as the recognition of a debt).

However, the rejection of abstract transactions does not mean that all transactions are causal. Transactions may be causal and non-causal. Cause is a concept that is only required in contractual obligations (Articles 1261.3, 1274), in the acquisition of ownership and limited real rights because of *traditio* and in donation (since Article 618 CC conceives gift as a gratuitous disposition). Hence, cause is a requirement for transactions based on freedom of will, which justifies a patrimonial transfer and which implies an economic sacrifice assumed voluntarily by the party. Only transactions intended to make a transfer require a cause, the cause being the foundation of the obligatory effects of the contract or of the transmission of ownership

186. On the three concepts of causa (causa of the attribution, causa of the obligation and causa of the contract) see TS 25 May 2007 (RJ 2007/3180).

or another real right. Therefore, family law and succession law transactions are non-causal. Family law transactions are non-causal because of the formal requirements that already limit the freedom of will, and because they do not produce any acquisition of rights. Succession law transactions are also formal, and the testator does not dispose of the estate voluntarily, but as a consequence of his/her death. Legal obligations (e.g., alimony) are also non-causal transactions.

141. The cause of the obligation can be deduced from Article 1274 CC: the counter-performance of the other party or the liberality (of the donor or the party who performs gratuitously). The cause of the contract is based on the economic function developed by such contract. Contracts may be onerous or gratuitous depending on the cause. The cause of onerous contracts is the exchange of the parties' performances, while in gratuitous contracts, the cause is the liberality that justifies a unique prestation without counter-performance. Article 1274 CC admits not only an actual performance but also the promise of a future performance. The requirement of a cause of the contract permits the distinction between the transactional agreement and the causal agreement. The transactional agreement is the one envisaged in Article 1254 CC: the contract is concluded once the parties agree to be reciprocally bound. Article 1262 CC also requires a causal agreement on the basis of the models set up in Article 1274 CC. This causal agreement does not need to be expressed in the contract, since Article 1277 CC presumes a valid cause in every contract, so that whoever is interested in the nullity of the contract must prove the absence of a true cause.

142. Traditio is the transaction whereby possession is transferred in a determined concept (concept of owner or another real right). The Spanish system of passing of property is based on title and mode. The obligational effect and the real effect take place by means of different transactions. We can think of sale.[187] According to Article 1445 CC, the consequences of sale are the obligation of the vendor to deliver the object and the obligation of the purchaser to pay the stipulated price. The sole contract of sale does not transfer ownership, but only originates the obligation to deliver the thing (title). A second transaction is required, that being *traditio*, the taking of possession (mode). The mere agreement of the parties is not enough to justify the real effect of the passing of ownership. Article 1901 CC reveals that *traditio* requires a cause. This cause can be an obligation, the intention of liberality or another *iusta causa* (fair cause). The concept of fair cause includes the *causa solvendi*, the *causa donandi* and the *causa credendi*.

A. *Functions of Cause*

143. Cause fulfils three distinct functions. On the one hand, cause works as a limit to the freedom of contract, constituting thus a legal control of transactions. Besides, cause is the final criterion to interpret contracts when the previous elements of interpretation (Articles 1281–1289 CC) do not suffice to unveil the content

187. *See* Part II, Ch. 4, paras 379 and 380.

of a contract. According to Article 1289 CC, if a contract is gratuitous, the doubt is solved in favour of the lesser transfer of rights, and if it is an onerous one, in favour of the major reciprocity. Finally, cause determines the application of the so-called *causal rules*. These rules watch over the typical consequences of contracts in order that the gratuitous or the onerous character of the contract is complied with. Onerous contracts ought to tend towards the major reciprocity of interests, hence the major equality of the parties must be pursued. The rules on lesion in Catalan law (Article 321 CDCC) or the rules on latent defects of the Civil Code (Articles 1474, 1475, 1478, 1483, 1553 CC) are thus causal rules, applicable to all onerous contracts of transfer of rights. Instead, the causal rules of gratuitous contracts tend to protect third parties (e.g., the rules on protection of creditors set out in Articles 1111 and 1297.1 CC – Paulian action – or 531-14 CCCat).[188]

B. *The Vices of the Cause*

144. Article 1275 CC refers to the absence of cause in the following terms: 'Contracts without cause produce no effect.' As mentioned, cause is a requirement for the validity of any contract (Article 1261.3 CC), hence the absence of cause makes the contract void. Nevertheless, Article 1277 CC presumes the existence of a valid cause, so that the burden of proof shifts to the debtor.

Article 1275 adds that contracts with an illicit cause are without effect either. An illicit cause is the one that contradicts the law or the good morals. However, the cause in its objective sense cannot be illicit or immoral, since it is typical (onerous or gratuitous). Therefore, unlawfulness has to refer to the causal agreement, to the purpose that has determined the parties to conclude the contract. The parties incorporate into the typical cause a purpose that makes the contract void. Hence, the subjective sense of the cause appears when the parties' purpose is unlawful.[189]

145. Still, according to Article 1276 CC, 'the expression of a false cause will make the contract void, unless a true and licit cause is proved'. The falseness of the cause embraces three distinct concepts: simulation, mistake as to the causal agreement and mistake as to the motives.

1. Simulation

146. Simulation occurs when the parties conclude an apparent transaction without a real intention and only to disguise another purpose. This purpose may be the intention not to enter into any transaction (absolute simulation) or to conclude a different transaction from the apparent one (relative simulation). Therefore, simulation presupposes an agreement between the parties, so that they conclude a transaction only in order to disguise a different transaction which is the one they really want to

188. *See* paras 222–224.

189. *See*, for example, TS 30 Nov. 2000 (RJ 2000/9319): recognition of a debt fifteen times the real debt in order to avoid a criminal prosecution.

enter into. A simulation agreement leads to the nullity of the disguising transaction, because it has only been concluded in pretence. The disguised transaction is not automatically void. However, the parties must prove a 'true and licit cause'. Hence, if all the requirements of the disguised transaction are complied with, such a transaction is valid. That includes formal requirements. The Supreme Court declares void contracts of sale concluded without any intention to claim the price and, thus, designed to disguise donations. The argument is that the cause is illicit.[190] By contrast, the Superior Court of Catalonia had accepted the validity of the disguised donation if its formal requirements have been fulfilled and the *animus donandi* is proved,[191] yet in the latest judgment it seems now to share the same approach as the Supreme Court and has declared void a disguised donation because the sale deed did neither express an *animus donandi* nor contain the donee's acceptation.[192]

2. Mistake as to the Cause

147. Mistake as to the causal agreement implies the lack of *consensus in idem* (one party thinks that he/she is renting a house whilst the other party thinks the contract is a sale). Therefore, the contract is void.

Nevertheless, Article 1301.2.2 CC establishes a four-year limitation period for the claim for contractual nullity in the case of falseness of the cause. Since Article 1301 CC envisages the voidability of the contract and not the absolute nullity, the legal provision refers to the mistake as to determining the motives of entering into the contract. Although the subjective motives of the parties are in principle irrelevant,[193] when the motives have been incorporated into the contract by means of a causal agreement, they are legally relevant and may lead to the nullity of the contract.[194]

C. The Cause as a Means of Qualification of the Contract

148. Pursuant to the cause, contracts may be classified as: onerous, and gratuitous. Nevertheless, there are also neutral contracts, since they admit both the onerous and the gratuitous cause, such as loan and mandate, depending on the pact of interest or the remuneration (Articles 1740.3, 1711 CC). The onerous cause tolerates a certain degree of manipulation in order to achieve other goals besides the

190. TS 28 Dec. 2007 (RJ 2007/9064), 5 Oct. 2007 (RJ 2007/6801), 23 Oct. 2002 (RJ 2002/9481), 2 Apr. 2001 (RJ 2001/6643). *See* para. 95.
191. TSJ Catalonia 22 May 2003 (RJ 2003/5396), 6 Feb. 1995 (RJ 1995/4463).
192. TSJ Catalonia 19 May 2008 (RJ 2010\1615).
193. TS 29 Jul. 1999 (RJ 1999/5722).
194. There are no coronation cases in Spain (*see*, in English law, *Krell v. Henry* [1903] 2 KB 740). Albaladejo, *Derecho civil*, I, 691, refers to the following case (a real case, he emphatically says). A woman bought a flat next to hers in order that her mother could live there and take care of her; the vendor knew the facts and that the buyer had an option to buy another flat, cheaper but quite far away. Unknown to the parties, the mother had already died. The contract is voidable on the grounds of mistake as to the motives of the contract.

typical one. Then we speak of indirect transactions. For example, where the parties also want to make a partly gratuitous attribution through an onerous contract (a sale under market price with the obligation to take care of the vendor).

The so-called fiduciary transactions have been accepted by case law.[195] A fiduciary transaction is the transaction whereby one party *fiduciante* transfers assets to another *fiduciario* who holds the right in the former's interest, either with a purpose of guarantee (*fiducia cum creditore*) or of administration or custody (*fiducia cum amico*). Case law considers that a fiduciary transaction enshrines two independent transactions: a real contract of transfer of ownership (with effects *erga omnes*) and an obligational transaction (with effects *inter partes*). The latter transaction gives rise to the obligation of transferring the asset back to the *fiduciante* or to a third party once the purpose has been complied with.[196]

II. The Object of the Contract

149. Besides consent and cause, Article 1261 CC requires a 'certain object' for the validity of the contract. It is not much clear what the CC understands as 'object', and in fact this requirement is alien not only to common law but also to the *PECL* (*see* Article 2:101) and the *Unidroit Principles* (Article 3.2). Articles 1271 and 1273 CC only seem to consider as object of the contract 'things' (even future things) and 'services'. But such dichotomy is unsatisfactory. What about the contract of civil partnership? What about compromise settlements, or the creations of the mind? Therefore, object of the contract is the piece of the social reality on which the parties agree. Whatever it may be, the object must be susceptible to private ownership (*intra commercium*, as Article 1271 CC puts it). Rights concerning personality are in principle outside the sphere of *commercium*. Nevertheless, rights of personality such as privacy and own image are often the object of contracts (exclusives sold to the magazines specializing in social gossip). By contrast, human organs cannot be the object of onerous contracts, since only donation is permitted.[197]

A. *The Object Must Be Determined or Determinable*

150. According to Article 1273 CC, the object of the contract has to be determined as to its kind. Indeterminacy as to the quantity does not affect the contract unless a new agreement between the parties is necessary. Therefore, it is enough if the contract contains the elements in order to determine the object;[198] for example, a generic thing. In that case, the quality of the thing becomes irrelevant, since the CC provides that the debtor is obliged to deliver a thing of medium quality (Article

195. *See also* above para. 66.
196. TS 7 May 2007 (RJ 2007/3559), 31 Oct. 2003 (RJ 2003/7977), 17 Sep. 2003 (RJ 2003/6419).
197. Act 30/1979 of 27 October, and Royal Decree Real Decreto 1723/2012, pf 28 December, on the regulation of the activities of extraction, clinical use and territorial coordination of the human organs for transplants. *See* Juana Marco Molina, 'El régimen jurídico de la extracción y del trasplante de órganos', *La Ley* no. 5343 of 3 Jul. 2001.
198. *See* TS 14 Jun. 1996 (RJ 1996/4772).

1167). Determination of the price and the quantity may be left to a third person appointed by the parties. The third person may decide on equity (*arbitrium boni viri*) or on the best of his/her knowledge (Article 1690 CC). If the third person does not decide, the contract is void.

B. *The Object Must Be Possible*

151. Article 1272 CC states that impossible things cannot be the object of any contract. The provision refers to an initial impossibility. The contract of which the object is impossible is null.[199] If impossibility is only partial, the creditor may rescind the contract or demand performance of the possible part of the obligation along with a reduction of the price (on the basis of Article 1460.2 CC). Nevertheless, when the impossibility is relative, that is, performance is only impossible for the debtor, the case must not be dealt with as one of impossibility but as a case of non-performance, since the debtor would otherwise profit from his/her own lack of diligence.

The requirement for the object to be possible does not exclude future things from being the object of a contract (Article 1271 CC). In this sense, future things comprise non-existent things at the moment in which the contract is concluded, but susceptible to come into existence, whether by natural reasons or by human acts.[200] Nonetheless, the law may occasionally exclude some concrete things from becoming the object of a contract; for example, future inheritance (Article 1271.2 CC).[201]

C. *The Object Must Be Lawful*

152. The requirement of lawfulness is expressed in two different ways depending on the object being a thing or a service. Things cannot be outside *commercium*, whilst services cannot contradict the law and the *bonos mores*. Things outside *commercium* include the public domain and the rights of personality as mentioned above. The unlawfulness of the object makes the contract void.

III. Initial Impossibility

153. Initial impossibility, as opposed to subsequent impossibility, renders the object impossible and, consequently, the contract void. Therefore, the rules on

199. Nullity is laid down in Art. 1460 CC dealing with sale, but the same solution can be applied to other contracts.

200. For examples, a flat to be built (TS 23 Feb. 2007, Roj: STS 811/2007), a potato crop (TS 23 Feb. 1999 (RJ 1999/1415), 31 Dec. 1999 (RJ 1999/9386)). Case law and doctrine distinguish between *emptio spei* and *emptio rei speratae*. *See* Part II, Ch. IV, para. 376.

201. However, a nuanced approach is to be found in TS 22 Jul. 1997 (RJ 1997/5807): Art. 1271.2 refers only to the inheritance as a *universitas*, not to concrete and existent assets belonging to the (in the future) *decujus*.

non-performance cannot be applied, since the contract is void and of no effect *ab initio*.[202]

IV. Illegality and Public Policy: Unenforceable Contracts

154. Article 1255 CC lays down 'public policy' as one of the limits of freedom of contract. However, Article 1275 CC establishes that contracts with unlawful cause produce no effect, the cause being unlawful when it contradicts the laws or the morals. In addition, Article 6.3 CC also deserves to be mentioned, since it states that any act against prohibitive or mandatory rules is void. The court is allowed to declare ex officio the nullity of any contract that contradicts public policy or mandatory rules.[203] Finally, public policy is also a limit to the waiver of rights (Article 6.2 CC).

Public policy may be defined as the rules and principles that in private law lay the legal, ethical, economic, public and private criteria essential for the conservation of the social order in a concrete society and time. Therefore, the concept of public policy is dynamic, for it changes as time goes by. The constitutional principles are now the cornerstone of the concept of public policy. Morality as well is a fluid concept.

Circumvention of the law, aiming at the achievement of a result prohibited by the law, whilst respecting the words of a specific legal provision, does not lead to nullity, but to the application of the law intended to be evaded (Article 6.4 CC).[204] A special intention to circumvent the law is not required.[205]

§4. The Consequences of a Defect of Consent or a Lack of Substantive Validity

I. Avoidance of the Contract: Nullity

155. The terminology of the CC as for the consequences of defects of consent or other validity requirements is rather imprecise. Frequently the contracts affected are qualified as void, but the significance of that qualification is not always univocal. First of all, from a dogmatic point of view, it is necessary to distinguish between

202. In this sense, TS 15 Feb. 1994 (RJ 1994/1316). By contrast, according to Art. 4:102 PECL, 'A contract is not invalid merely because at the time it was concluded performance of the obligation assumed was impossible, or because a party was not entitled to dispose of the assets to which the contract relates.' *See* now Luis Díez-Picazo, 'Sobre la imposibilidad inicial de la prestación', in *Homenaje al profesor Lluis Puig i Ferriol*, I (Valencia, 2006), 1087 et seq. The lower courts seem to be more favourable to deny nullity based on initial impossibility; *see*, for example, the decision of the Court of Appeal of Lleida handed down on 13 Sep. 2007 (JUR 2007/335298).

203. TS 20 Jul. 2006 (RJ 2006/4734), 12 Dec. 1990 (RJ 2000/9890), 24 Apr. 1997 (RJ 1997/3398).

204. For a concept of transactions in *fraudem legis*, TS 31 Oct. 2006 (RJ 2006/7122), 8 Oct. 2003 (RJ 2003/7224), 28 Sep. 2000 (RJ 2000/8128).

205. TS 20 Jun. 1991 (RJ 1991/4526), 20 May 1988 (RJ 1988/4323). Nevertheless, normally such intention will exist.

ineffectiveness and invalidity. Ineffectiveness consists in a lack of the normal consequences that the contract should produce. By contrast, invalidity means that the contract lacks some of the legal requirements for the formation of the contract. If we take the broadest sense of ineffectiveness, it is possible to distinguish three categories:

1. Nullity (radical or absolute nullity). Every contract, that due to a structural defect is unable to produce legal consequences, is void.
2. Avoidance (relative nullity, *anulabilidad*). Although all the legal requirements are complied with, the contract is affected by a vice that renders its effectiveness weak, in the sense that an action of avoidance can be brought into court in order to set the contract aside.
3. Rescission. The contract is perfectly valid and effective, but it causes a detriment to one party or to a third person, so that a declaration of ineffectiveness may be judicially obtained. Rescission will be analysed later on.[206]

156. Sometimes the concept 'non-existence' is also applied to legal transactions.[207] This category finds its roots in the French legal system, because the grounds for nullity constituted a *numerus clausus* (*pas de nullité sans texte*). The absolute lack of one of the requirements set down in Article 1261 CC could lead to the non-existence of the transaction (e.g., an absolute lack of object in a homosexual marriage). Nevertheless, this category is useless in Spanish law, for its consequences are not different from absolute nullity and from such transactions, a legal appearance may also originate that must be destroyed.

A. *Absolute Nullity*

157. A null contract, because of its structural defect, produces no legal consequences, in accordance with the old aphorism *quod nullum est nullum producit effectum*. Such ineffectiveness is *ipso iure*, without any need for a judicial declaration. Nevertheless, the transaction may have initiated a legal appearance that must be destroyed. The judgment merely declares the nullity. Therefore, the claim for the declaration of nullity is unprescribable. Everyone may invoke nullity, and the court is entitled to declare it ex officio. A void transaction is not susceptible to confirmation or validation[208] (ex Article 1310 CC). Moreover, the nullity of the contract provokes the nullity of any right or transaction based on it, unless the law specially protects third persons.

Among the grounds for nullity, it is worth mentioning:

1. any contradiction with the law, the morals or the public policy (Articles 6.3, 1255 CC);

206. *See* below paras 282 et seq.

207. For example, *see* TS 20 Nov. 2002 (RJ 2002/1026).

208. Exceptionally, the contract concluded in someone else's name without the power of attorney can be ratified by the principal (Art. 1259 CC), even tacitly (TS 10 Jul. 2002 [RJ 2002/7175]).

2. an absolute lack of the legal requirements of transactions (consent, cause and object, Article 1261 CC);
3. an unlawful cause or object;
4. an omission of the formal requirements, *forma ad substantiam.*

The action to declare a contract absolutely null is unprescribable.[209]

158. Given the general principle of conservation of transactions, conversion is a means of avoiding the total nullity of a contract through its transformation in a different transaction. Conversion requires that the void contract fulfils all the legal requirements of such a different transaction. Being an exceptional remedy to safeguard the contract, the law must expressly establish this possibility. Two sorts of conversion are permitted. On the one hand, formal conversion, which presupposes that despite the transaction being void because the formal requirements have not been complied with, the formalities of another transaction have been fulfilled.[210] On the other hand, material conversion, which is imposed by the law, provided that the subsequent contract still satisfies the practical purposes pursued by the parties.[211]

B. Partial Nullity

159. Nullity may be partial when the contract is deprived of its effectiveness only partially. The contract subsists without the null part. For example, the exemption of liability for eviction is null (Article 1476 CC), but it does not imply the nullity of the whole contract of sale.

C. Relative Nullity (Anulabilidad)

160. If, in spite of the concurrence of all the requirements for its validity as established in Article 1261 CC, the transaction is affected by any vice that renders its effectiveness weak, the transaction is relatively null or avoidable. But the action to avoid the transaction can only be prosecuted by the party affected by the vice (hence, validation of the transaction is permitted). Therefore, the transaction is normally effective until the claim for avoidance is successfully brought to court. The relative nullity may be invoked judicially by means of an action or a defence.

The grounds for avoidance may be classified twofold: on the one hand, the vices of the transaction in general, including vices of consent and vices of the cause. On the other hand, the incapacity of one of the parties to enter into the contract (minors of age, etc.).

209. TS 4 Oct. 2006 (RJ 2006/6429), 1 Apr. 2000 (RJ 2000/2504), 21 Jan. 2000 (RJ 2000/113).
210. For example, a closed will, which is void because of formal reasons, may be converted into a holographic will (Arts 715 CC and 422-6.2 CCCat).
211. For example, Art. 1741 CC lays down that a loan for use whereby the parties agree on paying a price is converted in a lease.

The claim for avoidance lapses within four years.[212] According to Article 1301, the period begins to run:

1. from the day when the conclusion of the contract took place;
2. from the day when violence or threats come to an end;
3. from the day when the party becomes of full age;
4. from the day when the marriage property system is dissolved or the spouse is aware of the transaction.

161. Validation of a relatively null transaction is possible by means of confirmation, the loss of the thing that was the object of the contract and the running of the limitation period.

Confirmation implies the purification of the transaction by the party entitled to claim for its avoidance (Article 1310 CC). Confirmation requires a relatively null contract,[213] the awareness of the ground for avoidance, the disappearance of the ground and the capacity of the party confirming the transaction. It entails a new unilateral transaction, as results from Article 1312 CC, and renouncement of the claim for avoidance. Its effects are *ex tunc* (Article 1313 CC). Confirmation may be express or tacit. Tacit confirmation results from acts of the entitled party that evidence the intention to renounce the claim, such as the collection of the price or the exercise of the rights derived from the transaction (Article 1311 CC).[214]

II. Retroactive Effect of Avoidance or Nullity

162. The effects of nullity are the same whether the nullity is relative or absolute, irrespective of the ground for the nullity.

A. *Effects Between the Parties*

163. The contract, being null, is in principle without effect *ex tunc*, and each party must make restitution for what he/she has received *quod nullum est nullum producit effectum*. Such retroactive effect is laid down in Articles 1303, 1307, 1308 CC. Furthermore, there can be no claim for performance of the contract. Nevertheless, concerning restitution, if the ground for avoidance was the incapacity of one party, the minor of age or the party lacking capacity to enter into a valid contract is only obliged to limited restitution (Article 1304 CC). The minor is liable only for his/her actual enrichment (Article 1304 CC). Besides, the claim for nullity will be dismissed if the parties cannot make restitution because of the loss of the object of the contract (Article 1314 CC).

212. The period is one of *caducidad* (lapse of rights), not of prescription. *See* for the distinction below para. 331.
213. In case of absolute nullity confirmation is not permitted (TS 18 Mar. 2008 (RJ 2008/3054), 20 Nov. 2001 (RJ 2002/1026), 26 Jul. 2000 (RJ 2000/9177)).
214. TS 14 Oct. 1998 (RJ 1998/8374).

B. Effects as Regards Third Parties

164. Since the contract is retrospectively null, a purported transfer of property in virtue of it is also in principle without effect. Nevertheless, if a third person acquires in good faith and by an onerous title in accordance with the Land Register (i.e., under the requirements of Article 34 LH), the acquisition cannot be challenged.

III. Damages

165. An effect of the nullity of the contract is that there may be a claim in tort for damage caused to the party who relied on the validity of the transaction, in the same way as there may be such a claim for damage caused by *culpa in contrahendo*. The defendant is liable for the negative interest.[215]

215. Albaladejo, *Derecho civil*, I, 879 and TS 29 Nov. 2007 (RJ 2007/8452).

Chapter 3. The Contents of a Contract

§1. The Different Clauses

I. Ascertaining of Express Terms

166. The expression 'content of the contract' refers to the rights and duties that contracts create. Assuming that a contract has been validly concluded, it is necessary to consider the extent of the obligations imposed on the parties of the contract. There may be some doubt about the interpretation of the contract, and resort will then have to be made to the rules of interpretation (*see* §2 below). The validity of the contract neither mean that all the clauses or stipulations agreed to by the parties are effective, nor that they all have the same impact on the effects of the contract. For example, standard terms may not have been deemed as being incorporated in the contract (*see* III.A below). However, the Civil Code recognizes different kinds of conditional obligations; time clauses are admissible as well (*see* §3 below).

II. Implied Terms

167. According to Article 1258 CC, agreements are not only binding in their express terms but also in 'all the consequences that, taking into account its character, are in accordance with the requirements of good faith, usage and the law'. Good faith implies the fair dealing of the parties not only by the conclusion of the contract but also during its execution. The exercise of the rights arising from the contract must conform to the requirements of good faith, as also stated by Article 7.1 CC.[216] The mention of the usage refers to usual business practices. It has to be borne in mind that Article 1.3 CC equates this usage to custom, which is one of the sources of the law. As for the law, the provision refers to non-mandatory rules, since every contract must comply with the requirements established by mandatory laws. The importance of non-mandatory law is remarkable when innominate contracts are considered.[217]

III. Standard Terms and Exemption Clauses

A. Standard Terms

168. The transposition of the Directive 93/13 into Spanish law took place through the *Standard Contract Terms Act*, of 13 April 1998 (hereinafter LCGC), which came into effect on 3 May 1998. The legal framework also includes the

216. According to case law, the contractual good faith, as a concretion of a general principle of the law, imposes a fair, lawful, honest and logical human behaviour, which cannot thwart the performance of the obligations undertaken (decisions of 13 Apr. 2004 (RJ 2004/2619) and 21 Nov. 2003 (RJ 2003/8085), which quote many other).

217. *See* above para. 43.

Royal Decree on the Register of Standard Contract Terms, of 3 December 1999, and the *Royal Decree on Standard Terms in Contracts Concluded by Phone and by Electronic Means*, of 17 December 1999. In addition, the LCGC amended the provisions of the LGDCU regarding standard terms, but now the LCGC has been partially substituted by Legislative Decree 1/2007 (the new LGDCU). Therefore, the transposition of Directive 93/13 has been carried out by means of two different statutes.

A standard term clause is a clause drafted in advance that one party imposes on the other party when concluding a contract, irrespective of who has materially drawn it up. One of the main features of standard terms is that they are provided for a plurality of contracts. Therefore, standard term clauses are uniform, prepared and imposed on a party. The adherent can be a professional, provided that he/she is not acting for purposes related to his/her activity. The requirements for standard terms to be incorporated into the contract are transparency, clearness, concretion and simplicity. The legislator tries to make sure that suppliers provide enough information to their customers and use fair terms and conditions in contract. The contract is not necessarily null where some clauses are deemed not to be incorporated, provided that the contract can subsist without them (the court may construe the contract and fill in the gaps in accordance with Article 1258 CC).[218] However, the provisions contained in the LGDCU will be applied not only to standard terms contracts concluded with consumers, but also to contracts that include prepared terms imposed and not specially negotiated, although they have not been drafted for all contracts.

In relation to the interpretation of standard terms, it has to be borne in mind that clauses individually negotiated prevail over them, unless standard terms are more favourable for the adherent. The principle of interpretation *contra stipulatorem* is strictly applicable.

Unfair terms concern consumers. All clauses that have not been individually negotiated are unfair if they imbalance in detriment of consumers the rights and duties arising from the contract. Moreover, the new LGDCU contains a black list of unfair terms (Articles 85–90). Not only can standard terms be unfair, but also any clauses drafted in advance to which the consumer adheres. Where one or more clauses have been individually negotiated, the statute applies to the rest of the contract. Unfairness must be decided taking into account the goods or services that are the object of the contract, the rest of the clauses and all circumstances surrounding the conclusion of the contract. Unfair terms are void, and the part of the contract affected has to be construed in accordance with the principle of good faith (Article 83 new LGDCU). The judge who declares the nullity of the terms will construe the content of the contract and will be entitled to moderate the rights and obligations of the parties, as well as the consequences of its ineffectiveness when the terms are detrimental to the consumer, if the contract subsists. The judge may declare the nullity of the contract when the surviving terms cause an imbalance in the position of the parties that cannot be rectified.

Finally, Article 12 LCGC contains collective actions to protect the interests of consumers against the use of standard terms by sellers or suppliers. The action of cessation seeks to obtain a judgment that ensures that the defendant eliminates the

218. *See* para. 180.

unfair terms in his/her standard terms and prevents the future use of such terms. The action of retraction tries to oblige the defendant, whether or not he/she was the person who prepared the contract, to retract from his/her recommendation to use the unfair terms of his/her standard term contracts and also to avoid recommending them in the future. The action of declaration pretends to recognize the unfairness of a standard term. The actions may be brought by professional organizations, Chambers of Commerce, registered consumers organizations and the National Institute for Consumers and other similar bodies in the Autonomous Communities, professional associations and the public prosecutor. The declaration of unfairness by the Supreme Court of a clause binds all courts in further proceedings where the same clauses prepared by the same supplier have been challenged.

Judgments concerning the nullity or non-incorporation of standard terms, the exercise of the actions of cessation, the retraction or declaration and the continued use of terms declared judicially void will be registered in the Register of Standard Contract Terms. Suppliers may voluntarily register their standard term contracts.

Some of the terms that case law has considered unfair include:

- the buyer of an immovable is obliged to pay the tax on the increase in value of urban land (TS 22 October 2014, Roj: STS 4429/2014);
- the floor clause in a mortgage loan (TS 8 September 2014, Roj: STS 3903/2014);
- the compulsory acquisition of a specific decoder supplied by the provider of Cable TV (TS 13 March 2012, Roj: STS 2543/2012);
- fee services charged to acquirers of electronic air tickets (TS 12 December 2011, Roj: STS 8850/2011).

If a term containing a penalty clause has been considered unfair, the court cannot moderate the penalty, yet the court may award damages provided that the loss is proved by the claimant.[219]

The law of standard terms has quickly evolved boosted by the European Court of Justice. In the *Aziz* case (2013), several clauses in a mortgage contract were considered unfair. When the Supreme Court had to decide on the consequences of the unfairness, it opted for a partial retrospective effect, so that despite the nullity of the clause, banks also had to reimburse the money paid by clients from September 2013 onwards. The European Court ruled in the *Gutiérrez Naranjo* case (21 December 2016) that unfairness implies radical voidness, so that retrospective effect cannot be restricted. The decision of the Supreme Court handed down on 24 February 2017[220] applies for the first time this solution. The object of the decision was a soil clause of a mortgage contract that was qualified as non-transparent. The subsequent decision of 9 March 2017,[221] again on a soil clause, reminds that individually negotiated clauses – even a soil clause – are not standard terms, and then the transparency control is not at stake. Only if the court faces a standard term, the transparency control is necessary in order to ascertain if that clause is part of the contractual content.

219. TS 11 Mar. 2014 (Roj: STS 1484/2014).
220. Roj: STS 477/2017.
221. Roj: STS 788/2017.

The clause is transparent when the bank, in the case, has given the necessary information to capture its economic consequences and the consumer has been able to really understand such consequences. However, there is a latent approximation between the control of transparency – standard terms – and vices of will – individually negotiated terms. It will be necessary to pay attention at further decisions on the issue. The decision of 25 May 2017,[222] assuming that unfairness cannot be excluded with the argument that the business acted in good faith. The Supreme Court points out that good faith does not mean that the business could not foresee that the interest rate would sink, but that the client would accept such a clause that imbalances so much her position in case she had all the information that the business disposed of. Also in the last decisions the Supreme Court clarifies that the first step is the control of transparency – whether the clause has incorporated or not to the contract – and the second step is the control of fairness. All in all, it must be taken into account that the vast majority of cases concern banks and that Spain has faced a huge crisis at the banking sector, therefore probably there will be more refinements in the next future.[223]

B. Exemption Clauses and Limitation Clauses

169. Spanish law allows the parties to validly diminish or exclude the liability which otherwise might be attached to them where an obligation has not been performed. However, it is necessary for a more nuanced approach. A debtor cannot free himself/herself from liability for his/her intentional non-performance, since Article 1102 CC states the nullity of the waiver for the claim for intentional breach of contract. Besides, any agreement on the exclusion or limitation of liability is subject to the general limitations of freedom of contract, that is, the clause cannot contradict the law, the morals or the public order. Spanish doctrine considers that liability based on fault cannot be excluded, for example, in the case of personal damages.[224] Such a clause would be void. Exemption clauses should be interpreted restrictively, and in case of doubt, against the exempted party, in accordance with the *contra stipulatorem* rule.

Specifically, exemption clauses in standard term contracts are subject to stricter limitations. The balance between the parties' position is safeguarded by consumer law. Thus, such clauses must be clear, understandable and available to the consumer,[225] and the latter must accept them.[226] In addition to this formal control of

222. Roj: STS 2016/2017.

223. *See* on the issue Sergio Cámara Lapuente, 'Las (seis) SS.T.S. posteriores a la S.T.J.U.E. 21 diciembre 2016. El control de transparencia sigue en construcción, muta y mutará aúan más: Hacia la transparencia subjetiva', *Boletín del Colegio de Registradores de España*, 42, pp. 1746 ff.

224. Adela Serra Rodríguez, *Cláusulas abusivas en la contratación. En especial, las cláusulas limitativas de responsabilidad* (Pamplona, 1996); Natalia Álvarez Lata, *Cláusulas restrictivas de responsabilidad civil* (Granada, 1998).

225. Article 80.1.a) and b) new LGDCU.

226. Article 5 Act 7/1998, of 13 April, on standard terms. *See* para. 168.

the clause, it must not contradict the principle of good faith and the balance between the parties' rights and duties.[227]

The legislature has also intervened on a number of occasions to exclude or limit exemption clauses in particular types of contract. For example, airfreight contracts might not exclude liability for loss or damage to the goods.[228] In Spanish domestic law, exemption clauses are not allowed in publicity contracts.[229]

170. Of special practical importance is the distinction between clauses limiting the rights of the insured party and clauses defining the risk in insurance contracts. The latter define the object of the insurance contract, so that any risk outside its scope will not be covered by the contract. The former restrict, condition or modify the right of the insured party once the risk object of the contract has occurred. The distinction laid down in Article 3 LCS has been widely developed by case law. Clauses defining the risk only need a generic acceptation, whilst clauses limiting the rights of the insured party need an express and specific acceptation.[230] It is not easy sometimes to distinguish them. A practical criterion is that limiting clauses do not define the risk but allow the insurance company to reject the claim of the party.

IV. Penalty Clauses

171. A penalty clause is an agreement whereby a party undertakes to pay a lump sum in case of non-performance of an obligation. It is normally a clause incorporated in a contract, but it can also be an independent transaction; it can also be negotiated subsequently to the conclusion of the principal contract, but always before it becomes enforceable. Therefore, the penalty clause is ancillary to the principal contract, so that its nullity entails that of the penalty clause (Article 1155 CC). By contrast, the nullity of the penalty clause does not render the principal obligation void. Non-performance must be attributable to the party; *casus* and force majeure exclude the effectiveness of the penalty clause unless it has been expressly stipulated.

Article 1152 CC considers that the function of the penalty clause is the substitution of the compensation for damages and interests. It works, thus, as a clause for the payment of liquidated damages. The creditor does not need to prove that he/she has effectively suffered any damage, since the clause is automatic. Nevertheless, the parties may shape the penalty clause in a different way. On the one hand, they can stipulate a penalty clause compatible with specific performance and damages, like a sort of private fine. On the other hand, the clause may entitle one party to withdraw from the contract (*pena* or *dinero de arrepentimiento*) by paying a sum (Article 1153 CC); the party may opt for the fulfilment of the obligation or the payment of the sum.

227. Article 80.1.c) new LGDCU.
228. Article 23 Warsaw Convention of 1929.
229. Article 13 Act 34/1988, of 11 November, General on Publicity.
230. *See* TS 28 Jan. 2008 (RJ 2008/227), 27 Nov. 2003 (RJ 2004/295), 17 Apr. 2001 (RJ 2001/5279), 2 Feb. 2001 (RJ 2001/3959).

The court shall moderate the sum to be awarded when the contract has been performed in part, according to Article 1154 CC. Case law has said that this moderating power has to be applied ex officio.[231] However, there must be a partial or irregular performance, since moderation is not possible in cases of total non-performance, even though the penalty is more than the damages effectively caused by non-performance.[232] Moreover, the court cannot moderate the sum when the parties have agreed on the punitive and the liquidative function of the penalty clause on the basis of freedom of contract.[233]

V. Earnest Money

172. Earnest money (*arras*) can be defined as the delivery of a sum of money or any other thing when the contract is concluded. According to its aim, earnest money can be classified threefold:

1. Confirmatory. When the delivery is aimed at confirming the conclusion of the contract. The sum that is delivered is a part of the total price.
2. Penance. Earnest money allows the parties to withdraw from the contract. If that is the case, the party who delivers the money loses it, whilst the party who receives it must pay back in double. This is a typical function in the sale of goods (Article 1445 CC).[234]
3. Penalty. Earnest money is now similar to a penalty clause, but does not allow withdrawal from the contract. In the case of non-performance, the aggrieved party is entitled to claim for it (if the party who does not fulfil delivered the earnest money, he/she loses it; if the party who does not fulfil received the money, he/she must return it in duplicate).[235]

VI. Arbitration Clauses

173. Clauses providing for the arbitration of future controversies arising out of a contract are valid. Each existing or future controversy about which the parties can make a contract of compromise can be submitted to arbitration by agreement. The only limitation refers to the issues of which the parties are not free to dispose of.[236] The submission to arbitration can be incorporated into a contract as one of its clauses, or it can be a separate contract. The new Act on arbitration makes it easier to the parties to submit their controversies to arbitration. The only requirement is that the agreement must be made in writing or available by an electronic medium.

231. TS 27 Apr. 2005 (RJ 2005/3769), 17 Feb. 1997 (RJ 1997/1239), 10 Mar. 1995 (RJ 1995/1852).
232. TS 17 Oct. 2007 (RJ 2007/7307), 28 Jul. 1995 (RJ 1995/6634).
233. TS 21 Feb. 2014 (Roj: STS 498/2014), 3 Dec. 2014 (Roj: STS 4842/2014).
234. TS 20 May 2004 (RJ 2004/3529), 5 Nov. 2003 (RJ 2003/8258). Nevertheless, the Supreme Court states that earnest money clauses must be restrictively interpreted, so that the express intention of the parties must be clear.
235. TS 11 Nov. 2010 (RJ 2010\8040).
236. Article 2 Act 60/2003 of 23 December, on Arbitration.

If the parties do not expressly agree that the arbitrators shall decide in equity, they must decide according to the law.[237] The parties may also stipulate the number of arbitrators and the place of arbitration. The number of arbitrators has to be an odd number; if the number of arbitrators is not agreed upon, there will be only one arbitrator.[238]

The courts are incompetent to adjudicate controversies covered by a valid arbitration clause. However, provisional relief may be granted by ordinary courts. In addition, the arbitration clause is waived if the defendant fails to demand dismissal at the beginning of an ordinary action.[239]

§2. Interpretation

174. Interpretation is an operation that aims at seeking out the true meaning of a contract entered into by its parties. It is necessary to ascertain the common intention of the parties. Interpretation entails at least two steps: on the one hand, the determination of the facts and the ascertainment of the expressed intention; on the other hand, the qualification of the contract that the parties have really entered into, irrespective of the name they have given to it. In addition, it may be necessary to fill the gaps of the contractual regulation by means of the construction of the contract.

175. As a general rule, the CC seems to prefer subjective interpretation over objective interpretation. The aim of the interpretation is apparently the ascertainment of the true intention of the parties. Intention prevails over the literal meaning of words.[240] Thus, Articles 1281 and 1282 focus – literally – on the 'intention' of the contracting parties, on their internal intention. Nonetheless, internal intention does not always prevail over the declared intention. In interpreting a contract, both parties must be considered. Therefore, the principles of reliance and responsibility temper the pre-eminence of the internal and true intention. Each party bears the consequences of the justifiable addressee's reliance on his/her statements, taking the principle of good faith always into account.

176. The first means of interpretation is the literal element, the concrete words used by the party to express his/her intention. Therefore, Article 1281 CC lays down that where the terms of a contract are clear and leave no doubt about the parties' intentions, the literal sense of its clauses shall rule.[241] Nevertheless, the rule *in claris non fit interpretatio* is not an absolute one, since the same provision highlights that

237. Article 34 Act 60/2003.
238. Article 12 Act 60/2003.
239. Article 11 Act 60/2003.
240. TS 8 May 2012 (RJ 2012\6117), with several references to European soft law.
241. Case law seems to highlight emphatically the prevalence of literal interpretation, in the sense that it is only possible to deviate from the wording when it is clear that the words do not reflect the intention (TS 13 Dec. 2000 (RJ 2000/10440), 13 Sep. 2000 (RJ 2000/7632)). However, the conclusion that the words do not correspond to the intention is only possible after interpreting the contract.

the intention prevails always over the words. The clauses must not be interpreted in isolation, but systematically. The contract has to be interpreted as a whole (Article 1285 CC). In addition, Article 1282 CC provides that attention must be paid to the parties' contemporaneous and subsequent acts. That includes drafts of the contract and the behaviour of the parties before, during and after the conclusion of the contract.

177. As for the criteria, besides the already mentioned preference for the subjective and the systematic interpretation, Article 1284 CC states *favour negotii* as a main rule. The contract must be understood in the most suitable sense to be effective. Article 1286 CC takes up the teleological element of construction, since words 'shall be taken in the meaning which may be nearest in accordance with the nature and object of the contract'. Article 1288 CC collects the *contra stipulatorem* rule: interpretation cannot favour the party that has introduced obscure clauses into the contract. Finally, Article 1289 CC introduces some subsidiary criteria for interpretation 'where it is absolutely impossible to resolve the doubts by the rules set forth in the preceding articles'. Thus, if the contract is gratuitous, it shall be resolved in favour of the smallest transmission of rights and interests, but if it is onerous, the doubt shall be decided in favour of the greatest reciprocity of interest.

178. Consumer contracts have their specific rules of interpretation.[242] In addition to the *contra stipulatorem* rule, some of the criteria are the prevalence of particular clauses to general clauses, the prevalence of the most advantageous clause for the consumer and the prevalence of the most important clause for the contract as a whole.

I. The Role of Good Faith

179. No provision within the Civil Code expressly states the necessity of taking into account the principle of good faith in interpreting a contract. Nevertheless, the *contra stipulatorem* rule laid down in Article 1288 CC is a concretion of such principle. Case law has admitted the role of this principle in the interpretation of contracts. It may develop three different functions:[243]

1. The declared intention prevails over the internal, true intention provided that the discrepancy is due to the party's carelessness, and the addressee has relied on the declaration in good faith.
2. If the addressee could have understood the real intention of the other party, in spite of the literal meaning of the words used, the true intention prevails.
3. The declared intention prevails where, in accordance with the usage and the principle of good faith, the addressee understands something different than the real intention of the other party.

---

242. Article 10 new LGDCU.
243. Díez-Picazo & Gullón, *Sistema*, II, 83. *See* TS 28 Dec. 1982 (RJ 1982/7985).

II. Construction of the Contract

180. Although the terms *construction* and *interpretation* are generally used as synonyms, they must be distinguished. Interpretation refers mainly to simply finding out the meaning of words, whereas construction (*integración*) is used when dealing with filling in the gaps of a poorly drafted agreement. The legal basis of construction is Article 1258 CC, according to which the parties not only undertake the obligations expressly stipulated but also all the consequences in accordance with good faith, the usage and the law. Hence, case law had already established before the enactment of specific consumer law that the content of publicity brochures is also enforceable.[244] The law refers mainly to non-mandatory legal provisions.

III. Much Restricted Control by the Supreme Court

181. The interpretation of contracts is considered a competence of the lower courts. Therefore, the interpretation given by judges of Court of First Instance and Courts of Appeal prevail unless the interpretation is illogical, absurd or arbitrary.[245] In practice, the interpretation given by lower courts is seldom reversed, since it is deemed to be more neutral and objective than the one suggested by the parties.

§3. Conditional Contracts

182. A condition is a provision that makes the existence of an obligation resulting from a juridical act – in the present context a contract – dependent on an uncertain event. The term 'condition' refers to both the limitation established in the declaration of will and the uncertain event on which the consequences of the contracts depend. As a general rule, all transactions admit conditions, unless otherwise provided; for example, family law transactions (specifically marriage, Article 45.2 CC) or, in the civil law of Catalonia, the appointment of an heir cannot be made under a resolutive condition (Article 423-12 CCCat).

The main feature of a condition is uncertainty. Article 113.1 CC refers to a 'future or uncertain event, or a past event unknown to the parties'. But every uncertain event is a future one. In addition, the admission of past events unknown by the parties reaffirms that the uncertainty is the core requirement. Therefore, future but certain events cannot be a condition (e.g., the death of a person, according to Article 1125.2 CC). Moreover, the condition must be voluntary, in the sense that it cannot be a legal requirement (the so-called *conditio iuris*; e.g., marriage in the marriage contract).

183. The condition may be either suspensive, where the obligation will not exist unless and until the event occurs, or resolutive, where the obligation will cease to

244. *See* now Art. 61 new LGDCU.
245. TS 17 Mar. 2011 (RJ 2011\2884), 1 Mar. 2011 (RJ 2011\2612), 21 Dec. 2007 (RJ 2008/335), 12 Nov. 2003 (RJ 2004/203), 1 Oct. 2001 (RJ 2001/7137).

exist if the event occurs (Article 1114 CC). Whether a particular condition is suspensive or resolutive is sometimes a matter of construction, and even the law can establish a rebuttable presumption on the kind of condition (e.g., as for the sale based on approval, Article 1453 CC presumes a suspensive condition).

I. Condition and Term

184. If it is certain that some event will happen, we are not dealing with a condition but with a term (*dies*). The event is a future one, but certain, even though the precise moment in which it will happen is unknown (*dies certus an, incertus quando*: the day when someone will die). The term determines the moment in which the effects of a transaction begin (initial or suspensive term) or cease (final or resolutive term). Term (time clause) is also voluntary; if not, it is an essential requirement of the transaction (e.g., loan for use is necessarily temporal, Article 1740 CC). Exceptionally, some transactions do not admit a time clause; for example, the appointment of an heir in the civil law of Catalonia (Article 423-12 CCCat).

A suspensive term differs from a suspensive condition in that it does not suspend an engagement but only delays its execution. Therefore, the parties have an expectancy protected by the law (Article 1129 CC) because the event will happen. Besides, if the debtor mistakenly performs before the term has arrived, he/she cannot claim restitution (Article 1126 CC). If the term is a final one, the transaction produces its effects normally until the *dies* arrives.

The Civil Code considers the term as a benefit for the contractual parties. Article 1127 presumes that it constitutes a benefit for both parties, so that neither the debtor is entitled to perform nor the creditor is entitled to demand performance before the term has arrived. Nevertheless, the party autonomy permits the insertion of a time clause in favour of only the debtor, so that the creditor may not demand performance before the *dies* has arrived but the debtor can freely perform, or conversely in favour of the creditor.

II. Casual, Mixed and Potestative Conditions

185. Article 1115 CC makes a threefold distinction between conditions which are *casual*, *mixed* and *potestative*. A casual condition depends on chance or the will of a third person. A potestative condition depends for its fulfilment on the will of one of the parties. A mixed condition depends upon either chance or the will of a third person and the will of one of the parties. Casual and mixed conditions are valid. As for potestative conditions, authors and case law[246] distinguish between the 'purely potestative' condition and the 'simply potestative' condition. A simply potestative condition is one which depends for its fulfilment on the will of one of the parties expressed in the accomplishment of a certain act (e.g., I will sell you my house if you write a poem in my honour). A purely potestative condition is the one

246. TS 6 Feb. 2004 (RJ 2004/217), 3 Dec. 1993 (RJ 1993/9830), 30 Sep. 1993 (RJ 1993/6663).

which depends merely on the will of one of the parties. It is necessary here to distinguish between succession law and contract law. In succession law, purely potestative conditions are admitted, since the heir is free to accept or reject the inheritance (Articles 795, 800 CC, Article 423-12 CCCat). In contract law, purely potestative conditions on the part of the debtor are null, since the effectiveness of the contract will otherwise merely depend on the will of one party, a result that Article 1256 CC forbids.

III. Impossible and Unlawful Conditions

186. Impossible and illicit conditions are void. Article 1116 CC declares the obligations void depending on such conditions, although this does not necessarily mean that the whole contract is void. If the nullity refers to only a clause of the contract, the remainder of the agreement is still valid. However, the impossible or illegal condition affecting the whole contract renders it void.

IV. The Effect of a Condition

187. In order to describe the effects of a condition, one has to distinguish three possible periods of time: *pendente conditione* (pending the occurrence of the event), *eveniente conditione* (the condition is satisfied) and *deficiente conditione* (the condition will not be definitively fulfilled).

A. Pendente Conditione

188. 'Pendency' covers the period during which the condition is not satisfied but can be satisfied. In the case of a resolutive condition, *pendente conditione* the contract is fully effective – although not definitively – and enforceable. By contrast, in the case of a suspensive condition, the contract is not enforceable. No property passes and the debtor can claim restitution if performance has been mistakenly rendered. Nevertheless, the contract has been validly concluded. The parties have an expectancy that the obligation would become effective. Such expectancy is protected by the law. According to Article 1121.1 CC, the creditor is entitled *pendente conditione* to take whatever steps are necessary in order to protect his/her right. The expectancy is susceptible of transmission. Obviously, neither the debtor nor the creditor may withdraw from the contract.

The moment when the condition is fulfilled is a matter of fact, but the CC devotes two articles to it (Articles 1117 and 1118). If the parties stipulated a period in which the condition should be satisfied and the time period expires, the condition has failed to materialize. If there is no time fixed, the condition must always be fulfilled, unless it becomes evident that the event will not happen. However, in such a case the intention of the parties needs to be construed and, according to Article 1118.2 CC, the event must occur within the time presumably intended by the parties, taking into account the character of the obligation, that is to say, the function of the transaction and the aims pursued by the parties.

B. Eveniente Conditione

189. The satisfaction of a condition usually has a retroactive effect. The uncertainty disappears and, therefore, in the case of a suspensive condition, the transaction produces its effects, while in the case of a resolutive condition the effects cease. Nevertheless, retroaction is not absolute. Article 1120.1 CC establishes a compensation between fruits and interests, and Article 1120.2 lays down that the court would determine the retroactive effect concerning obligations to do and not to do. The acts of disposition carried out under a suspensive condition become definitive, whilst if the condition was resolutive the acquirers lose their rights (unless they deserve special protection based on the ignorance of the existence of the condition; e.g., the condition was not registered, and the purchaser of the immovable bought it in good faith). Acts of administration by the interim owner are binding on the definitive owner, unless in intentional or grossly negligent detriment of the latter.

190. The satisfaction of a condition is imposed as a sanction to the party intentionally preventing the fulfilment of the event (Article 1119 CC).

191. Article 1123 CC deals with the destruction or the deterioration and the improvement of the thing to be delivered under a conditional contract. The creditor bears the risk of destruction or deterioration alien to the debtor. Natural improvements benefit the creditor. Negligent destruction of the thing entitles the creditor to claim damages. The creditor has the option to claim either termination or performance, plus damages, if the debtor negligently deteriorates the thing.

C. Deficiente Conditione

192. If the condition fails to materialize, uncertainty also disappears. In the case of a suspensive condition, the transaction produces no effects. In the case of a resolutive condition, the effects will not cease, and the expectancies based on the possibility of the fulfilment will vanish.

Chapter 4. Privity of Contract

§1. The Rule of Privity of Contract

I. Third Parties and the Contract

193. According to Article 1257.1 CC, a contract produces effects solely between the parties (Article 1091 CC) and their successors, unless, in the latter case, the rights and obligations stemming from the contract are not transferable (res inter alios acta, *aliis nec nocet nec prodest*).[247], [248] However, the contract may also produce consequences in respect of a third party (a non-contracting party), in the sense that it may make him/her acquire rights (Article 1257.2 CC), undertake obligations, or cause him/her damage. Another case in which the effectiveness of a contract with regard to third parties is questioned is in the field of agency without power of attorney. In any case, a contract exists even in respect of non-contracting parties, and in this sense it can affect the rights of third parties. Privity of contract only means that third parties cannot acquire rights or incur obligations under a contract without their consent.

194. Where someone acts in the name of another without authority (*falsus procurator*), Article 1259.2 CC considers that the contract is null and void (*rectius*: ineffective), unless there is subsequent ratification by the principal. This party, until such ratification takes place, is merely a third party – not a contracting party – and, therefore, not bound by the agreements between the agent acting without authority and the other party, who are the sole subjects of the contractual relationship. Hence, only the other party, who does not know that the agent is acting without authority, could escape the contract (Article 1259.2 CC), but not the *falsus procurator*. The principal is only bound after ratification, by retroactively taking over the contractual effects. In this case, the intermediary who has acted without authority may be released from his/her contractual obligation with the person he/she has entered into the contract with.

II. Contract for the Benefit of a Third Party

195. Article 1257.2 CC regulates the stipulation in favour of a third party (in fact, the entire contract may be on behalf of the third party, and not just one clause), according to which a party is obliged to fulfil an obligation to the benefit of someone alien to the contractual relationship. For example, an insurance contract (Articles 83–99 LCS), a life annuity contract (Article 1803.2 CC), or a gift with reversional clause (Article 641 CC).[249] It is necessary that the parties confer directly a right on the third party, so that the latter can claim it[250] (if not, the third party is

247. Sections I–V have been written by Esther Arroyo i Amayuelas (University of Barcelona).
248. TS 16 Feb. 2010 (RJ 2010\1780), 23 Jul. 1999 (RJ 1999/6355).
249. For these and other examples TS 1 Jul. 1996 (RJ 1996/5548), 6 Oct. 1994 (RJ 1994/7464).
250. TS 9 Mar. 2006 (RJ 2006/5710).

merely an *adjectus solutionis causa*, someone only entitled to receive performance).

The indication of the beneficiary is essential at the time the debtor assumes to perform in his/her favour, but the designation is also allowed to take place at a subsequent time. The third party does not even have to be the person determined at the time of conclusion of the contract. In these cases, unless the beneficiary refuses to accept the right, he/she will only acquire it if he/she has the legal capacity when the obligation is to be performed. The beneficiary does not need to accept expressly; he/she only 'adheres to a legal act', which can be qualified as a non-contractual declaration binding upon receipt, given that the beneficiary is not a contractual party (the only parties are the promisor and the stipulator). Before such 'acceptance' takes place, only the stipulator – who has the right to designate the third party – may revoke the stipulation or the contract; after this, the beneficiary may claim performance from the promisor.[251] The stipulator can revoke the benefit conferred on the beneficiary as long as the third party has not accepted. The right to revoke passes to the stipulator's heirs. Revocation and acceptance are not subject to any formal requirement. In fact, acceptance can be tacit, resulting from the claim of the right.

196. The relationship between the stipulator and the promisor is a 'coverage' relationship, either onerous or gratuitous, according to which the former may require performance from the latter in favour of the beneficiary, or termination of the contract for breach. By contrast, the promisor can force the stipulator to execute the main contract (e.g., to pay the insurance premium). Between the promisor and the beneficiary, there is a typical relationship between creditor and debtor. The promisor can avail himself/herself of the purely objective defences, stemming from the character of the obligation, and of those which are personal to the debtor in respect of the beneficiary. Lastly, between the stipulator and the beneficiary, there is a 'valuta' relationship – the subjacent relationship – which may have gratuitous, *solvendi* or *credendi causa*.

III. Contract for Person to Be Designated

197. Legal doctrine and case law admit the contractual clause whereby one of the parties – the stipulator – is granted the option, during a specific period of time (as agreed between the two parties or, in any event, prior to performance), to indicate a person to replace him/her in his/her contractual position.[252] This choice has retroactive effects from the moment of conclusion of the contract so that, once done, it works as if the initial party – now replaced – had never existed. The person designated is a third party, in respect of the contract concluded between the person undertaking to accept the third person as a future party, and the person who has the power to replace himself/herself. If the designation does not take place, the initial party then becomes the final party. This is why some authors consider that this case

251. *See* TS 6 Jun. 2003 (RJ 2003/5341), 21 Nov. 1997 (RJ 1994/8094).
252. *See* TS 2 Mar. 2007 (RJ 2007\2525), 9 Mar. 2006 (RJ 2006/5709), 15 Dec. 2003 (RJ 2004/73), 21 Nov. 1997 (RJ 1997/8094).

is not one of the consequences of the contract in respect of third parties, but rather a type of contract whereby one of the parties is designated on an alternative basis. Once chosen, the third party must have the necessary capacity to become a party; furthermore, he/she must consent to become one of the contractual parties.

The only example to be found in the CC is Article 1766 CC concerning the contract of deposit. Article 7.9 of Act 28/1998, of 13 July, on sale on instalment, lays down, in relation to the obligations arising from the contract, the option of agreeing that the seller reserves the right to assign his/her rights to an unspecified person. Usually, if the clause 'for person to be designated' is incorporated into a contract of sale, the aim is to avoid paying the taxes twice.[253] In relation to judicial auctions, and, in particular, to specific performance, Article 647.3 LEC allows the executor to adopt the position in the auction with the faculty to assign it to another person.

IV. Contract Damaging a Third Party

198. This is a contract that, when entered into, causes damage to a person, whether or not deliberately, and who is not obliged to bear. There must exist causation between entering into the contract and the damage. This is a qualified application of the abuse of rights doctrine (Article 7.2 CC) in the sphere of contractual law. For example, cases where an exclusivity pact or agreement is infringed.

V. Contracts Which Impose Obligations on Third Parties

199. One party may undertake the obligation that a third person will give, do or not do anything in favour of the other party. The third party must accept such obligation. If this is not the case, the promisor is liable for breach of contract because, in respect of the other contractual party, he/she has guaranteed the fulfilment of such obligation. This contract is implicit in Article 1828 CC, for the provision refers to the obligation of providing a surety which the principal debtor undertakes in respect of his/her creditor.

VI. Direct Action

200. The adjective 'direct' implies that a person can sue another although they are not parties in the same juridical relationship. Direct action is a legal guarantee of the right of credit that entitles a creditor to exercise some rights of credit that his/her debtor may have against a third party. Direct action is a means of protection of the right of credit because the creditor in some specific cases may not only sue his/her own debtor but also the debtor of his/her debtor, although they have not concluded any contract. Only the law can grant such protection on the basis of the connection between the two obligations. The result of this connection is that the

253. Xavier Cecchini Rosell, *La cláusula 'por sí o por persona que se designará'* (Valencia, 2000), 281–284.

debtor pays at the same time his/her own debt and the debt of his/her immediate creditor. The connection is subjective and objective. Subjective because the debtor in the first legal relationship is the creditor in the second one. Objective because both relationships arise from the same object.

The most significant examples in the Civil Code are:

1. Article 1722: the principal against the agent's substitute.
2. Article 1522: the lessor against the sub-lessee.
3. Article 1597: the subcontractor against the owner of the building work.[254]

§2. TRANSFER OF CONTRACTUAL RIGHTS

201. Contracting parties may in certain circumstances assign or pass their rights to others. The change in the position of the creditor does not extinguish the legal relationship; on the contrary, the same relationship remains with a new creditor. There are two means that allow the change of the creditor: subrogation and assignment. Moreover, assignment may refer to the contractual position (*cesión de crédito*) of the creditor and to the whole contract.[255]

I. Assignment of Credits

202. The Civil Code regulates assignment of rights under the chapter devoted to the contract of sale. The assignor transfers the right that he/she has against the obligor, based on the contract, to the assignee. This transfer may be done by means of transactions other than by sale. In fact, assignment embraces any transaction whereby the object is the credit, aimed at changing the person of the creditor (including, thus, not only sale, but also donation, assignment in order to discharge a debt, etc.).

The object of the assignment may be any right of credit (Article 1112 CC), unless the debtor and the creditor had agreed that an assignment should not be permitted or the assignment is forbidden by law.[256]

The transaction chosen by the parties determines the form of the assignment (if it is a donation, it is subject to Article 632 CC, which requires the transaction to be done either orally with simultaneous delivery of the thing or in writing). In general, Article 1280.6 CC requires a public deed when the right assigned raises from an act documented in a public deed, but it must be reminded that the cases foreseen in Article 1280 are not of *forma ad solemnitatem*.[257] However, the legislator may impose a certain form exceptionally (e.g., to assign a mortgage credit, Article 149 LH).

254. *See* below Part II, Ch. 5, para. 418.
255. *See* on the different modalities of transfer of contractual rights TS 5 Mar. 2004 (RJ 2004/1811).
256. For example, Art. 151 CC forbids the assignment of the claim for the payment of alimonies.
257. *See* para. 93.

203. Claims relating to debts embodied in negotiable instruments are subject to a less restricted method of assignment. Negotiable instruments may be classified threefold: titles issued to bearer, to order or nominative. Titles issued to a bearer are transferable by simple delivery (Article 545 CCom) following a causal transaction, although mere possession entitles the right documented in the title to be exercised since the bearer appears to hold the right. Titles to order are transferable by endorsement followed by delivery (Article 19 LCCh requires a chain of endorsements). Concerning nominative titles, shares and similar titles require setting the transfer down on the title, the delivery of the title to the acquiror and its registration in the register book; cheques require delivery and setting down the transfer on the same title (Articles 14.2, 120.3 LCCh).

A. *General Principle*

204. The parties in the assignment of a right are assignor and assignee. The debtor is not a party in the transaction, since he/she does not need to accept the assignment.[258] In fact, the person of the creditor is, in principle, irrelevant for the debtor, since he/she must perform in any case. The immediate effect of the assignment is the replacement of the old creditor by the new creditor. When a public deed is not required, it is essential to know exactly when the transfer was completed. As for the date of private documents in relation to third parties, Article 1227 CC has to be taken into account. According to it, the date of a private document would not be effective against third parties until it is recorded in a public register, until the death of one of the parties who signed the contract or until it was delivered to a public servant.

In consumer contracts, the ineffectiveness of the consumer contract extends to the financial consumer credit even if the credit has been assigned to another financial company.[259]

B. *Effects of the Assignment*

205. Although not being a party in the assignment, and despite the fact that the assignment is valid and effective once agreed by assignor and assignee,[260] the debtor is only bound by the assignment from the moment he/she has been notified (Article 1527 CC). The law protects the debtor's interest in knowing to whom he/she must pay. If the debtor is not aware of the assignment and pays to the former creditor or assignor, he/she performs satisfactorily and discharges the obligation (Article 1527 CC). Therefore, the assignor is burdened to notify the assignment, since otherwise

258. TS 13 Oct. 2014 (Roj: STS 3909/2014), 30 Sep. 2015 (Roj: STS 4339/2015). This is the main difference with assignment of a contract, because the assigned party to a contract has to express his/her consent to the assignment.

259. TS 19 Feb. 2010 (RJ 2010\1787), 25 Nov. 2009 (RJ 2010\145).

260. TS 6 Nov. 2013 (Roj: STS 5875/2013). The moment when the credit is paid is irrelevant in that sense.

he/she would be liable for damages against the assignee. Nevertheless, the debtor may renounce to be notified (Article 242 RH in relation to mortgage credits). After notification, payment made to the former creditor will not free the debtor any longer. Only the assignee is entitled to enforce the assigned claim. Assignment does not need any form of *tradition* to be effective (TS 30 September 2015).

206. The change of the creditor does not only affect the debtor, but also the legal position of third parties, such as the assignor's creditors, new assignees. Once the assignment has taken place, the credit is also transferred to the assignee with respect to third parties. The problem that then arises is one of opposability of the transfer. This problem will be considered below in subsection C.

207. As for the defences available to the debtor against the new creditor, the general principle is that the assignee cannot be in a better position than that of the assignor. Although the debtor is not a party in the assignment, it cannot be in his/her detriment. Therefore, as a general rule, the debtor can avail himself/herself against the assignee of the same defences as it would have against the assignor (Article 1528 CC).[261] In general, the debtor can oppose to the new creditor all objective defences against the former creditor, such as prescription, payment, nullity. These exceptions are inherent to the assigned credit. Concerning set-off, the debtor can avail himself/herself of that defence as far as he/she does not consent to the assignment (Article 1198.2 CC), except in consumer credit contracts, where set-off is always available according to Article 31 of the new Act on consumer credits. In addition, where the debtor does not know about the assignment, Article 1198.3 CC allows the debtor to oppose the set-off of the debts incurred with the assignor subsequently to the assignment but prior to its notification or knowledge. The same is applicable to other personal defences of the debtor against the assignor.

208. The Civil Code regulates the relationship between assignor and assignee in Articles 1529 and 1530. The assignor, if in good faith, guarantees the existence and the validity of the credit *veritas nominis* transferred to the assignee, but not the solvency of the debtor unless his/her insolvency is previous and notorious, or at least known to him/her (Article 1529 CC). The assignor is not liable where the credit was assigned as uncertain, that is, where the assignee is aware of the risk of nullity of the credit. The *veritas nominis* refers to the time when the assignment took place, not to subsequent events. But if the assignment was gratuitous, the assignor is not liable. As far as the solvency of the debtor *bonitas nominis* is concerned, unless expressly stipulated, the assignor is only liable where the insolvency was previous and notorious (Article 1530 CC). Nevertheless, it is far from clear why the assignor is responsible where the debtor was notoriously insolvent, since the assignee could know (diligently) of it. Hence, the provision must be interpreted as the fraudulent concealment of insolvency by the assignor.

261. *See also* Art. 31 Act on Consumer Credit 2011.

209. The doctrine[262] distinguishes two kinds of assignment: assignment *pro soluto* and assignment *pro solvendo*. Where the assignment is *pro soluto*, the assignor discharges his/her obligation against the assignee merely by means of the transfer of the credit he/she holds against a third person; the assignor is only liable for the existence and validity of the credit. If the assignor's debt is only discharged when the assignee collects the assigned credit, the assignment is *pro solvendo*. The latter is to be presumed.

210. If the assigned credit is a contentious one, in the sense that its existence or validity is under dispute, the debtor is allowed to free himself/herself from the obligation by paying the price tendered by the assignee (Article 1535 CC). The law tries to avoid the speculation in the purchase of credits at a lower price. The so-called *retracto de créditos litigiosos* must be exercised within nine days from the day the assignee claims for payment. Nevertheless, cases in which the assignee has an interest in the assignment are excluded from the range of application of the rule (Article 1536, which covers coheirs or the assignment as a means of payment of a debt). It is also excluded the case of a bulk assignment of credits (TS 1 April 2015,[263] in the case the assignment of the credits within the framework of bank mergers in Spain).

C. *The Transfer as Against Third Parties (Other than the Debtor)*

211. The assignment has also effects concerning third parties such as the assignor's creditors. But, according to Article 1526 CC, the assignment will not be effective against them until its date is certain in accordance with Articles 1218 and 1227 CC.[264] If the credit concerns an immovable, the assignment is only effective against third parties from the date it is recorded in the Land Register.

II. Subrogation

212. The concept of 'subrogation' describes a legal effect, that of the maintenance of the credit in spite of the change of the creditor. A new creditor takes the place of the former. As it consists in the maintenance of the credit, this subsists with all its ancillary warranties (Article 1212 CC). Subrogation can be a legal effect of the payment made under certain requirements or an express agreement between the creditor and the subrogating party. Subrogation excludes the normal effect of payment, which is the extinction of the obligation. Such payments must be done by a third party or by a non-exclusive co-debtor (e.g., the solidary co-debtor, because when he/she performs the whole obligation, then at the same time pays his/her – partially – own debt and – also partially – alien debt).[265]

262. Díez-Picazo & Gullón, *Sistema*, II, 239–240.
263. Roj: STS 1420/2015.
264. *See* above paras 100–101.
265. That is, the share of each co-debtor in the whole debt.

213. Subrogation has three possible sources:

1. The law (an *ipso iure* effect), in cases where the surety pays the principal debt and therefore subrogates in the creditor's position (Article 1837 CC) and where the insurer compensates the damages caused and subrogates in the victim's position against the tortfeasors (Article 43 LCS).
2. The agreement between creditor and third party who performs the obligation (Articles 1209.2, 1211 CC *in limine a contrario*).
3. The unilateral decision of the debtor who performs with foreign money (Article 1211 CC).[266]

III. Assignment of Contract

214. Assignment of a contract is the transaction whereby a third person substitutes one of the original parties in its whole contractual position. This transaction aims at the transmission of contractual relationships as a whole, avoiding the transmission of its active (assignment of credits) or passive (assumption of debt) elements. This modality of assignment is not expressly regulated in the Civil Code, but it has been accepted by doctrine and case law.

The parties in the transaction are the assignor, the assignee and the assigned party. The assignee takes the position of the assignor in the contract and assumes the rights and duties inherent to that position. The object of the assignment is hence the whole contract, so that ancillary rights and warranties remain.

215. The requirements of the assignment of a contract are the following:[267]

1. The contract must be a synallagmatic one, because if only one of the parties has to perform, only a credit or a debt would be the object of the assignment and not a complete contractual position.
2. The obligations arising from the contract must not have been completely performed, since otherwise it would be impossible to assign the contractual position.
3. The consent of the original parties and the assignee, as well as the capacity of the latter to assume the contractual position.
4. The observance of form requirements of the contract to be assigned.

216. As for the effects of the assignment, the assignor is free from the obligations under the contract, but also loses any right deriving from it. The assignee and the assigned party become the contractual parties. The assigned party has to accept

266. This provision has been developed in the Act 2/1994 of 30 March, on subrogation in mortgage credits, aiming to foster subrogation in the case of financial institutions in order that the debtor could benefit from competition between banks and lower interest rates. This Act has been modified by Act 41/2007, of 7 December.

267. TS 8 Jun. 2007 (RJ 2007/3465), 19 Feb. 2004 (RJ 2004/1427), 9 Jul. 2003 (RJ 2003/4619), 19 Sep. 2002 (RJ 2002/8561).

the assignment. According to the Supreme Court, the assignment of the contract may be agreed beforehand in the same contract that is later assigned or in a different contract.[268] Both parties may avail themselves of the defences they have against each other, but they cannot oppose the defences they might have against the assignor, unless otherwise provided. The assignor is liable for the existence and the validity of the contract, but liability for performance has to be expressly stipulated.

§3. Subcontracting

217. Subcontract is a modality of contract whereby one party, on the basis of the legal position resulting from the contract in which he/she is a party, concludes a contract of the same kind with another person, so that both contracts coexist. The peculiarity is that the same person assumes in each contract a different contractual position. For example, the lessee concludes a new lease and subleases a part of the dwelling. Hence, the lessee creates a new legal relationship whereby he/she acts as a lessor (sub-lessor) in front of the lessee (sub-lessee). The Civil Code regulates two subcontracts: sublease (Articles 1550–1552) and sub-mandate (Articles 1721–1722).

218. However, Spanish law allows the parties to use the services of third persons, with whom, in turn, they make a contract, in order to perform their own obligations. This right of subcontracting, which is quite usual in building contracts, can be nevertheless reduced or excluded by law or by express agreement; it can also be excluded by the nature of the contract *intuitu personae*. Where a subcontract is concluded, the law provides the subcontracting party with a direct action against the main party.[269]

§4. Oblique Action, Paulian Action and Direct Actions

219. The property of a debtor is the common pledge of his/her creditors (Article 1911 CC). Although creditors may not enjoy special securities, the law finds ways to protect their interests. Under the expression 'legal guarantees of the right of credit' Spanish doctrine gathers different remedies granted to the creditor to ensure the collection of a debt. By contrast to personal – suretyship – or real – mortgage, pledge – guarantees, which need to be expressly stipulated, legal guarantees are granted directly by the law. However, those legal guarantees do not have the same effectiveness. Whilst direct action is an ordinary remedy, oblique action and Paulian action are extraordinary means of protection, since they both involve the reconstruction of the debtors' assets, as a consequence of the debtor's insolvency.

268. TS 25 Feb. 2013 (Roj: STS 4760/2013).
269. *See* paras 200 and 418.

I. Oblique Action

220. Article 1111 CC entitles the creditors to exercise all rights and actions of the debtor in the latter's name but in their own interest. The ground for this remedy is that the debtor's patrimony is not enough to satisfy all the creditors in relation to its possible amount. The debtor would be solvent – at least, more solvent – if he/she was already prosecuting the claims he/she holds against his/her own debtors. Therefore, oblique action is an extraordinary remedy to which the creditor can resort where he/she has no other means to be satisfied. It is not a new action or claim of the creditors against their debtor or against a third party, but simply the legal permission to exercise the debtor's rights and action in their own interest.

Oblique action requires a payable credit, and that all assets of the debtor had been pursued in vain. Nevertheless, case law has interpreted this requirement in a flexible way, so that the creditor does not need to prove an absolute lack of assets, but only the lack of known assets even in the same proceeding in which the oblique action has been brought into court.[270] This action entitles the exercising of any right or action belonging to the debtor, except those which are purely personal (such as the action to revoke a gift for ingratitude or the claim for damages for pain and suffering).

221. Two modalities of the oblique action can be distinguished. The first one lies on the mere inactivity of the debtor; the intervention of the creditors, then, changes the composition of the debtor's patrimony, by means of the transformation of 'rights' into 'assets'. The second one presupposes the extinction of rights, such as the rejection of an inheritance (Article 1101 CC, Article 23 CS) or the renunciation of *usucapio* (Article 1937 CC). In this case, the creditors exercise the right (e.g., they accept the inheritance in the name of the debtor) or the defence available to the debtor.

Any creditor can resort to the oblique action, it is not necessary that all the creditors act together. But the creditor who brings the oblique action does not thereby obtain any priority with regard to what is recovered, as long as the action is successful. The property recovered simply falls into the general estate of the debtor in favour of all creditors, therefore it cannot be adjudicated in payment to the creditor that has resorted successfully to the oblique action.[271] However, as the creditors exercise the rights of the debtor, any defence opposable to the latter can be opposed to the creditors; the same applies to the defences that have become available after the bringing of the oblique action.

II. The Paulian Action

222. Article 1111 CC defines the action for revocation or Paulian action as 'the legal power granted to the creditor to dispute the acts that the debtor has carried out

270. TS 18 Oct. 2007 (RJ 2007/8661), 26 Feb. 2002 (RJ 2002/1909), 16 May 1995 (RJ 1995/3919).
271. TS 6 Nov. 2008 (RJ 2008\5900), 25 Nov. 1996 (RJ 1996/9119). As the Supreme Court puts it, the action is oblique, not direct.

to the detriment of his/her right, where the debtor's net worth is insufficient to settle the credit'.[272] In addition, within the same general contract law theory, and based on severance, there are precepts that develop it, specifically Articles 1291.3, 1292, 1294, 1295, 1297, 1298 and 1299 CC. The general rule is stated in Article 1291.3 CC, according to which contracts concluded to the detriment of creditors are cancellable where the latter cannot collect what is owed to them by any other means.

223. Prior to the dispute, there has to be a credit in favour of the plaintiff and it has to be payable, since the creditor can only bring the Paulian action after having pursued the assets the debtor has in his/her possession (*see* Article 1111 CC). Moreover, the debtor must have committed a valid act that provides an asset advantage to a third person. After these basic prerequisites have been fulfilled, the concurrence of the following requirements is demanded:

1. Significant prejudice to the debtor's solvency. For these purposes, damage consists of the fact that the act or contract carried out causes a decrease in the debtor's net worth, to the point that he/she cannot settle the creditor's interest. This is the so-called *eventus damni*, which means frustration of the credit, and it is only confirmed if the creditor has no other means to collect what he/she is owed. The Supreme Court refers to a 'Paulian perjudice' in the sense of an unjustified lesion to the creditor's reasonable expectations to be paid.[273]
2. Any alienation that does not lead to a consideration of the debtor's patrimony is considered prejudicial to his/her solvency. Thus, donations, sales or rentals at absurdly low prices. However, this is not the case of payment of own debts or concluding new contracts if there is a balance in the provisions.[274] It is not necessarily a total insolvency; the court must be satisfied if there are no sufficient known assets of the debtor.[275]
3. That the act disputed is fraudulent, Recent case law tends however to highlight the objective character of the action, in the sense that intention to cause a prejudice is not necessary.[276] Establishing the participation of the third party in the fraud is more difficult (*consilium fraudis*), but it is indisputable that the act will be fraudulent if the third party knows that the debtor is deceiving his/her creditors.[277]

Due to the difficulty of proving fraudulent conduct, the legislator establishes some presumptions. To be specific, fraud is always presumed in gratuitous disposals

272. Written by Isabel Espín Alba, University of Santiago de Compostela.
273. TS 26 Oct. 2016 (Roj: STS 4646/2016).
274. TS 24 Nov. 1988 (RJ 1988/8705), the decision of 22 Apr. 2004 (RJ 2004/2082) emphasizes the requirement of a transaction aimed at the disposal of assets.
275. TS 27 Jan. 2004 (RJ 2004/46). Along the lines of the oblique action already seen above, the creditor does not need to prove an absolute lack of assets (TS 19 Nov. 2007 [RJ 2007/8456], 21 Apr. 2004 [RJ 2004/2080], 31 Dec. 1002 [RJ 2002/9735]).
276. TS 3 Nove 2015 (Roj: STS 4471/2015).
277. Nevertheless, the Supreme Court has considered that *consilium fraudis* is not a requirement, but the court must be satisfied with the awareness of the potential detrimental character of the transaction (TS 13 Jun. 2003 [RJ 2003/4304]).

(Article 1297.1 CC, *iure et de iure* [irrebuttable] presumption). Fraud is also presumed in any onerous disposal that has been carried out by people against whom a verdict of guilt has been pronounced in any action or where an embargo has been issued (*see* Article 1297.2 CC, *iuris tantum* [rebuttable] presumption). In any case, the creditor can always try to prove fraud by all the means recognized in law.

On this point, it is interesting to refer to the differences between the Paulian action and the action for simulation. In theory, simulation implies fictitious asset transfers, which are radically void (Article 1261 CC). Therefore, action for absolute simulation seeks the nullity of the act and the declaration that the assets continue in the debtor's patrimony. By contrast, the Paulian action disputes real transfers carried out by means of transactions that meet the essential requirements of validity, but are revocable due to the fact that they frustrate the creditor's right to collect the debt. The practical consequence is obvious since, while action for absolute simulation does not expire, the Paulian action is subject to a limitation period of four years. However, due to the difficulty in proving lack of cause, which is essential to bring the action for simulation, it is advisable to bring the Paulian action collaterally at the same time.[278] The limitation period runs from the day when the creditor knew or could have known of the transaction carried out by the debtor.[279]

However, the recent case law has softened those requirements; for example, the credit need not be immediately payable, but it can be a future one;[280] the subsidiary character has been adjusted, and a complete insolvency is not required.[281] All in all, the Supreme Court makes easier rescission.

224. As for the effects of the Paulian action, Article 1295.1. CC determines that rescission makes the return of the items that were the object of the contract obligatory, together with their profit and of the price with its interest. As a result, it will only be possible to carry this out when the person who has claimed it can return that for which he/she has an obligation. Nonetheless, in accordance with the majority position in Spanish doctrine and case law, the main effect of the Paulian action is the relative or subjective ineffectiveness of the act disputed. It is a system of special ineffectiveness marked by subjective relativity (it only reaches the disputing creditor) and objective limitation to the extent of the financial damage.[282] Therefore, the Paulian action is not aimed at restoring the debtor's patrimony, and the alienated asset is not available for the remaining creditors.

278. TS 30 May 1997 (RJ 1997/4118), 7 Jul. 1995 (RJ 1995/5594), 7 Jun. 1990 (RJ 1990/4742).
279. Therefore, if the transaction has been recorded in the Land Register, prescription runs from that day, according to TS 30 May 2003 (RJ 2003/5324) and 8 Mar. 2003 (RJ 2003/2564).
280. TS 21 Dec. 2016 (Roj: STS 5526/2016).
281. TS 25 Jun. 2010 (RJ 2010\5413), 12 Nov. 2009 (RJ 2009\405), 25 Jun. 2008 (RJ 2008\3235).
282. *See* TS 21 Oct. 1998 (RJ 1998/8230), 24 Jul. 1998 (RJ 1998/6139), 28 Nov. 1997 (RJ 1997/8430). This is still more obvious in Art. 531-14 CCCat. This provision is based on the non-opposability of the detrimental transaction to the creditor, who may act as if the challenged donation did not exist. Non-opposability constitutes a mechanism of solving the conflict created between the third party and the owner in relation to the same good. The donatee has acquired ownership of the object donated, in conflict with the donor's creditor – who, alien to the donation, counted on that good as guarantee of his/her credit. The solution of this conflict involves granting primacy to this guarantee – the creditor's – above the donatee's ownership, inasmuch as the change of ownership does not

However, where the property that has been alienated cannot be brought back, rescission is replaced by a merely compensatory effect. To be precise, Article 1295.2 CC establishes that rescission will not take place 'where the assets, the object of the contract, are legally in possession of third parties that have not acted in bad faith'.[283] Article 1298 CC states that 'the person that has acquired the assets disposed in bad faith in detriment of creditors will have to compensate the latter for the damage that the disposal may have caused, as long as it is impossible to return them for any reason'.

III. Direct Action

225. A direct action is the possibility given to a creditor to sue directly a third party debtor of his/her own debtor. Direct action is a means of protection of the right of credit because the creditor in some specific cases may not only sue his/her own debtor but also the debtor of his/her debtor, although they have not concluded any contract. Only the law can grant such protection on the basis of the connection between the two obligations. The cases in which a direct action is granted have been already considered above in paragraph 200.

---

affect and is not detrimental – is non-opposable – to the creditor. The basis, thus, of non-opposability lies in the precedence of the credits protected. Therefore, we can say that the precedent guarantee prevails over the subsequent ownership resulting of the gratuitous alienation. This approach corresponds to a common trend in comparative law, on which Antoni Vaquer, 'From Revocation to Non-opposability. Modern Developments of the Paulian Action', in *Regional Private Laws and Codification in Europe*, ed. Hector MacQueen, Antoni Vaquer & Santiago Espiau, 199 et seq., 'Traces of Paulian Action in Community Law', in *New Features in European Contract Law*, ed. Reiner Schulze, 421 et seq. However, the Superior Court of Catalonia has strictly sticked to the requirement that the credit has originated previously to the insolvency, hence leaving some creditors unprotected (decision of 19 Nov. 2015, STSJ CAT 11219/2015).

283. TS 24 May 2010 (RJ 2010\3712).

Chapter 5. The End of the Contract

§1. Payment and Breach

I. Payment

226. Payment or performance of an obligation consists in its undertaking on the part of the debtor of the prestation or in carrying out the conduct owed to the benefit of the creditor, in such a way that the interest of the latter is satisfied.[284] This requires that the conduct actually undertaken by the debtor matches the prestation as set out in the obligation. Consequently, the conduct must meet all of the circumstances and requirements foreseen in the obligation. Several precepts of the CC confirm this: Article 1166 CC, which excludes the possibility of payment where one attempts to hand over something different from what is owed or substitute the property owed for another (*identity of payment*); Article 1157 CC, which binds payment of the debt to the 'complete' hand over of the property or fulfilment of the prestation (*totality of payment*); or Article 1169 CC, which rejects that a creditor may be compelled to 'partially receive the prestation' (*indivisibility of payment*).[285]

The requirement for strict identity between the prestation owed and the conduct undertaken also extends to the time (Articles 1125.1 and 1100 CC) and place of performance. With regard to the latter, if this has not been designated, Article 1171 CC establishes that in obligations to supply a certain good, payment shall be made wherever the relevant good existed at the time the contract was entered into, whereas in the remainder of cases it shall be the domicile of the debtor.

A. *Who May Pay?*

227. The subjects of performance are those that undertake the obligation and those that benefit from it. When considering this criteria, a distinction is usually made between the *active subject of payment*, who executes the conduct owed, and the *passive subject*, the recipient or beneficiary of such conduct.

The *active subject* of the payment is, in the first place, the debtor, who has a legal duty to perform. In addition to the required capacity to act in order to assume the legal position of a debtor, the CC places an obligation on him/her in order to render

284. Written by Santiago Espiau (University of Barcelona, Spain), except subs. C and D.

285. An exception to the principles of *totality* and *indivisibility* of payment is provided by the so-called *legal* appropriation of payment, to which Art. 1174.2 CC refers. 'Appropriation of payments' presupposes the existence of various debts of the same nature between a sole debtor and a sole creditor. In such cases, by performing a conduct able to satisfy any of those debts, the debtor may state the debt to which this payment should be applied, unless the creditor does so on accepting such conduct, and the debtor does not oppose such appropriation (Art. 1172 CC). However, in the absence of any such statement on the part of the debtor or creditor, the Civil Code establishes three subsidiary criteria for appropriation. In the first place, preferential appropriation for interest before capital (Art. 1173 CC); second, appropriation for the most burdensome or onerous debt (Art. 1174.1 CC); and finally, of an equal nature, pro rata appropriation for all of them, which shall – by law – result in partial and incomplete payment even though the same consequences as payment shall be applied to this solution.

the property transferable: 'the free disposition of the property owed and the capacity to dispose of it' (Article 1160 CC). Assuming the existence of an obligation, the debtor must fulfil the said obligation once demanded, unless the debtor has been 'legally ordered to withhold the debt' (Article 1165 CC). In such cases, a *prohibition* shall exist that not only legitimizes an opposition to its performance, but also, in addition, if paid, this payment shall not be valid. Finally, the debtor shall be responsible for any fraud or negligence arising from performance (Article 1101 CC). The debtor also assumes a burden of diligence demanded by 'the nature of the obligation and corresponding to the circumstances of the persons, of the time and of the place', or, in its absence, 'that corresponding to a good *paterfamilias*' (Article 1104 CC).

228. In addition to the debtor, a third person can be the *active subject* of the payment. Any third person is legitimated to pay someone else's debt. The intervention of this third person is allowed in spite of the possible unawareness of the debtor or even where the debtor opposes this conduct (Article 1158.1 CC).[286] The only limitation placed upon performance by a third person is in the case of a 'highly personal' obligation that can be performed by only the debtor (Article 1161 CC). Yet the effects of the payment conducted by a third person depend on the position of the debtor and of the interest of this third person. When the payment is objected by the debtor, the third person can only recoup the amount that has been useful to the debtor. When the debtor does not object, the *solvens* can opt for reimbursement or for subrogation. Surrogation depends on reaching an agreement with the creditor (conventional subrogation) or having a specific interest (legal surrogation) in the payment (the third person wants to extinguish the obligation: the mortgagor who is not the debtor but sees the property threatened in case the debtor does not pay the mortgage) or in the obligation (the third person is willing to aquire the credit, e.g., in order to improve her rank)

B. Whom Should One Pay?

229. As far as the *passive subject* of payment is concerned, this is at all times, solely and exclusively the creditor or the person authorized to receive on behalf of the creditor (Article 1162 CC). Payment to someone other than the creditor shall not extinguish the obligation or discharge the debtor, except in exceptional circumstances in which the good faith of the paying party is decisive, or where the usefulness of this may finally be beneficial to the creditor. For instance, where the payment has been made to whoever is in possession of the credit (Article 1164 CC), or where the payment has been made to a creditor who has assigned his/her right unknown to the debtor (Article 1527 CC).[287] Apart from these cases, the performance carried out by someone different from the creditor would be ineffective to

286. TS 12 Mar. 2010 (RJ 2010\2344), 20 Dec. 2007 (RJ 2007/9055), 5 Mar. 2001 (RJ 2001/2564), 18 Dec. 1997 (RJ 1997/8819).

287. As far as usefulness to the creditor is concerned, *see* Art. 1163.2 CC.

discharge the obligation, even though this may give rise to an obligation in restitution for undue payment (*see* Articles 1895 et seq. CC).[288]

Assuming that payment is made to the creditor, the CC demands that the latter has, at least, the capacity to act in the administration of his/her assets; otherwise, the payment made shall not be valid, unless it becomes useful to him/her (Article 1163.1 CC).

230. Not only the creditor has the right to demand performance, but he/she can also be compelled to receive it. The creditor certainly has the authority to demand performance; however, if he/she fails to do so, since the obligation is payable, the debtor may similarly perform and compel the creditor to accept it. In this respect, the creditor owes a *burden of collaboration*, which corresponds to the interest of the debtor in being discharged. Therefore the debtor may 'compel' his/her creditor to accept performance, and this refers to both obligations *in dando vel in faciendo* (*see* Articles 1161, 1166.1 and 1169.1 CC, *to the contrary*).

Developing this principle, the Civil Code regulates 'deposit' as an instrument that allows the debtor to discharge the obligation where the creditor does not wish or cannot accept performance, as well as where such discharge may prove difficult owing to certain circumstances (Article 1176 CC). Deposit consists of placing the property owed at the disposal of the legal authorities (Article 1178.1 CC) and authorizes the debtor to ask the judge to cancel the obligation (Article 1180.1 CC). *See below* paragraph 250.

C. *What to Pay?*

231. As mentioned above, a creditor may not be forced to receive anything other than what is due to him/her, even though the value of the thing offered is equal or even greater than the amount due. The creditor may avail himself/herself of the defences of identity and totality of the payment against the tender made by the debtor to fulfil the obligation with a different object. However, it is obvious that the creditor may accept any performance as payment, as it will be seen.

In the case of a generic obligation, the debtor is released if he/she hands over a thing of average quality (Article 1167 CC).

The creditor does not have to accept part-performance unless either a specific law or the contract obliges him/her to do so. If the debtor tries to pay in instalments, the creditor is entitled to reject the first instalment without incurring *mora creditoris*.[289]

D. *Special Rules as to Payment of Money Debts*

232. The genuine monetary debt is the sum debt, whereby the debtor undertakes the obligation of handing over a certain amount of money to the creditor irrespective of the concrete 'signs' he/she uses (notes, coins, etc.). The main feature of this

288. *See* below Part II, Ch. 13, §3.
289. *See* below para. 250.

obligation is that its fulfilment cannot become impossible, since an official currency will always exist. Non-performance of the obligation causes a detriment to the creditor, who is then entitled to claim the legal interest (Article 1108 CC).

Obligations to pay a sum of money are governed by the nominalist principle. Consequently, the debtor discharges the debt by paying the nominal amount of the debt fixed in the contract, regardless of the fact that the currency has depreciated in value since the contract was concluded (Articles 1170 and 1754 CC).[290] The parties, however, may resort to clauses incorporating indices of prices or other clauses to avoid the inconveniences of the monetary fluctuations.

233. A Spanish court can pass judgment for an amount expressed in foreign currency. The exchange rate is the one published by the European Central Bank. If the stipulated currency could not be delivered, it must be exchanged for the legal currency in Spain (Article 1170 CC).

The creditor cannot be compelled as a rule to take payment by cheque. If he/she takes it, Article 1170.2 CC establishes that the obligation is then not released until the cheque is cleared.[291]

234. The obligation of interest is accessory to the obligation of returning or handing over the capital. The accessory character is apparent since the stabilization clauses stipulated for the capital are not applicable to the obligation of interest; the guarantees of the principal include the interest, and the payment of the principal also extinguishes the obligation of interest. Any payment done by the debtor is preferentially appropriated to any outstanding interest in full and then to the principal. Interest may be either legal or conventional. Legal interest is determined by the economic authorities. Conventional interest is limited by the statute against usury.

E. Payment with Subrogation

235. Subrogation in its largest sense implies that a person (personal subrogation) or a thing (real subrogation) in a defined legal situation are replaced by another person or another thing without extinction of the legal relationship. Articles 1209 et seq. CC refers to personal subrogation in relation to payment, so that in some cases the person who pays does not extinguish the obligation but takes the position of the creditor vis-à-vis the debtor.

236. The effects of performance shall be produced on the satisfaction of the creditor's interest at which the payment is aimed. At this point, the debtor discharges his/her obligation (Articles 1164, 1175 and 1176 CC).

However, the effects of performance shall vary depending on whether such performance has been undertaken by the debtor or by a third person. Certainly, if

290. Only exceptionally the Supreme Court admits that the nominalist principle yields in abnormal events (TS 17 Oct. 2002 [RJ 2002/8765]: the devaluation of the ruble after the fall of the Soviet Union).
291. TS 1 Jul. 2002 (RJ 2002/5833), 28 Jan. 1998 (RJ 1998/119), 4 Jan. 1989 (RJ 1989/95).

payment has been made by the debtor, the obligation shall be extinguished, and the debtor is discharged. However, no discharging effect will be produced in all cases where payment has been made by a third person. If the third person pays with the consent or the approval of the debtor, or by holding an interest in performance, he/she subrogates in the rights of the creditor; the obligation subsists, without resulting in the debtor being discharged (*see* Articles 1159, 1210.2 and 3 CC). In any other case, the third person's payment extinguishes the obligation and gives rise to a new obligation between the third person and the debtor. By virtue of this new obligation, the former may demand from the latter either whatever has been paid to the original creditor[292] or whatever has been useful for the debtor in cases where the third person had acted contrary to the express will of the debtor (Article 1158.2 and 3 CC).

II. Non-performance

237. In Spanish law, the expression 'non-performance' is a key concept applicable to any situation where a party does not perform under the terms originally agreed.[293] Non-performance may consist in a failure to perform, in a defective performance or in a performance carried out too early or too late. Therefore, 'non-performance' (*incumplimiento*) has various meanings. Besides, the concept of non-performance pays no attention to the causes of the breach of contract, since the failure may or may not be imputable to the debtor or to the creditor – when non-performance is due to an impediment unconnected to them. Nevertheless, these facts are not irrelevant for the consequences of non-performance. When non-performance is imputable to the debtor, the creditor can claim performance and damages. In the case of synallagmatic contracts the aggrieved party may either terminate the contract (*facultad de resolución*) or claim performance (in both cases damages can also be claimed). When non-performance is not imputable to the debtor, part of these rights cannot be claimed.

These situations (non-performance of the obligation, cases imputable to the debtor and their consequences) are established in Article 1101 CC. This provision is not very clear – it can also be said to be technically incorrect, because the provision mixes up the situations of irregularities of performance with the criteria of imputation. The article states that the party who commits fraud, fault or delay or violates the obligation in whatever way is obliged to compensate. But it must be noted that fraud and fault are criteria of imputation, whereas delay and violation of obligation are cases of non-performance.

A. *Debtor's Delay*

238. The first type of irregularity of performance expressly regulated in the CC is the debtor's delay or debtor's default. According to Article 1100.1 CC, 'debtors

292. Not the total amount of the debt; *see* TS 5 Mar. 2001 (RJ 2001/2564).
293. Written by María Paz García Rubio (University of Santiago de Compostela).

who are obligated to give or to do something incur in delay from the moment the creditor claims performance of the obligation – whether judicially or extrajudicially'.

'*Mora debitoris*' is a delay in performing the obligation subject to certain conditions:

1. First, the delayed obligation must be an obligation to give or do something. In negative obligations, *mora* does not exist, because non-performance cannot possibly be delayed. This obviously implies that non-performance is always definitive in negative obligations.
2. Second, delay in legal terms can only exist where the obligation is demandable. Thus, there is no delay if a deadline has been set, and it is not yet over. In the case of monetary obligations, it must be liquidated (*in illiquidis non fit mora*). Generally, the obligation is not liquidated if the creditor does not claim a specific amount of money. As Article 572 LEC states: 'Any amount of money expressed by means of characters, figures or digits in the enforceable title will be considered 'liquidated' in case of specific performance.' Only a reasonable discrepancy with the total amount of the debt allows resorting to the *in illiquidis non fit mora* principle in order to avoid payment of interest, according to case law.[294]
3. Finally, the debtor must be notified by means of a warning or notice of default (*interpelación*). This warning is a duty of the creditor, and consists in a unilateral declaration made by the creditor; the debtor must receive it. The notice can be a judicial or an extrajudicial demand, which does not require specific form. Its purpose is to clarify that the creditor has an interest in the performance of the obligation, and it is a manifestation of the principle of favouring the debtor. Nevertheless, Article 1100 CC states that, even without formal warning, *mora* is incurred (automatic delay (*mora automática*)):
   a. where the obligation or the norm clearly specifies a fixed date for performance (Some situations of automatic delay are described in Articles 63.1 CCom, or 284, 1682.1, 1744, 1770.2 and 1896 CC.);
   b. where the period for performance is essential to the obligation (Article 1100.2, paragraph 2).

The interpretation of this part of the article is difficult. It cannot refer to the essential period of performance, because in these obligations, the creditor no longer retains an interest in performance, when the period is over, and delay means definitive non-performance. Some authors interpret this paragraph of Article 1100.2 as referring to the situations where performance is still useful in case of delay, although it may be urgent in the mind of the parties. Others point out that this paragraph must be analysed from the perspective of the allocation of risks in the obligation; for instance, when the debtor is obligated to prevent a danger to the creditor. In this case, the debtor must choose the moment of his/her activity, and no notice of default is needed.

294. TS 10 Dec. 2010 (Roj: STS 7345/2010), 6 Apr. 2009 (Roj: STS 1644/2009).

239. The effects of delay in Spanish law are similar to those in other European legal systems. They are basically two as follows:

1. The debtor's obligation to perform remains unaffected, if still possible.
2. The debtor must repair the damage caused by his/her delay in performing, in accordance to Article 1101 CC. The measure of damages is stated in Article 1107 CC. Concerning monetary obligations, damages are agreed by the parties and, if the stipulation of interest does not exist, the debtor must pay the legal interest (the statutory rate), pursuant to Article 1108 CC. So, the monetary obligation is a privileged obligation, because the creditor does not need to prove damages. However, the difficulty in interpreting this article arises when deciding whether the moratory interests are fixed damages or if, alternatively, the creditor can demand compensatory and not merely moratory damages. Most authors favour this second possibility, though in this case the burden of proof falls on the creditor.

The third effect of the debtor's default is *perpetuatio obligationis*, that is to say, the enhancement of the debtor's responsibility. This implies that the debtor is liable even for fortuitous cases, as stated in Articles 1096.3 and 1182 CC. This aggravation of liability reveals a punitive attitude, which is inconsistent within the Spanish system of contractual responsibility.[295]

240. The debtor's default is especially relevant in obligations arising from synallagmatic contracts. Article 1100.2 CC states that in synallagmatic obligations, a party does not incur *mora* if the other party does not perform his/her own obligation. A party's default runs from the moment the other party fulfils his/her obligation. The classical interpretation of this article considers that in synallagmatic obligations with simultaneous performance, performance by one party implies automatic delay for the other party – and no formality to put it into default is needed. In this sense, performance stands in for the warning. By contrast, other authors consider that default starts when the requirements (warning included) are fulfilled, but enforceable obligations must also be performed. Thus, in synallagmatic obligations warning is not excluded. It must be pointed out that Spanish courts have not been very conclusive on this point.[296]

241. The debtor's default finishes with performance, when the creditor or a provision gives him/her additional time to perform, and when the debtor is able and willing to perform, but the creditor does not accept performance (*mora creditoris*). In these cases, the consequences of the debtor's default during the time of the delay persist.

'*Purgation*' of the default means the elimination of its effects. This situation arises where the creditor waives the rights derived from the default.

---

295. Fernando Pantaleón, 'El sistema de responsabilidad contractual (Materiales para un debate)', ADC (1991): 1019.

296. Manuel Albaladejo, 'La mora en las obligaciones recíprocas', RCDI (1968): 10–11. *See* TS 26 Dec. 2001 (RJ 2001/1233).

242. It is worth mentioning Directive 2000/35/EC of the European Parliament and of the Council of 29 June 2000 on combating late payment in commercial transactions. The Directive is limited to payments made as remuneration for commercial transactions and does not regulate transactions involving consumers. For the purpose of the Directive 'commercial transactions' means B2B transactions or between business and public authorities, which lead to the delivery of goods or the provision of services for remuneration. 'Late payment' means exceeding the contractual or statutory period of payment. No other requirement is necessary. The Act 15/2010, of 5 July, has newly transposed not only the European Directive affecting businesses but also public administrations and has established long adaptation deadlines.

B. Definitive Non-performance: Permanent Impossibility to Perform

243. Non-performance of the obligation can be definitive if the object of the obligation becomes permanently impossible. According to Spanish authors, this case is called supervening impossibility (*imposibilidad sobrevenida*). This situation exists if the object of the obligation was possible when the obligation arose but it subsequently became impossible.

244. According to Article 1156.2 CC, the loss of the thing is a ground for extinction of the obligation. Nevertheless, within the CC, impossibility only extinguishes the obligation and terminates the link between the debtor and the creditor if it is a consequence of 'force majeure', and it is not imputable to the debtor. This means that in unilateral obligations, the creditor bears the damage. However, in these unilateral obligations, failure to perform caused by impossibility imputable to the debtor does not release him/her, but the obligation subsists, and it is for the creditor to claim performance and damages.

In case of synallagmatic contracts, the creditor can always resort to synallagmatic remedies (right to terminate the contract and right to withhold performance). This means that in bilateral obligations, both parties suffer the consequences of non-performance. In fact, the creditor of an impossible obligation cannot claim its performance, but the debtor cannot claim the counter-performance.

245. Concerning obligations to do something, Article 1182 CC considers that when a certain and determinate thing that is the object of an obligation, happens to perish or is lost, the obligation is also extinguished if the thing would have perished or would have been lost without the debtor's fault, and before he/she was in delay. According to Article 1183 CC, when the thing is in the debtor's hands the loss is presumed to have happened by fault and not by fortuitous event (*caso fortuito*). In obligations to do and not to do, according to Article 1184 CC, the debtor will be discharged where performance would be unlawful or impossible.

Impossibility not imputable to the debtor can also be only partial. In these cases discharge of the debtor is limited to the part of the obligation affected by the impossibility. In the case of a partial impossibility of a synallagmatic obligation, the creditor can choose between claiming partial performance, with the reduction of his/her own obligation, or terminating the contract.

However, according to Article 1186 CC, where the thing has perished without fault on the part of the debtor, if there are any claims or actions for indemnity in reference to such thing, they belong to the creditor. Spanish authors think that the transfer of actions to the creditor is not automatic, but the debtor is bound to yield them to the aggrieved party. This article must be applied in every case of obligations to give. Nevertheless, the rule must be qualified in the synallagmatic obligations. In these cases, if the creditor of the lost thing claims termination of the contract, he/she is not entitled to the debtor's actions mentioned by Article 1186. Both remedies, termination and actions for loss of the thing against third persons, are incompatible.

C. *Defective Performance*

246. In Spanish law, non-performance may consist of a defective performance. There is defective performance in cases where the debtor carries out acts of performance, but performs in a way that does not satisfy the creditor's interest, or it is not conforming with the contract. Among other cases, there are situations of defective performance where the debtor performs the obligation in due time, but he/she does not perform an accessory but important duty (e.g., the seller delivers the computer to the purchaser, but does not deliver the instructions about its use). There is also a defective performance if the debtor delivers a defective good or carries out the service but in a negligent way.

The CC does not rule this topic systematically. There are some articles dealing with non-performance in general, such as Articles 1101 or 1098 (to contravene in any way the obligation), and others included in the chapters devoted to the contract of sale (Articles 1484 et seq.) or the contract of work. This lack of a systematic approach is one of the crucial problems in the codified Law of Obligations in Spain and probably it needs an important and a general reform.

Taking into account the provisions of the Civil Code, the most interesting consequences of a defective performance of the obligation are, first, that the creditor bears the burden of diligently examining the performance of the obligation. If the creditor accepts performance and he/she knows or should have known that it is defective, acceptance saves the nonconformity, and the debtor is freed. Second, the creditor has the right to refuse defective performance. This right is not clearly expressed in the Civil Code, but its existence is deduced from Articles 1166, 1169 and 1176, which concern the payment of the obligation.

247. If the creditor has accepted performance, but has reserved the right to claim for its defective character, or if the defect becomes known for the creditor after the reception of the thing, he/she can resort to different remedies. However, the creditor can claim specific performance. In relation to obligations to give something, specific performance can amount to repair the defect or to replace the defective good. The CC does not clearly recognize the two possibilities of specific performance.

Article 119 new LGDCU dealing with durable consumer goods, however, recognizes both of them. Both remedies are also expressed in the Convention of Vienna about International Sale of Goods, ratified by Spain. At this moment, Article 3 of Directive 1999/44 recognizes repair and replacement (at the consumer's choice) for all consumer goods and free of charge; the Directive was been transposed into Spanish law through the Act 23/2003 of 10 July and now has incorporated into the new LGDCU. However, the debtor is also liable for the damages caused by a defective performance if these damages are imputable to him/her. The concept of nonconformity is still not present in the CC, but the proposal prepared by the Commission on Codification considers it a goal that needs to be achieved.

248. Spanish writers discuss the possibility of terminating the contract or withholding performance where defective performance concerns a synallagmatic contract. Some authors argue that termination should be an exceptional remedy and that, generally, it is not appropriate in the case of a defective performance.

However, it is necessary to consider the case where the seller has delivered defective goods. In Spanish law, in the first place, delivery of defective goods may amount to non-performance of the contract and may also render the seller liable under the '*latent defects*' guarantee. This guarantee includes an action for termination or reduction of the price, but only within six months after delivery of the good. Spanish authors and case law have believed that this period of time is too short. This is why liability for defects in goods is often subject to general regime of breach of contract, so even the purchaser can terminate the contract where non-performance is fundamental. Some authors also argue that it must be possible to claim reduction of the price during the general period of prescription. Price reduction and termination are the two remedies of the Directive 1999/44, as well as in Article 121 new LGDCGU – through which the Directive has been transposed into Spanish law – when replacement or repair are not possible.

Spanish authors consider that the buyer can always withhold performance where he/she has been supplied with defective goods.

The CC Cat has instead resorted to the notion of non-performance. European private law alike, nonconformity in an inclusive concept ensrhrining any deviation of the assets in respect to the reasonable expectations of the debtor according to the contract. Quantity, quality, type and package determine conformity (Articles 621-20 ff CCCat). Fault on the debtor is unnecessary. Although the regulation is far from perfect, conformity depends first on the common intention of the parties to the contract as to the characteristics of the thing; this common intention may be express or implicit, provided that the seller admits the specific use claimed by the acquiror. When the seller has presented a sample to the acquiror, the thing must gather all the attributes of the sample. Conformity also takes into account the statements made by or attributable to the vendor, including any publicity. In the last term, the thing must fulfil the standard quality. Incorrect installation also leads to nonconformity when the item was intended to be installed by the consumer and the incorrect installation was due to a shortcoming in the installation instructions. Under Catalan law, any acquiror, whether business or consumer in C2C contracts, is obliged to inspect the delivered goods; only consumers in B2C contracts must not. Additionally, the acquiror has to communicate the nonconformity of the assets. Ignoring these two burdens prevents the acquiror from alleging nonconformity.

D. Imputable and Non-imputable Non-performance and Their Consequences

249. Non-performance may either be imputable to the debtor, or it may not be imputable to him/her. In the first case, the debtor is liable for non-performance, in the second he/she is not. Failure to perform can be imputed to the debtor by fraud (*dolo*) or by fault (*culpa*). Failure cannot be imputed to the debtor on the basis of fortuitous event. Between '*dolo*' or '*culpa*' and fortuitous event, there are situations not attributable to the debtor according to the traditional criterion. Nevertheless, the debtor is liable. These are the cases where the risk of non-performance falls on the debtor.[297]

III. Creditor's Default

250. Sometimes the debtor cannot fulfil his/her obligation by himself/herself, that is, his/her performance is bilateral rather than unilateral. If the activity is unilateral, the debtor alone can perform; for example, an obligation to transport goods. If the activity is bilateral, by contrast, the debtor needs the creditor's cooperation. This cooperation may assume different forms: for example, allowing the obligor to enter a house that the debtor is contractually obliged to paint, or taking delivery of the goods from the debtor. Failure to cooperate may cause delayed performance or even non-performance on the side of the debtor. If an obligor's delayed performance results from his/her creditor's unpreparedness or unwillingness to accept a performance tendered on time, then the creditor incurs *mora creditoris*. It goes without saying that a creditor is not obliged to accept a performance tendered by the debtor. If the creditor was so obliged, the debtor could compel him/her to accept, for example, the delivery of the goods. On the contrary, the debtor has no right to fulfil his/her obligation by forcing his/her performance upon the creditor. Nevertheless, the law still finds ways to protect the debtor. The debtor has a direct interest in discharging his/her obligation. Running of interest, penalties, risk of deterioration of the goods, figure among the disadvantages that the debtor's timely performance would avoid. Therefore, when the creditor prevents the debtor from fulfilling his/her contractual obligations, all legal systems entitle the debtor to set up as a defence a refused tender of performance. The defence is accompanied by a deposit of the money or the goods with a tribunal in order to completely discharge his/her obligation (Articles 1176 et seq. CC). The key point here is, that the debtor is not prejudiced by the creditor's refusal. While the debtor cannot compel his/her creditor to accept, the creditor's recalcitrance should nevertheless put on the debtor no risks of negative consequences.

The concept of *mora creditoris comprises* a variety of effects. First, by tendering performance, the debtor cannot be in delay (*mora debitoris*).[298] If the debtor's

297. *See* para. 169 above.

298. TS 13 Nov. 2013 (Roj: STS 5471/2013), 22 Oct. 2003 (RJ 2003/7405).

performance is delayed, a conforming tender (in that case, including moratory interest) brings the consequences of *mora debitoris* to an end (*purgatio moræ*). The main consequence of *mora creditoris* is doubtless the alleviation of the debtor's liability. The debtor no longer bears the risk of accidental destruction of the property due. Therefore, if the specific thing perishes, the debtor is discharged. Of course, if the thing belongs to a genus, the conclusion might be a different one, because *genus nunquam perit*. Nevertheless, another effect that can be linked to a conforming tender of performance is the specification of the generic obligation, so that after the tender, the generic thing due is deemed to be a specific one.[299] Roman law relaxed the debtor's liability, holding him/her responsible for only *dolus* and *culpa lata*.[300] But this alleviation of responsibility is not accepted in Spanish law.

The debtor's responsibilities may be alleviated to an extent, but the debtor is not freed from his/her obligation. In spite of the relaxation of his/her responsibility, he/she may be interested in a full discharge of his/her duties. The law allows the debtor to deposit the money or the property due. Regulation of deposit has been amended in 2015. This deposit has to be judicial or notarial and a proper tender has to precede it; however, deposit without or against the will of the creditor is only effective provided that it is judicial. Deposit without tender is completely ineffective unless the creditor is absent or unable to collect the payment, several creditors pretend to be entitled to collect the payment[301] or the document entitling to collect the debt is lost (Article 1176 CC). Deposit must be validated by the judge.

Finally, two other consequences of tender of performance can be linked to the concept of *mora creditoris*. If one party tenders performance, he/she acknowledges that he/she is the debtor, and that the debt exists. Consequently, as a way of recognizing the debt, a tender interrupts prescription (Article 1973 CC, Article 121-11.d CC Cat).

Because the obligation has not been discharged, the creditor is still entitled to claim performance. Therefore, the debtor must remain ready and willing to perform, for if he/she does not fulfil the contract upon the creditor's demand, he/she falls into delay (*mora debitoris*) and the positive effects of his/her previous tender vanish. The debtor has to be ready to perform until the extinction of the obligation.

§2. Impossibility, Frustration and Hardship

I. Irresistible Force

251. Some provisions of the CC exclude the liability of the debtor where non-performance is caused by force majeure (*fuerza mayor*)[302] or fortuitous event.[303] There is no express definition of those terms, and they are even mentioned indistinctly, for example, in Article 1602 CC. Following Article 1105 CC, they may be

299. Article 1452.3 CC.
300. Zimmermann, *The Law of Obligations*, 819.
301. TS 11 Oct. 2011 (Roj: STS 9343/2011).
302. Articles 1096 and 1891 CC.
303. Articles 1602 and 1777 CC.

defined as unforeseeable events (fortuitous event) or irresistible events (force majeure). Therefore, they are events beyond the debtor's control: external circumstances that cannot be imputed to him/her and exclude the debtor's fault.[304] Among these events one can mention wars, earthquakes, storms, lightning, etc.[305] The consequence of irresistible force is the extinction of the obligation with no liability from the debtor. However, the debtor will be liable if such events concur while he/she is in unlawful possession of the thing owed; for example, the possessor in bad faith, that is, whoever is aware that the thing must be returned to its owner (Article 457 CC). Also in tort law, the courts will not be ready to exonerate the defendant if any fault in the prevention of the risk can be imputed to him/her.[306]

II. Impossibility

252. Impossibility of performance is one of the ways to terminate an existing obligation included in Article 1156 CC, although it is referred to as 'loss of the indebted thing' (*pérdida de la cosa debida*). Nevertheless, if we want to cover all kinds of obligations, we must talk of impossibility of performance.[307] Such is the usual expression, used, for example, in Article 1184 CC, and which states the discharge of the obligation to do (*ad faciendum*) where 'performance is impossible in law or in fact'. Articles 1182–1186 CC present impossibility of performance as a cause of discharge under the title 'loss of the thing due'. The provisions deal mainly with the destruction of a particular thing, and only Article 1184 CC regulates impossibility in relation to the obligation to do something. However, the requirements and effects of impossibility, as an excuse for non-performance, apply to all types of obligations.

III. Absolute or Practical Impossibility

253. In order to consider impossibility of performance as a basis to terminate a contract and discharge the debtor of his/her obligation, it must comply with certain requirements.[308] First, impossibility must be ex post facto and not initial. Second, it must be an impossibility for which the debtor is not responsible, that is, not due to the debtor's fault. Finally, impossibility must be objective, not subjective. Let us analyse each and every requirement in turn.

304. Therefore, if the concrete cause of a fire is unknown but the tortfeasor was not completely diligent in order to prevent the damage, he/she cannot invoke fortuitous case (TS 18 Jul. 2006 [RJ 2006/5345], 4 Mar. 2004 [RJ 2004/1805]).

305. TS 25 Jun. 2002 (RJ 2002/5368) considers as a fortuitous case a bacterial infection caused by *Staphylococcusaureus*; TS 14 Feb. 2007 (RJ 2007/1378) considers a case of force majeure the damage caused by high alumina cement since it was allowed in construction during the 1970s. TS 18 Dec. 2006 (RJ 2006/9171) alternatively considers as fortuitous case or force majeure a violent work strike.

306. For example, TS 27 Oct. 2003 (RJ 2003/8718), 20 Oct. 2003 (RJ 2003/8242), 31 Mar. 2003 (RJ 2003/2839).

307. Written by Juan Antonio Fernández Campos (University of Murcia).

308. Written by Juan Antonio Fernández Campos (University of Murcia).

A. *Subsequent Impossibility*

254. Impossibility of performance that discharges the obligation should be subsequent, not initial, for example, due to a cause arisen after the conclusion of the contract.[309] In the event of an initial impossibility, impossibility would be deemed as a reason of nullity of contracts, since 'possibility' is one of the requirements of the object both of an obligation and a contract (Article 1272 CC). Sometimes the Supreme Court has confused initial impossibility and ex post facto impossibility, as can be seen in the decision of 1 May 1950.[310]

B. *Impossibility for Which the Debtor Is Not Responsible*

255. The debtor is released by supervening impossibility as long as it is not his/her fault. Such is the provision in Article 1182 CC: loss or destruction of a specific thing to be delivered should take place 'without the debtor's fault' (*sin culpa del deudor*). If destruction or loss of the subject matter of the contract or impossibility of performance is due to a cause for which the debtor is responsible, he/she will not be discharged, and the creditor may claim compensation for non-performance.

In such cases, performance being impossible, the creditor cannot claim specific performance (*ejecución forzosa en forma específica*), but the debtor's fault entitles the creditor to damages for breach of contract. Such situation, in which impossibility is due to the debtor's behaviour, is described as '*perpetuatio obligationis*'. Therefore, in spite of the impossibility, the obligation persists but instead of specific performance, the aggrieved party can claim pecuniary compensation.

In order to establish the burden of proof of the debtor's fault, Article 1183 CC presumes it when the supervening destruction of a specific thing necessary for performance occurs while in the debtor's possession.[311]

Likewise, it should be emphasized that, provided that the debtor had already been considered in default, no discharge of obligation would be deemed if the thing were lost or destroyed by a cause for which the debtor is not responsible, as it is established under Article 1182 *in fine*.[312]

309. TS 18 Jan. 2013 (Roj: STS 679/2013). The decision adds the idea that the impossibility must not be linked to the debtor. In the case, the debtor alleged that he could not obtain a credit from a certain bank, yet the Supreme Court considers that the debtor could have applied to other banks.
310. RJ 994/1950. *See* TS 19 Jul. 1993 (RJ 6165/1993), 15 Feb. 1994 (RJ 1316/1994) and 11 Oct. 1995 (RJ 6360/1997).
311. On the concept of fault in Arts 1182–1183 and 1104 CC, *see* Ferran Badosa Coll, *La diligencia y la culpa del deudor en la obligación civil* (Bolonia, 1987); *ibid.*, *Comentarios del Código Civil*, Vol. II, sub Art. 1183 (Madrid, 1993).
312. With regard to the requirement of absence of breach of contract, *see* TS 29 Oct. 1996 (RJ 1996/7484), 30 May 1994 (RJ 1994/3763), 25 Mar. 1993 (RJ 1993/2232), 20 May 1991 (RJ 1991/9817). In the event of concurrent breaches, discharge of obligation and, consequently, the debtor's release may not be considered but only the amendment of the debtor's liability (TS 29 Oct. 1996). For an overview of case law, *see* TS 21 Apr. 2006 (RJ 2006/1875).

C. Objective Impossibility

256. According to authorized opinions,[313] impossibility is to be deemed objective where it depends upon a hindrance inherent in the contents of the performance; it should be deemed subjective where hindrances are relative to the debtor himself/herself, and not linked to the subject matter of the contract. In accordance with this statement, if performance is of an exclusively personal character, impossibility could be objective if non-performance is linked to anything inherent to the debtor himself/herself (i.e., the illness that prevents the soprano from singing). Nonetheless, it is sometimes difficult to ascertain whether the impossibility is objective (hence the obligation being discharged) or subjective.

D. Partial Impossibility and Temporary Impossibility

257. As for partial impossibility to fulfil an obligation, there is no provision in our Civil Code regulating this matter specifically (as opposed to other foreign civil codes). Some writers consider that, in case of impossibility that only partially affects performance, partial discharge of the obligation should take place. However, other authors point out that each solution depends upon each particular case. Specifically, provided that there are no contractual provisions on this matter, if the obligation has gratuitous *causa*, partial impossibility shall give rise to partial discharge; however, if the obligation has onerous cause, partial or total discharge will take place depending upon the creditor.[314]

Another case that deserves particular attention is that of temporary impossibility of performance. In the event that impossibility of performance was not definitive but temporary, discharge of obligation would obviously not be deemed. In the additional event that the cause of impossibility is not the debtor's fault, even if fulfilment is not on schedule, the debtor will not be considered by default, so the creditor will bear the eventual damages caused by the delay. However, in the event of breach under the specified schedule, provided that late performance would not satisfy the creditor's interest, definitive impossibility and discharge of obligation would occur (as if, e.g., the soprano loses her voice momentarily and recovers it once the date of the performance is overdue).

Impossibility of performance due to the scarcity of supplies and infrastructure problems arising from the Spanish Civil War and the Second World War, forced the Supreme Court to soften the requirements of this cause of discharge. In some cases considering a sale of goods to be specific and not generic (a certain item of oil)[315] in order to terminate the contract and discharge the debtor. In other cases, using temporary impossibility as a ground to, at least, modify the initial schedule of the contract, if not to discharge the obligation.[316]

313. Díez-Picazo, *Fundamentos*, II, 651.
314. Albaladejo, *Derecho Civil*, II, 301.
315. TS 2 Jul. 1948 (RJ 1948/1116).
316. TS 27 Apr. 1943 (RJ 1943/559). On the subject of transitory impossibility, *see* TS 13 Jun. 1944 (RJ 1944/893), 9 Jan. 1951 (RJ 1951/581) and 3 Mar. 1984 (RJ 1984/286).

However, some authors point out that transitory impossibility does not discharge the obligation automatically (not being a definitive impossibility). On the contrary, regarding reciprocal obligations, the creditor should be entitled to terminate the contract (under Article 1124 CC), provided that the present uncertainty prevents the creditor from satisfying his/her interest by other means, as for instance, approaching another debtor who could offer a similar counter-performance.[317]

Impossibility should not be, eventually, definitive, as in TS 23 February 1994,[318] which gathers a case of rejection of licence that prevents the contractor from performance: the Supreme Court chose discharge for impossibility, avoiding to put the debtor in an indefinite delay in fulfilment.

IV. Loss of Subject Matter

258. The 'loss' of a particular thing is defined in Article 1122.2 CC as perishment, disappearance or legal impossibility (*cosas fuera del comercio*).[319] It states that if the debtor is responsible for the loss, he/she is liable for damages. In consequence, 'loss' has three different meanings. First, when a particular thing cannot be found or is not available, which could be due to theft or because it has been passed on to a third person (i.e., the debtor sold it to somebody else), from whom it cannot be recovered. Second, it applies to cases of material destruction, either by fortuitous perishment or caused by a third party. Third, the expression 'things out of trade' (Article 1122.2 CC) refers to a prohibition or 'legal impossibility' which frustrates the contract, as performance is illegal.

Where disappearance or destruction is due to a third party, two questions arise. First, who can claim against the third person responsible for the loss, the debtor or the creditor? Second, is the creditor entitled to any of the remedies the debtor may have against the third person, although it implies a substantial change of the original subject matter of the contract? Article 1186 contains specific provisions on this matter, and we will deal with it *below* paragraph 260.

The above-mentioned legal definition of 'loss of a particular thing' is deemed insufficient to embrace the broad constellation of cases of impossibility. Some authors define the impossibility of performance as any event that makes it impossible to fulfil the contract, regardless of the present circumstances, and of the debtor's or any other person's personal hindrances.

259. When the subsequent impossibility is due to an intervention of a third person (the case considered by the Civil Code is that of the loss or destruction of the thing that the debtor had the obligation to deliver), Article 1186 foresees a device of protection of the creditor by virtue of which this impossibility due to a third party (without breach on the debtor's side, it is understood)[320] determines the discharge

317. Albaladejo, *Derecho Civil*, II, 302.
318. RJ 1994/683.
319. Written by Juan Antonio Fernández Campos (University of Murcia).
320. That is, the debtor's diligence does not require him/her to have foreseen and prevented the loss or destruction of the thing due to the action of a third person.

of the obligation. Once the said obligation has been discharged, the creditor will be entitled to any action that the debtor should have had against the third person liable for the loss or destruction (or in general, of the impossibility).

The remedy looks simple, but the authors discuss about its foundation and the instrument or legal means upon which it is embodied. The majority understands that, once the obligation is discharged, there is a legal and an automatic assignment to the creditor of whatever rights the debtor may have against the third person. A minority, however, assumes that we face an assignment of actions on the debtor's side, so that he/she is not automatically entitled to resort to the remedy.

260. Indeed, some authors consider that Article 1186 CC contemplates an automatic transfer of the actions that correspond to the debtor against the third person responsible for the destruction of the particular thing or the impossibility of performance, so there is no need for the debtor himself/herself to assign them. Likewise, it is argued that the obligation from which such duty on the debtor's side could arise, has been discharged.[321] This assignment *ope legis* is foreseen to set-off the losses suffered by the creditor; if the debtor is immediately released from his/her obligation because he/she is not responsible for the impossibility, the creditor should likewise receive automatically whatever rights the debtor accrued against the third person.[322] The remedy provided by Article 1186 is based on the following argument: if the creditor has to bear the risk of non-performance due to a third person, he/she should be entitled to those actions that might alleviate the prejudicial consequences (*commodum representationis*).[323]

The legal legitimacy to act against the third person responsible for the debtor's non-performance is the fair ending to the initially foreseen consequence: discharge of the obligation despite the fact that the debtor has still actions under command to obtain the thing itself (action of replacement against who stole it or against who failed to return it), or an action to claim the amount corresponding to its value (action in tort against the third person, or actions for breach of contract if such were the case).[324]

This argument has led to the argument that we actually face a case of real subrogation (*subrogación real*). This would mean an automatic change of the object due to the creditor, no longer being the specific thing but the action against the third party (to obtain the thing itself or its value). To verify that initial impression, let us analyse the rule more closely, and let us distinguish among several cases. Indeed, despite being unable to deliver the owed thing, the debtor does occasionally have actions against the third person who causes the impossibility, either because the loss of the thing is due to theft (a replacement action would arise) or because of destruction (an action in tort would arise) or because the third person, in its turn, has engaged to transfer it to the debtor (in which case a contractual action of specific performance or damages for breach of contract would arise).

321. Pedro De Pablo Contreras, et al., in *Curso de Derecho Civil. Derecho de Obligaciones* (Madrid, 2008), 202.
322. Albaladejo, *Derecho Civil*, II, 304.
323. Díez-Picazo, *Fundamentos*, II, 657.
324. Other examples could be actions against the insurance company to claim for compensation, or to ask for fair price in the case of a compulsory purchase.

V. No Doctrine of Unforeseen Circumstances

261. Spanish authors and also the Supreme Court have distinguished between impossibility of performance and the extraordinary difficulty to comply with the same performance, inasmuch as only the former is the cause of discharge of obligation (when, additionally, the other requirements are fulfilled).[325]

Extraordinary difficulty of performance takes place in cases where modification or alteration ex post facto of circumstances breaks the contractual balance as agreed by the parties beforehand in long-term contracts or contracts for continuing or periodic performance, thus involving excessive onerosity as far as one of the parties is concerned. Many legal systems have introduced some sort of mechanism to balance the hardship that one of the parties suffers due to supervening events or change of circumstances. Such remedies have been first introduced by case law and eventually by statute.

Change of circumstances has been taken into account in different countries and thus, the *théorie de l'imprevision* in France, the *Lehre der Wegfall der Geschäftsgrundlage* in Germany, or the theory of excessive onerosity in Italy. These remedies are based on different arguments; in some of them there is a subjective view, dealing with the would-be will of the parties; in others, they have an objective basis, which tend to remedy an unjust result that is deemed contrary to the principle of good faith. The latter, according to our general view, must be the support of the '*rebus sic stantibus*' doctrine under Article 1258 CC.

The possibility of a contract revision due to change of circumstances constitutes an exceptional basis for modifying a contract, as contrary to the principle of *pacta sunt servanda*. It is a remedy created by case law and developed by different authors but still not incorporated by statute. Therefore, it requires a sensible and an accurate implementation of requirements that the courts have gradually defined:

1. extraordinary alteration of circumstances;
2. unforeseeable alteration;
3. as a result, a major imbalance in the contract.[326]

The traditional restrictive approach of case law to hardship has been modified by the judgment handed down by the Supreme Court on 30 June 2014.[327] The decision, in a context of a crisis of huge proportions in Spain, normalizes the *rebus sic stantibus* doctrine within contract law. Inspired by the regulation in the soft law that is cited, the court links hardship with good faith: 'when, beyond the pacts between the parties and without fault, the circumstances that constituted the basis or goal of the contract unexpectedly change, the performances which the parties could await in good faith may be adapted' (author's translation).

---

325. Written by Juan Antonio Fernández Campos (University of Murcia).
326. *See* TS 10 Feb. 1997 (RJ 1997/665), 15 Nov. 2000 (RJ 2001/9214), 28 Dec. 2001 (RJ 2002/1650), 27 May 2002 (RJ 2002/4573), 25 Jan. 2007 (RJ 2007/592), 1 Mar. 2007 (RJ 2007/1618).
327. Roj: STS 2823/2014. *See* Jorge Castiñeira Jerez, 'Hacia una nueva configuración de la doctrina rebus sic stantibus: a propósito de la sentencia del Tribunal Supremo de 30 de junio de 2014', *Indret*, 2014/3. Along the same lines, TS 15 Oct. 2014 (Roj: STS 5090/2014), reducing a 29% the rent of a lease for hotel project.

Hardship which arises from ex post facto alterations after the celebration, since these do not imply an impossibility of performance itself, does not lead to the discharge of obligation but offers a basis to demand the modification of the contract. Only when its modification or judicial revision is not possible, discharge will be deemed.

Different arguments support this measure. First, the principle of good faith, as laid down in Articles 7 and 1258 CC, which is always required in the performance and enforcement of the parties' obligations. Second, even if the Civil Code deals solely with impossibility, this does not exclude some sort of appropriate measure in case of supervening extraordinary difficulty due to unforeseeable change of circumstances. Finally, we must consider that case law has applied the same doctrine, even in cases in which there was no reciprocal obligation.[328]

VI. The Doctrine of Good Faith

262. As mentioned above,[329] the principle of good faith is a theoretical basis that allows the exceptional recourse to the doctrine of unforeseen circumstances in Spain. The revision of a contractual relationship could be demanded where the unmodified continuation of the relationship under the initial conditions would be unfair because of the change of the circumstances.

VII. Contractual Allocation of Risk

263. The agreements providing an alteration of the legal regime of liability are valid if they do not contradict the limitations established in Article 1255 CC of the freedom of contract. Concerning legal limitations, it has to be borne in mind that Article 1102 CC declares void the renunciation of the action to claim liability for intentional breach of contract (*dolus*). As for fault, the parties are allowed to specify a certain degree of diligence within the terms of Article 1104 CC.[330] The parties are also free to allocate risk deriving from force majeure or fortuitous case (Article 1105 CC).

VIII. Administrative Contracts

264. The principle of good faith is equally applicable to administrative contracts (Article 3.1.e Act 40/2015). The doctrine of the *imprévision* is not alien to administrative contracts either. As contractual equilibrium needs to be protected in order to ensure the maintenance of administrative contracts, for they may affect public services, two sorts of facts, the so-called *factum principis* and the exceptional

328. Albaladejo, *Derecho Civil*, II, 303–304.
329. *See* paras 179, 261 above, and also 67 et seq.
330. *See* para. 169.

change of circumstances, allow the revision of administrative contracts (art. 205.2.b Act 9/2017 on contracts of the public sector).

IX. Consequences of Force Majeure

265. The consequences that force majeure may provoke have been considered in precedent subsections.

§3. Discharge by Agreement

266. The parties may agree on ways of fulfilling an obligation other than payment.[331] In addition, the creditor may unilaterally extinguish the obligatory relationship if he/she disposes of his/her right of credit. The following subsections will focus on some of these ways.

I. Release

267. Release (Articles 1187–1191 CC) or remission (Articles 1143 and 1146 CC) is the unilateral declaration of the creditor that discharges the debtor without receiving anything in exchange. This demonstrates the creditor's power of disposal of the total obligatory relationship. Being a gratuitous act, the rules on donations apply. Specifically, the rules on *inoficiosidad*, that is, when the deceased's actual assets are insufficient to satisfy the compulsory share (Article 1187 CC), which include the possibility of reduction (Articles 654–656 CC) and revocation (Article 644 CC).

Concerning the formal requirements of the declaration, release may be expressly or tacitly granted. When it is expressly granted, form of donation applies, and therefore if the object of the obligation is an immovable, a public deed is required. Moreover, the CC presumes release from the concurrence of certain circumstances, independent of whether there was an intention of the creditor (Article 1191 CC).[332] Another distinction is usually made between total release and partial release.

Also distinct from release or remission is the *waiver* of the right of credit. This also gives grounds to the extinction of the obligation and arises from a unilateral act or declaration of the creditor. However, it does not affect the legal position of the debt, but the right of credit. The general rules on renunciation of rights contained in Article 6.2 CC apply to this.

The principal effect of release is the extinction of the obligation. Suretyship also extinguishes if the obligation is released, but release of the suretyship does not extinguish the principal obligation.

331. Written by Santiago Espiau (University of Barcelona).

332. The accessory obligation of pledge is presumed to have been released if the pledged thing is on the debtor's hand (Article 1191 CC), the guardian's credit against the person in care in case the debt is not included in the initial inventory (Article 222-22.2 CCCat).

II. Confusion of Rights

268. Article 1192 CC defines 'confusion of rights' as a ground for the extinction of an obligation that occurs where the position of creditor and debtor with regard to one and the same obligation merge 'in the same person'. The obligatory relationship requires the presence of two distinct and opposing legal positions – credit and debt – that are possessed by different subjects; should one of these disappear by means of the other occupying both positions, the obligation shall logically and structurally disappear.[333] Extinction by confusion is not automatic, since it must be alleged by the interested party.

Confusion usually arises by virtue of hereditary succession, where the creditor is the debtor's heir and conversely, wherever the inheritance has not been accepted with the benefit of inventory (*see* Articles 1192.2 and 1023 CC). This may also occur in relation to legal persons, where, through the existence of one or several obligatory relationships between them, one of them succeeds, merges with or absorbs the other. Confusion also takes place in the case of assignment of credits made by a creditor in favour of his/her debtor, or in the event that the latter acquires a credit in the procedure of specific performance.

III. *Datio in Solutum*

269. The Civil Code does not specifically regulate *datio in solutum*, although some articles do presuppose its existence (namely Articles 1521, 1636 or 1849 CC), as being admissible under the principle of freedom of contract.[334]

In fact, even if Article 1166 CC excludes payment by means of property or conduct other than that foreseen in the obligation, it implicitly accepts so if both debtor and creditor agree to it and, more specifically, if the latter accepts it. The fundamental question raised by *datio in solutum* – and not regulated by Spanish law – is one of determining the effects derived from the loss of the property given in payment, by virtue of eviction, or as a consequence of an action of recovery based on a previous right. Scholars offer two possible solutions. On the one hand, the application of the rules on eviction (Articles 1475 et seq. CC). On the other hand, some authors consider that *datio in solutum* does not discharge the obligation, thus allowing the creditor to claim performance or to claim damages for non-performance.[335] Since the Supreme Court has considered *datio in solutum* as an agreement intended to extinguish the obligation by means of a different performance,[336] eviction must be treated as a case of non-performance.

333. *See* TS 19 May 2006 (RJ 2006/3047).

334. TS 1 Oct. 2009 (RJ 2009\7263), 6 Jun. 2007 (RJ 2007/3423), 27 Sep. 2002 (RJ 2002/7877), 23 Sep. 2002 (RJ 2002/7837).

335. Alabaladejo, *Derecho civil*, II, 152.

336. TS 16 Dec. 2014 (Roj: 5694/2014).

IV. Payment by Transfer of Property

270. The Civil Code dedicates only Article 1175 CC to payment by transfer of property. According to this provision, the debtor authorizes the creditor or creditors to dispose of his/her property and to set its value off against the debt owed. Thus, the transfer does not discharge the debtor; this only occurs once the disposal has been verified, and the sum has been set-off against the corresponding debt or debts.[337] In cases where such sum does not fully set-off the obligation, creditors reserve the right to charge the outstanding proportion of the obligation. If the sum obtained is greater than the value of the obligation or obligations that have given rise to the transfer, the excess or surplus sum must be given back to the debtor.

V. Set-Off

271. Article 1195 CC establishes that 'set-off occurs where two persons, by their own right, are reciprocally the creditor and debtor of each other'. Article 1202 CC adds that 'the effect of set-off is the extinction of both debts by the coinciding sum, even if the creditors and debtors have no knowledge of this'. Therefore, if the debts are equal, being identical sums, both shall be extinguished; if they are not of equal sums, the smaller shall be extinguished and the greater reduced. The CC configures set-off as a *defence* opposable by the interested party (Articles 1197 and 1198 CC); however, its extinguishing effect shall occur immediately and automatically at the moment in which the debts to be compensated coexist.[338]

272. In order for set-off to be applicable, certain requirements of a subjective and an objective character must concur. As far as the first are concerned, reciprocity between the subjects affected is required, in the sense that both must be creditor and debtor (Articles 1195 and 1196.1 CC). As for the second, set-off requires homogeneity of the prestations, the object of which must necessarily be fungible goods of the same kind and the same quality (Article 1196.2 CC), while the obligations must be liquid payable (Article 1196.3 and 4 CC).

273. Even though all requirements concur, set-off does not occur in three cases: First, where any of the obligations are burdened by retention or claim by a third person, who has duly notified the debtor (*see* Article 1196.5 CC and TS 17 March 1977).[339] Second, where any of the debts originated from deposit or from the obligations of the depositary or borrower (Article 1200.1 CC). Finally, the debtor cannot resort to the defence of set-off in the case of a gratuitous obligation of alimony (Articles 151 and 1200.2 CC).

337. *See* TS 28 Jun. 1997 (RJ 1997/5403).
338. *See* TS 9 Apr. 1994 (RJ 1994/2739), 21 Nov. 1988 (RJ 1998/9039), 20 Jun. 1986 (RJ 1986/3786), 7 Jun. 1983 (RJ 1983/7000).
339. RJ 1977/1241.

Set-off is automatic once the mentioned requirements concur, yet the person interested in the extinction of the obligation must invoke it (TS 15 April 2014).[340] This declaration of will does not need any form. The guarantor may also declare set-off (Article 1853 CC).

§4. Novation

I. Conditions for Novation

274. How can a contract be modified or changed in Spanish law? There are three possible answers, either you modify the parties to the contract (subjective modification), or the object or conditions (objective modification), or, finally, both of them (mixed modification).[341] The Civil Code, following the traditional approach, shows the difference between objective modification, modification of the debtor and that of the creditor. According to Article 1203 CC:

> Obligations can be modified:
>
> 1. By change of object or their principal conditions.
> 2. By substituting the person of the debtor.
> 3. By subrogating a third party in the rights of the creditor.

There is a lack of reference here to mixed modification, which signifies that when modifying a party to a contract at the same time as the object, both regulations should be applied concurrently.

To change a contract objectively, you can either celebrate a modification contract or a classical novation. The modification of the contract is a new contract itself, and therefore must include the three necessary elements, consent, object and consideration (Article 1261 CC). It also must comply with the Statute of Frauds (Articles 1278, 1279 and 1280 CC).

In contrast to what happens in common law countries, in Spanish law, the term *novación* can encompass both subjective and/or objective modification. In the civil law, there are three kinds of subjective novations: where the debtor and the creditor remain the same, but a new debt takes the place of the old one; where the debt remains the same, but a new debtor is substituted; where the debt and debtor remain, but a new creditor is substituted. You should also notice that the idea is that when you simply modify a contract, the rest of the background status of the parties remains unchanged, and also other ancillary obligations, terms and conditions of fulfilment, etc. It is even possible that the sureties and guarantees will remain if there is only a minor change. To the contrary, when you novate a contract, a new one is created at the same time as an original is extinguished (*see* Article 1156 CC), and, therefore, all the background clauses of the first and any sort of ancillary or subsidiary obligations are also eliminated.

340. Roj: STS 1405/2014.
341. Written by Miguel Ángel Adame (University of Sevilla).

275. The Civil Code only devotes one section to the objective novation of the contract. Article 1204 states that 'In order that an obligation may be extinguished by another which substitutes it, it is necessary that it should be so expressly declared, or that the old and the new be absolutely incompatible.' The idea is twofold. On the one hand, the presumption goes against the novation of the contract; novation is never presumed, hence it must be expressly declared or the new obligation and the former one must be fully incompatible.[342] On the other hand, this presumption does not operate when the quality or quantity of the change is so important as to justify the creation of a new obligation that substitutes and at the same time extinguishes the former. The concept of incompatibility includes change in the object of the contract (STS 31 July 2015),[343] change in the type of contract – for instance, a bailment that becomes a sale –, the change of the payment modality,[344] etc.

II. Delegation

276. The delegation of duties can be accomplished in Spanish law by the assumption of debts (*asunción de deudas*). The bottom line that qualifies the *asunción de deudas* is that the parties to the assumption want to maintain the status created by the contract, and by modifying the person who is the debtor. Other accessories and determinations of the debt assumed, at least *inter partes*, are to remain the same. In contrast to this, when you novate a contract, you destroy one obligation to create another, extinguishing the whole programme of the previous contract.

The *asunción de deuda* is not explicitly regulated in the Civil Code, but there is repetitive case law that admits this institution, and applying to the situation Articles 1203, 1205, 1206 and 1207 CC. In particular, Article 1203 allows the modification of the debtor that does not extinguish the obligation. There are many cases on the issue. Some cases are the following decisions from the *Tribunal Supremo*: 3 September 2007 (RJ 2007/4709), 14 February 2005 (RJ 2005/1671) and 4 June 2004 (RJ 2004/3982). Case law insists that delegation may not be tacit or presumed.[345]

277. There are two types of assumption of debts, the *asunción delegatoria* and the *asunción expromisoria*. In general, the concept *delegación* is reserved to label a change of debtor when the original debtor (*delegante*, delegating party) has ordered another (*delegado*, delegate) to do or pay[346] the other party to the original contract

342. TS 6 Mar. 2012 (Roj: STS 4184/2012), 22 Oct. 2012 (Roj: STS 8033/2012).

343. Roj: STS 4002/2015.

344. TS 11 Feb. 2016 (Roj: STS 352/2016).

345. TS 19 Nov. 2014 (Roj: STS 4616/2014).

346. If the *delegado* just pays the debt, then there is no contract between the creditor and the *delegado*. This situation is called *delegación depago* or *delegación solutoria*. In Spanish law, any third party can pay an obligation, according to Art. 1158 CC, but with differences on what can be recovered by him/her, depending upon the debtor's consent or lack of it. The payor might even benefit from the *subrogación* (subrogation in the position of creditor) explained in the text.

to whom he/she owed something or to whom he/she wants to gift (*delegatario*, obligee). It should be noticed that the term *delegación* is more specific than the concept *delegation of duties* of the common law.[347] A delegation can be novative, but it can also be intended by the parties to maintain the former contract as much as possible, without the extinction/creation mechanism of the novation.

The *asunción delegatoria* is the contract by which the debtor agrees with a third party that the latter will step in and assume the position of the debtor. As a matter of fact, one must distinguish whether there is assent/consent of the creditor. Without the creditor's consent to the assumption, there is neither liberation of the debtor nor privity of contract between creditor and the third party. If after the delegation, there is an agreement between the third-party delegate *asumente* and the creditor *acreedor*, the former debtor can be freed of the obligation if expressly agreed upon. If not, the delegating party remains liable, and the delegate can also be liable to the obligee, in accordance with the agreement. In contrast to what happens in common law countries, a delegation for consideration itself does not create a third-party beneficiary obligation. This is a question of construction of the agreement between the old debtor and the party assuming the obligation.

278. Article 1206 states that:

> The insolvency of the new debtor, who has been accepted by the creditor, shall not revive the action of the latter against the original debtor, unless said solvency has been prior, public and known to the debtor when he transfers his debt.

This provision recognizes the passive delegation, and also includes one exception to the lack of liability of the debtor for the insolvency of the third party that substitutes him/her. Article 1206 is the parallel of Article 1529 CC for the assignment of credit.

279. The new debtor can oppose defences based on the new agreement with the creditor. Real defences that affect the obligation assumed are also valid, but neither personal defences of the former debtor, nor defences that the third party had against the former debtor (this is only applicable in the *asunción delegatoria*, where there is the agreement of delegation between these two) are enforceable.

III. Novation on Initiative of the New Debtor

280. The concept *asunción de deuda* (assumption of debts) can also be accomplished in another way: a simple agreement between a creditor and a third party that assumes the obligation, and liberates the former debtor, (*asunción expromisoria*). It should be noticed that, according to Article 1205 CC, not only is there no need for the consent of the former debtor to it, but also he/she need not know about the agreement.

---

347. *See* Black's Law Dictionary, 426: Delegation.

IV. Effect

281. There are two provisions devoted in general to the effects of novation of obligations. According to Article 1207 CC:

> When the principal obligation is extinguished by effect of the novation, the accessory obligations shall only subsist in so far as they benefit third parties who have not given their consent.

This provision means, according to the majority view, that after a novation, third parties that have rights granted by the contract, rights that have been vested, cannot be deprived of them. To the contrary, third parties that have duties to the parties of the main particular contract, are freed of them once the conditions change by virtue of the novation.

Article 1208 states that:

> Novation is null and void, if the original obligation is also so, unless the cause of nullity can be claimed by the debtor only or the ratification gives validity to acts which were null in their origin.

This provision reflects the way novation operates, the mechanical destruction of the novated obligation and the correlative creation of a new one.

§5. Rescission

282. Rescission is a remedy aimed at repairing the economic detriment caused by the contract to certain persons. Rescission puts an end to the effectiveness of the transaction. The contract is valid but, because of the detriment caused to those persons, it may be rescinded. Rescission is an exceptional and subsidiary remedy. The plaintiff can only resort to it where the law expressly establishes it, and there is no other remedy available (Articles 1290 and 1294 CC).

283. Article 1291 CC enumerates the contracts that may be rescinded:

1. Contracts concluded by guardians without judicial authorization if the ward has suffered a lesion in more than one-fourth of the value of the object of the contract. This remedy goes back to the Roman *restitutio in integrum minorum.*
2. Contracts concluded in representation of absent people under the same lesion.
3. Contracts concluded to the detriment of creditors. It refers to the Paulian action, which has been analysed above.[348]
4. Contracts regarding litigious items if they have not been approved by the parties to the contract or the court.

348. Paragraphs 222 et seq.

284. The party who has suffered the detriment, and its successors may claim rescission. It is nevertheless required that they can make restitution of the object of the contract (Article 1295 CC). Restitution is therefore the main legal consequence of rescission. If restitution is not possible, the plaintiff can claim damages.

The limitation period of prescription is four years. The period is one of lapse of rights.[349]

§6. WITHDRAWAL

285. The term withdrawal (*desistimiento*) is employed to designate the power granted to one or both parties for them to unilaterally extinguish the legal relationship. Withdrawal only depends on the will of the party who has the power to extinguish the relationship. The CC does not regulate withdrawal systematically, but some examples can be found in it and in some statutes:

1. Article 1750 CC, dealing with simple loan, states that where neither the duration of the contract nor a concrete use have been stipulated, the lender can demand restitution at will.
2. Article 1755 CC entitles the bailor to ask for the restitution of the bailment, even when the period stipulated in the contract has not elapsed.
3. As far as consumer law is concerned, Articles 68 et seq. new LGDCGU regulates withdrawal in general terms, whilst Articles 101 and 102 LGCDU regulate withdrawal in distant contracts and 110 in contracts concluded away from business premises; Article 10 Act on timesharing, Article 9 Act on sale on instalments regulate other rights of withdrawal. Withdrawal is granted here as a means of consumers' protection.
4. Articles 11 and 12 Act on Urban leases.

Nevertheless, the proper scope of withdrawal is to be found in contracts of successive performance (lease, supply, distribution, etc.) lacking a specific period of time and provided with a certain *intuitu personae* character. According to case law, withdrawal cannot be arbitrary. Notice must be given within the time scheduled, and if no period was stipulated, within a reasonable time in accordance with the principle of good faith.[350] If notice is not given or is given in contradiction with the contract or the principle of good faith, the aggrieved party is entitled to damages.[351] In case of leases, the amount of the compensation relates to the period in which the dwelling or the premises have remained unoccupied.[352] Another field where withdrawal plays an important role is consumer law. Now withdrawal has a general regulation in Articles 68 et seq. new LGDCU, and additionally certain consumer contracts

349. *See* below para. 331.
350. TS 16 Nov. 2016 (Roj: STS 5103/2016), 30 Apr. 2008 (RJ 2008/2687), 16 Dec. 2003 (RJ 2003/8605).
351. TS 16 Mar. 2016 (Roj: STS 1207/2016), 30 Dec. 2010 (RJ 2011\149), 20 May 2004 (RJ 2004/2786), 13 Apr. 2004 (RJ 2004/2619).
352. TS 20 May 2004 (RJ 2004/2710), 15 Jul. 2002 (RJ 2002/6048).

have a specific regulation of withdrawal (e.g., Articles 101–102 new LGDCU [distance contracts], Article 10 Act 32/1998 [timesharing], etc.).

When both parties want to withdraw they can agree on terminating the contract. In Spanish this is called '*mutuo disenso*'. According to the Supreme Court,[353] it is an extinctive contract where the parties agree to bring to an end the contract. Although it not explicitly regulated, its admission is based on freedom of contract (Article 1255 CC). The agreement may also be implicit and expressed separately by the parties.[354]

353. TS 5 Dec. 2013 (Roj: STS 5820/2013).
354. TS 22 Oct. 2013 (Roj: STS 5102/2013).

Chapter 6. Remedies

§1. General Provisions

286. If the debtor does not fulfil his/her obligation voluntarily, the creditor may resort to different remedies.[355] Generally, the creditor may claim either specific performance or damages or both of them. In the case of synallagmatic obligations, the aggrieved party has also the synallagmatic remedies, namely, termination of the contract, reduction of his/her obligation and withholding performance.

In order to determine which remedy or remedies the creditor may use in Spanish law, it is necessary to know if the debtor is responsible for non-performance. The question whether the debtor is liable for non-performance or whether he/she is excused, has been considered in the previous chapter. In the first case (imputable non-performance to the debtor), the aggrieved party may resort to any of the remedies mentioned above, including the synallagmatic ones in the case of synallagmatic contracts. In the second case, damages are usually excluded. If an act of the aggrieved party has caused the other party's non-performance, generally this party may not resort to any of the remedies. This last rule is not expressed in the CC, but it results from the general principle of good faith and fair dealing in the formation, performance and enforcement of the parties' duties under a contract.

Some of the above-mentioned remedies are compatible and can be cumulated. Far from it, other remedies are incompatible with each other. For instance, the party pursuing specific performance or termination of the contract is not precluded from claiming damages. Nevertheless, he/she cannot claim specific performance and termination at one and the same time. However, an election of a remedy is sometimes definitive and will preclude later elections of incompatible remedies. For instance, if a party terminates the contract, he/she may not claim performance afterwards; by contrast, he/she can first claim performance, and if this is not possible then resort to termination. The parties can exclude the accumulation of compatible remedies. Some remedies, particularly termination, require a relevant non-performance.

The Spanish Commission on Codification has launched (2009) a proposal for a thorough amendment of the *Código civil* that takes into account the developments in European Community law and soft law, but for the time being it is not going to be considered by the Spanish government.

§2. Faulty Behaviour of the Debtor

287. Generally speaking, breach of contract requires that the promised result is not attained, and that the breach is imputable to the debtor. The imputation to the debtor is the foundation of his/her liability. The criterion of imputation in Spanish law is subjective, since it is based on unlawful conduct by the debtor. This unlawful conduct can derive from the intention not to fulfil the obligation (intentional breach of contract or fraud) or from a faulty behaviour. Therefore, the breach is neither

355. Written by María Paz García Rubio (University of Santiago de Compostela).

imputable to the debtor if it is caused by an outside cause (fortuitous event, force majeure) nor it is imputable if the parties have agreed on a lower degree of diligence in performing the obligation, and the conduct of the debtor corresponds to a higher level. In addition, the debtor is responsible if the breach is imputable to a third person for whom he/she is answerable, such as persons who helped him/her in performing (Articles 1551 and 1597 CC).

288. Fraud means the intentional breach of contract: the debtor does not want to fulfil his/her obligation. A specific intention to harm the creditor is not required. Liability based on fraud cannot be excluded by the parties (Article 1102 CC). The consequence of an intentional breach of contract is liability for all damages, whilst the faulty debtor is only liable for foreseeable damages (Article 1107 CC).

289. According to Article 1104 CC, fault implies the omission of the diligence required by the nature of the obligation and corresponding to the circumstances of the persons, time and place. Therefore, the concretion of fault depends on the parties. In general terms, it can be described as the lack of foresight of what should have been foreseen. If the parties do not stipulate a certain degree of diligence, the law imposes that of a good father of a family. The courts may moderate the responsibility based on fault (Article 1103 CC).

The creditor bears the burden of proving fault even where the obligation is *de résultat*. Nevertheless, the Supreme Court has reversed the burden and, once non-performance is proved, it is the debtor who bears the burden of proving that he/she was not negligent.[356]

§3. Specific Performance and Injunctions

I. Specific Performance

290. Where a party does not perform, performs defectively or does not perform within time for performance, and these situations are imputable to the debtor, Spanish law entitles the other party to specific performance or *in natura* performance.[357] If specific performance is not possible any more, Spanish law changes this obligation into an obligation to give the monetary equivalent of the non-fulfilled prestation. As long as performance remains possible, the creditor is not obliged to content

356. This is especially frequent in cases of medical malpractice, where the Supreme Court has occasionally reversed the burden of proof in cases of 'reparative medicine' where a certain result is intended (TS 26 Mar. 2004 [RJ 2004/1668]). The burden of proof is also reversed in cases of 'disproportionate result', that is, the patient is seriously injured although his/her pathology was not so important; sometimes the Supreme Court even mentions the rule res ipsa loquitur (TS 14 May 2008 (RJ 2008\3071), 16 Apr. 2007 (RJ 2007\4332),15 Sep. 2003 [RJ 2003/6418]). Finally, it is worth mentioning that the Supreme Court resorts to the consumer legislation (specifically Arts 26 and 28 former LGDCU, currently 148 and 149 new LGDCU), which is based on strict liability (e.g., TS 26 Mar. 2004 and 19 Jun. 2001 [RJ 2001/4974]).

357. Written by María Paz García Rubio (University of Santiago de Compostela).

him/her with the monetary substitute. Before the Civil Procedure Act, lawyers considered that specific performance was a right of the debtor, because specific performance is, in principle, the primary remedy in Spanish Civil law; consequently, the creditor could not claim damages before the specific performance. However, Article 706 LEC states that the creditor can choose between performance *in natura* or damages, if the debtor does not perform voluntarily.

291. Specific performance can be obtained with an order by the judge upon demand of the person to whom the obligation is owed (voluntary procedural execution). If the debtor refuses to perform, the judge will order forced execution. The sort of forced execution depends on the type of obligation.

Concerning the obligation to give (e.g., to deliver property, to pay a sum of money), Article 1096 CC states that where a specific thing must be delivered, the creditor has the rights recognized by Article 1101 and also the right to compel the debtor to deliver the thing. In case of a generic obligation, the creditor can request performance of the obligation at the expense of the debtor. Articles 701–704 LEC contain detailed rules on delivery of tangible movables, generic things and immovables. Concerning the obligation to pay a sum of money, the rule is contained in Articles 705 et seq. LEC.

According to Article 1098.1 CC, if a person does not fulfil an obligation to do something, the judge may order performance at his/her expense. Article 1098.2 applies the same rule where the debtor did something in breach of the obligation; besides, the judge can order destroyed what has been done in breach of the obligation (*see also* Article 706 LEC, if the obligation has not a personal character). In case of obligations with a personal character, Article 709 LEC replaces the obligation with the monetary equivalent. Article 708 LEC, following the doctrine of the Supreme Court about pre-contract, entitles the judge to replace the declaration of the will of the obliged party.

Article 1099 CC deals with obligations not to do something. The creditor has the right to demand the destruction of anything done in breach of the contract, notwithstanding the claim for damages and the right to the future debtor's abstention. These rules must be completed with Article 710 LEC.

292. Specific performance is also possible in case of defective performance. It admits two modalities: repair and replacement of the defective goods. Both remedies were already recognized in the Consumer Protection Act of 1984 for durable goods, but they were not incorporated into the Civil Code. Both remedies are included in several international enactments, like the Directive 1999/44/CE on certain aspects of the sale of consumer goods, which was transposed into Spanish law by means of the Act 23/2003 of 10 July, *de Garantías en la Venta de Bienes de Consumo* and now in Articles 116 et seq. new LGDCU. Repair and replacement are general remedies in the CC Cat (Article 621-37.a). It is expressly stated that specific performance cannot entail additional costs for the aggrieved party. Exceptionally, specific performance is not available when it is impossible or illegal – which must be strictly construed – and when its cost is disproportionate in relation to the benefit to the creditor. Moreover, the debtor is entitled to cure performance as long as there is no definitive non-performance (Article 621-39), unless (a) the right to cure cannot be exercised without delay or detriment to the creditor; (b) the creditor may reasonably believe that the debtor is not going to perform or that is going to perform regularly; (c) the delay entails an essential non-performance. Self-reparation is not ruled and case law is far from unanimous.

II. *Astreintes*

293. *Astreintes* or injunctions were not regulated in Spanish law. Currently, however, there are some provisions that allow the court to put economic pressure on the debtor in case he/she does not want to perform an obligation. For example, according to Article 709.1 LEC, within the judicial procedure of specific performance of non-pecuniary obligations, if the debtor is recalcitrant in performing the obligation of personal character, the court can impose upon him/her a fine, which amount is determined by Article 711 LEC. Article 710.1 LEC also provides the possibility of imposing a fine in case of an obligation not to do.

III. Seizure

294. If the debtor does not voluntarily perform an obligation to do, where the property is movable and ascertained the creditor may be put into possession of it (Article 701 LEC). In order to avoid the frustration of specific performance, the creditor may resort to the provisional remedy of the exhibition of the thing (Article 256.1 LEC) and subsequently its attachment. When it is of a generic character, the creditor may also be allowed to buy the goods at the debtor's expenses (Article 702 LEC). In cases where specific performance in such a way becomes impossible, the creditor may claim damages pursuant to Article 712 LEC.

Seizures may also lead to the sale of the property (embargo) in cases of pecuniary obligations. Embargo confers on the court the power to dispose of the debtor's good in order to sell it (usually auctioning it) and pay the creditor with the price of the sale. Preventive embargo (Article 727.1 LEC) is a provisory remedy in order to guarantee a future specific performance of a pecuniary obligation, which tries to avoid the negative consequences of the debtor's insolvency. It implies the provisory attachment of certain assets of the debtor. It can also be applied to conditional obligations.

§4. Termination

295. The right to terminate the contract is expressly recognized in Article 1124 CC. According to this provision, 'a resolutory condition is always understood in synallagmatic contracts for the case where one of the parties does not fulfil his/her obligations'.[358] In this case, the aggrieved party has the choice between forcing the other party to perform or claim termination, both with a right to damages. The aggrieved party may also terminate the contract, after claiming performance, where the performance is impossible. The court must order termination, except if the court, according to the circumstances, fixes an additional period for performance. The rights of the third party are regulated by Articles 1295 and 1298 and by the *Ley Hipotecaria*.

The rules on termination appear to follow the model of the French Civil Code, but with some important differences. In this sense, termination is considered like an implied term of the contract, a resolutory condition (*condición resolutoria tácita*). Nevertheless, the courts confirm that termination is not a clause of a contract, but a legal right in synallagmatic contracts. Besides, in Spanish law termination is deemed to be retrospective, in contrast with other perspectives, and a source of restitution.[359]

296. According to Spanish lawyers, the basic rules for termination are the following:

1. The right to terminate the contract concerns synallagmatic contracts. As opposed to other systems, termination may not be applied to multilateral contracts,[360] and it is only a synallagmatic remedy.
2. The obligation must be enforceable (*exigible*), although Spanish Code recognizes some cases of anticipatory non-performance (e.g., Article 1503). The obligation of the party who terminates the contract does not need to be enforceable.
3. Non-performance must be serious. Termination is only permitted if the non-performed obligation is of such kind that its breach would entitle the other party to escape from the contract. This requirement is expressly recognized in Article 25 United Nations Convention on the International Sale of Goods (CISG) (essential non-performance) and in Article 9:301 PECL (fundamental non-performance) and has been assumed by Spanish case law.[361] This requirement means that a simple delay or a slightly defective performance does not entitle termination, except if time of performance is of the essence. Usually, the courts consider that in case of breach of a minor obligation or term of the contract (*obligaciones accesorias*), termination is not permitted.[362] Nevertheless, in some particular contracts, a party is entitled to terminate the contract even on the basis of non-performance of an incidental obligation.[363] The parties are free to shape a certain non-performance as a fundamental one.[364] Non-performance is fundamental when the aggrieved party is deprived of its contractual expectations and the goal of the contract becomes frustrated.

---

358. Written by María Paz García Rubio (University of Santiago de Compostela).
359. TS 12 Feb. 2012 (RJ 2012\4054).
360. TS 20 Jun. 1991 (RJ 1991/4528).
361. For example, TS 4 Sep. 2014 (Roj: STS 4607/2014), 23 May 2014 (Roj: STS 2404/2014), 16 May 2012 (RJ 2012\6351).
362. TS 21 Mar. 1994 (RJ 1994/2560).
363. It is the case of the contract of edition (Art. 45 Intellectual Property Act).
364. TS 12 Nov. 2014 (Roj: STS 4442/2014): non-payment of a single instalment.

4. The party who terminates must have performed or have tendered his/her own performance. The courts consider that the party who does not fulfil loses the right to terminate the contract,[365] unless his/her non-performance is a consequence of the non-performance of the other party.[366]
5. Non-performance must be 'true and suitable' (*incumplimiento verdadero y propio*). This requirement sets out some problems in cases of partial execution of the obligation. Generally, the doctrine considers that a partial non-performance does not permit termination of the whole contract, unless the partial non-performance is essential in relation to the synallagmatic contract as a whole. A partial non-performance permits a partial termination of the concerned part of the contract.[367]

297. Partial non-performance has a particular interest in cases where the seller has delivered defective goods. Spanish law has a special body of rules concerning the delivery of defective goods. These are the '*aedilitian remedies*' that render the seller liable under the '*guarantee for latent defects*'. This action has a brief period of limitation (six months). Under the '*garantía*' the purchaser can claim either termination of the contract or a reduction in price. This special body of rules has some problems of coordination with the general rules on breach of contract. The most traditional literature considered that in cases of defective performance the special regime on '*guarantee for latent defects*' excluded the general rules on breach of contract. The modern doctrine and case law state that the seller who delivers defective goods, delivers an *aliud pro alio*. Consequently, the buyer has the right to choose between the two possibilities: either the special guarantee *for latent defects* or termination based on Article 1124 (as well as the right to performance ex Article 1101).[368] This alternative choice is very important because the period of prescription of general actions for performance and termination is pretty long: fifteen years (Article 1964 CC). Currently Community law – the Directive 1999/44 -– is transposed without amending the Civil Code in the new LGDCU, in particular in Articles 118 et seq. It has regulated the four remedies for non-performance: repair and substitution, on the one hand, and reduction of price and termination, on the other hand.

298. Reduction of price in case of defective performance (*actio quanti minoris*) has concrete applications, for example, in Article 159 new LGDCU in relation to package travels.

299. During a long time, the doctrine and the decisions of the courts demanded a subjective requirement in order to terminate the contract: either the deliberate intention of non-performance or the definitive impossibility of performance.

365. TS 8 Apr. 2000 (RJ 2000/2354). Non-performance of one party neutralizes non-performance of the other (TS 29 Jul. 1999 [RJ 1999/6217]).
366. TS 5 Jul. 1999 (RJ 1999/4980).
367. A similar rule is to be found in Art. 9:302 PECL.
368. A similar rule is to be found in Art. 9:302 PECL.

Nowadays this subjective requirement is forgotten, and the courts confirm that frustration of the aim of the contract is enough.[369]

300. The right to terminate does not require the debtor's default. It also does not demand the imputation of the non-performance to the debtor. The authors recognize that a party may terminate the contract if performance becomes permanently impossible.

Case law admits extrajudicial termination.[370]

I. Exercise of the Right to Terminate

301. In the Spanish legal system, termination is not automatic. Unlike French law, termination may be judicial, extrajudicial and by means of an informal notice to the party.[371]

Nevertheless, in cases of extrajudicial or notified termination not accepted by the party, the courts must declare the lawful character of termination because it is a necessary judicial control of non-performance.[372] During this period of time, the creditor can withhold performance. The judgment subsequently declares the termination of the contract. The plaintiff is the aggrieved party, and the defendant is the non-performing party. The period of prescription of the action is fifteen years since there is no specific period in the Civil Code.[373]

302. Termination and specific performance of the contract are two incompatible remedies. According to Article 1124.2, the aggrieved party can choose one of the two possibilities, but he/she cannot resort to both remedies at the same time. However, Article 1124.2 does not preclude the alternative or the subsidiary accumulation of the remedies.[374] The actor may also change the remedy. If, after having claimed specific performance, he/she becomes aware that the other party has not performed or is not likely to do so within a reasonable time, the aggrieved party may terminate the contract (*see* Article 1124.2).[375] However, opting for termination is definitive and will preclude resorting to other remedies.[376] These rules are in accordance with Article 8:102 PECL and with Articles 45 and 61 CISG.

303. Article 1124.3 CC allows the court to grant the debtor a *délai de grace* (*término de gracia*) that means a last chance to perform if there are 'justified

369. For example, TS 17 Feb. 2010 (RJ 2010\1284, quoting Unidroit Principles), 23 Jul. 2007 (RJ 2007\4702, quoting Unidroit Principles and PECL), 7 May 2003 (RJ 2003/3886).
370. TS 14 Feb. 2012 (Roj: STS 1303/2012), 11 Dec. 2013 (Roj: STS 6175/2013).
371. Similar rules are to be found in Arts 9:303 PECL and 26 CISG.
372. TS 26 Nov. 2001 (RJ 2002/1038), 15 Nov. 1999 (RJ 1999/8213).
373. TS 9 Sep. 2014 (Roj: STS 3812/2014).
374. TS 17 Jan. 2000 (RJ 2000/67).
375. TS 29 May 2000 (RJ 2000/3944).
376. But *see* TS 26 Dec. 2001 (RJA 2002/1038), which allows to claim performance after a claim for termination.

reasons' (*causas justificadas*).[377] The court fixes this additional period for performance. The purpose of this additional period, unlike the *Nachfrist* of German law in which Article 8:106 PECL was inspired, is to give the other party one last chance to fulfil his/her contractual obligations. This sort of additional period can be fixed voluntarily in a clause of the contract. This clause is very usual in the sale of immovable property and is governed by Article 1504 CC.[378] Nevertheless, courts have recognized this voluntary additional period beyond Article 1504, like in contracts of agency.[379]

II. Consequences of Termination

304. The consequences of termination in the CC are not comprehensively regulated. The Code forgets two principal effects. First of all, termination releases both parties from their obligations. Besides, if performance has been carried out, both parties must return benefits received from the other or make restitution of their value. Doctrine and case law admit both effects. Generally, they consider that termination acts retroactively and consequently it produces the same retroactive effect as nullity: the contract had never existed. Nevertheless, if contractual obligations are to be performed over an extended period of time (*contratos de tracto sucesivo*), termination has only prospective effects. But, in my opinion, the CC does not contain any rule on the retrospective effect of termination. Moreover, this retrospective effect is unnecessary and introduces a lot of difficulties concerning restitution between the parties.[380]

305. The principal consequence of termination is restitution of property. This consequence is not mentioned in the Civil Code. However, it is clear that if the parties of a synallagmatic contract have already performed, in whole or in part, termination imposes on them a reciprocal obligation of restitution. When property that should be recovered has deteriorated or is improved, the provisions on usufruct apply. Nevertheless, some difficulties may arise in two situations. First, in the case where restitution *in natura* becomes impossible, for example, because the property has been destroyed or the performed prestation was a service. Second, when third parties have become interested in the property. The first case is not regulated by the Civil Code. According to some opinions, the aggrieved party can terminate the contract and claim for the monetary equivalent of the impossible restitution. However, this solution does not solve the problem of the aggrieved party, for example, when the debtor is bankrupt. The second difficulty arises if possession of property has been transferred to a third party; Article 1124 refers to Articles 1295 and 1298 CC.

377. *See* 22 Mar. 2000 (RJ 2000/1498). This judicial additional period is also established in Art. 11.1 of the Sale on Instalment Act (Act 28/1998 of 13 July).
378. Among others, TS 29 Dec. 1999 (RJ 1999/9494), 22 Sep. 1997 (RJ 1997/6858).
379. TS 11 Oct. 2000 (RJ 2000/7723).
380. *See* my commentary to TS 13 Oct. 1995 (1996) *RDP* 561.

Namely, the third person who has acquired in good faith keeps the acquired property. The acquirer in bad faith loses the acquired property, and the aggrieved party recovers the property. The rules of the *Ley Hipotecaria* must be also applied.

306. According to Article 1124 CC, termination and damages are compatible remedies. Nevertheless, the claim for damages is only possible if failure to perform was imputable to the debtor. The creditor may claim for patrimonial and non-patrimonial damages.

307. Although the distinction between expectation (positive interest) and reliance (negative interest) does not seem to be recognized in the Spanish Code, it is used by the doctrine in relation to the termination of the contract. According to some authors, damages after the termination of a contract are limited to the negative interest including expenses as well as the loss of opportunities to conclude the contract with third parties;[381] furthermore, the reliance interest may not exceed the positive interest. According to another opinion, the plaintiff may claim for expectation interest (positive interest);[382] in other words, the creditor is to be put into the position he/she would have been if the contract had been performed.

The parties of a synallagmatic contract can modify the right to terminate the contract. For example, if they establish penalty clauses.[383] The same applies to other clauses such as arbitration clauses and clauses which limit one party's liability (except in case of '*international non-performance*').

308. Termination is ruled in Article 621-41 CCCat as an alternative to specific performance, subject to the creditor's right to cure. Termination is available when non-performance is fundamental; intentional non-performance is always fundamental. It is also available when the party declares or somehow makes evident that she is not going to fulfil the contract. It is expressly stated that termination by notice is effective. Notice does not need any formal requirement, but it is necessary to terminate the contract. Restitution after termination is not regulated.

§5. *Exceptio Non Adimpleti Contractus* (The Defence of Non-Performance by the Other Party)

I. *Exceptio Non Adimpleti Contractus*

309. Once termination has been considered, there is another specific remedy for synallagmatic contracts: withholding performance.[384] As opposed to termination, which refers to the right to refuse the performance by the other party and to escape

381. Jesús Delgado Echeverría, in Lacruz, *Elementos*, vol. II, 204; F. Jordano Fraga, 'Comentario a la STS 26 Nov. 1987', CCJC, no. 15, 5183–5207.
382. Ángel Carrasco Perera, 'Comentario a la STS 30 July 1989', CCJC, no. 21, 885–894; Fernando Pantaleón Prieto, 'Resolución por incumplimiento e indemnización', ADC (1989): 1143 passim; Díez-Picazo, *Fundamentos*, II, 727.
383. TS 22 Sep. 2000 (RJ 2000/7026).
384. Maria Cruz Moreno, *La exceptio nona dimpleti contractus* (Valencia, 2004).

from the contract, withholding performance (*exceptio non adimpleti contractus*) is the aggrieved party's right to refuse to perform some or all of his/her obligations until the other party has performed his/her obligations, or at least until he/she is willing to perform them. The foundation of both remedies lies in the link between the obligations of the parties (functional synallagma).

The right to withhold performance allows a party to refuse to counter-perform in a synallagmatic relationship. The *exceptio non adimpleti contractus* is an expression of this idea in the procedural sense of the term. Nevertheless, in the Spanish system, it is not necessarily a judicial remedy. Withholding performance has its sense for the party who must perform simultaneously or after the other party.

310. This remedy is expressly recognized by several codes, and it is also contained in Article 71 CISG and in Article 9:201 PECL. The Spanish Code, however, does not expressly establish a general rule on the right to withhold. Nevertheless, there are some miscellaneous precepts dealing with it (e.g., Articles 1466, 1467, 1500, 1502). Spanish authors remark that the rule is a consequence of Articles 1100 (no party incurs *mora debitoris* while the other party does not perform) and 1124 that regulates termination of the contract. In a broad sense, the right of retention of the creditor is a sort of withholding performance. In the cases provided by the law, the party has the right to suspend the performance of his/her obligation of restitution to the owner of the thing until the obligation is fulfilled.[385] Spanish courts have allowed the defence of non-performance in many different cases.[386]

According to Spanish doctrine and case law, the requirements for the defence of non-performance are three. First, it must be a synallagmatic obligation. Second, non-performance must refer to fundamental obligations. Third, the defence must be used in good faith. There is no good faith if the defendant has caused the other party's non-performance or if non-performance is not fundamental. By contrast, Article 621-40 CCCat lays down a basic regulation. This remedy does not require a fundamental non-performance. The debtor is entitled to withhold when both performances must be carried out simultaneously and when she reasonably believes that the other party will not perform her obligations and notifies withholding.

311. The principal effect of the right to withhold performance is the provisional suspension of the creditor's counter-performance. This means that his/her obligation is suspended, but not extinguished.

Spanish writers and Spanish courts have argued in favour of a partial right to withhold where the circumstances of non-performance do not justify withholding the whole performance.[387]

385. Below, para. 313.
386. For example, TS 22 Oct. 1997 (RJ 1997/7410).
387. TS 27 Mar. 1991 (RJ 1991/2451) and later, with a very formal criterion, stating the difference between *exceptio nonadimpleti contratus* and *exceptio non riteadimpleti contractus*, TS 3 Feb. 2000 (RJ 2000/621).

312. It must be remarked that Spanish courts have confirmed that the right to withhold cannot be excluded by the parties.[388] This criterion is opposed to the general rules about clauses excluding or restricting remedies, and it does not match with Article 8:109 PECL either. Moreover, some precepts in the CC admit the exclusion of the *exceptio* by the parties (e.g., Article 1502).

II. Lien

313. The right of retention is the debtor's right to retain the property that must be delivered or given back, until the creditor to whom he/she is obliged to deliver or restitute performs his/her own obligation. The regulation of the right of retention is rather fragmentary in the CC. Retention is allowed in a number of cases, either on the grounds of expenses carried out in the retained thing (Articles 453, 502, 1780 CC) or as a guarantee of certain debts (Article 464). It is also discussed if it is a real right,[389] although the doctrine favours its *erga omnnes* effectiveness. The retainer cannot use the retained thing. He/she is only entitled to reject delivery or restitution. Retention extinguishes when the obligation is fulfilled.

By contrast, the right of retention is comprehensively regulated in the civil law of Catalonia (Articles 569-3 et seq. CC Cat). It is expressly shaped as a real right. Its main feature is the *ius distrahendi* recognized by the retainer: under certain formal requirements, the retainer is allowed to sell the retained thing in order to get paid. If the value of the retained thing is less than EUR 2,000, the law alleviates the formal requirements of the sale (e.g., auction is not necessary). The law also authorizes the substitution of retention by another guarantee (a real security or a solidary suretyship), in order to avoid the owner from being deprived of the possession of productive assets (trucks, machinery, etc.).

The right of retention can be used as a defence against the claim of the owner, but it is more than just a defence, since it is a real right. Therefore, it is also possible for a claim based on the right of retention.

§6. Restitution

314. The consequence of contractual ineffectiveness in a broad sense (i.e., including nullity and termination) is the restitution of property passed under the contract (Article 1303 CC). Termination has retrospective limited effect *ex tunc*,[390] because restitution concerns only the legal consequences resulting from instantaneous prestations (not those stemming from enduring prestations).[391] The general rule is that property must be returned with its fruits and price with legal interests.[392] Restitution is imposed on both parties. If a third party has acquired in good faith the

388. For example, TS 9 Jul. 1991 (RJ 1991/5336).
389. The judgment handed down by the Supreme Court on 7 Jul. 1987 (RJ 1987/5185) stated that it is a real right, but this configuration is by no means unanimously accepted.
390. TS 2 Apr. 2004 (RJ 2004/1670), 5 Dec. 2003 (RJ 2003/8786), 5 Feb. 2002 (RJ 2002/2884).
391. TS 30 Apr. 2013 (Roj: STS 5873/2013).
392. TS 17 Jun. 1986 (RJ 1986/3554).

property, restitution *in natura* becomes impossible, and the party has to return the value of the property. Concerning contracts with successive obligations, restitution has effects *ex nunc*, since restitution *in natura* is not possible, and therefore it operates for the future.[393]

§7. Damages

I. The Concept of Damages (*daños y perjuicios*): Types of Damages

315. Non-performance imputable to the debtor gives the creditor a right to recover damages.[394] The claim for damages is compatible with a specific performance and with the termination of the synallagmatic contracts.

Some authors consider that the claim for damages is an accessory claim, because it depends on the previous existence of a principal obligation. It is also believed that it is a monetary obligation, because it consists in delivering a sum of money (*see* Article 713 LEC). Nevertheless, in my opinion, although usually damages must be repaired by paying money, it is also usual that actual reparation is possible and more appropriate than payment of a sum of money. This last possibility of reparation *in natura* is admitted in Articles 110 and 112 CP and in Article 141.4 Legal Regime of Public Administration and Administrative Procedure Act of 26 November 1992.

316. The borders between reparation of damages and the monetary equivalent of performance are not clearly settled (*see* Article 1101 CC). According to some authors, the equivalent of performance is a part of the obligation to repair damages. Other authors believe that performance by equivalent must be distinguished from damages, because the obligation to repair damages only arises if actual damage exists and, generally, the aggrieved creditor may claim both, specific performance and damages. Now the difference is clearly recognized in Articles 712 and 717 LEC.

Article 1101 CC regulates the foundations of the claim for damages (its grounds and the criterion of imputation). Article 1106 CC expressly describes the concepts covered by damages: the loss suffered by the aggrieved party and the gain he/she had been deprived of.

317. According to case law, the plaintiff has to prove the damage and the causal link between it and non-performance.[395]

The damage can be either patrimonial or non-patrimonial (pain and suffering, '*daño moral*'). Patrimonial damage comprises both, the loss suffered by the creditor and the profit he/she has been deprived of (*daño emergente* and *lucro cesante*) (Article 1106 CC mentioned above). The distinction between both concepts comes from Roman law. Nevertheless, the distinction between expectation (positive interest) and reliance (negative interest) damages, known to both English and German

393. TS 20 Mar. 2007 (RJ 2007/2622).
394. Written by María Paz García Rubio (University of Santiago de Compostela).
395. TS 12 Dec. 2003 (RJ 2003/9285), 17 Sep. 1987 (RJ 1987/6063).

laws as well as the PECL (Article 9:502) does not seem to be recognized by the CC, but it is increasingly accepted by the doctrine.[396]

The '*daño emergente*' is the loss suffered by the aggrieved party. It includes, for some authors, the monetary substitute of the non-performed obligation. It also covers the expenses made by the creditor that non-performance turns useless. Finally, '*daño emergente*' includes loss in other goods of the creditor, caused by non-performance and resulting from the particular circumstances of the case (Pothier's classic example: the sick animal that transmits the illness to the other animals of the creditor). The net value added tax that the claimant has to pay to a third person has to be included in the assessment of the damage.[397]

The '*lucro cesante*' is the gain of which the creditor has been deprived[398] (the description in Articles 63 and 65 LCS is interesting). Spanish courts are very strict in the establishment and the proof of the '*lucro cesante*'. Case law confirms that the obligation to repair the '*lucro cesante*' cannot result from simple possibilities or unsure and uncertain results.[399] Compensation for 'dreams of gains', according to the expression of Dernburg, must be rejected.[400] Burden of proof of *lucrum cessans* rests with the claimant, even in the case of delay in delivery of a building for lease purposes, since a *damnum ex re ipsa* is not presumed.[401]

318. As mentioned above, the aggrieved party may claim not only for patrimonial damage but also for moral (non-pecuniary) damage. Article 1106 CC does not exclude non-pecuniary loss (*daño moral*). *Daño moral* is every pain and suffering, inconvenience and mental distress resulting from the failure to perform the obligation. Since a famous judgment by the Spanish Supreme Court handed down in 1912 and for a long time after, non-pecuniary loss was considered only in tort law (*responsabilidad extracontractual*). Nowadays, *daño moral* is also recognized in contractual liability. In the Spanish legal system, there is no statutory limitation to compensation for non-pecuniary loss, and it is possible to claim it without a specific legal authorization. In the context of certain contracts, this sort of damages is particularly frequent. That is the case of the package travel contract regulated by the Package Travel Act of 6 July 1995, complying with the Directive 90/314/EEC on package travel, package holidays and package tours.[402] In this contract, it is possible to claim compensation for non-pecuniary loss, including disappointment over spoiled holidays and mental distress caused by the delay in the return flight.[403]

---

396. Díez-Picazo, *Fundamentos*, I, 683 and 726; Fernando Pantaleón, 'Resolución por incumplimiento e indemnización', ADC (1989): 1143, passim; M.P. García Rubio, *La responsabilidadprecontractual en el Derecho español* (Madrid, 1991), 230 et seq.
397. TS 21 Oct. 2014 (Roj: STS 4236/2014).
398. TS 15 Jul. 1998 (RJ 1998/5550). *See also*, TS 14 Jul. 2003 (RJ 2003/4629) and 26 Sep. 2002 (RJ 2002/8094), which consider the basis for '*lucro cesante*' its foreseeable character. *See* Elena Vicente Domingo, *Ellucro cesante* (Madrid, 2014).
399. TS 29 Dec. 2001 (RJ 2001/1474), 8 Jun. 1996 (RJ 1996/4831).
400. TS 1 Mar. 2011 (RJ 2011\2615).
401. TS 10 Sep. 2014 (Roj: STS 3907/2014).
402. M.P. García Rubio, *La responsabilidad contractual de las agencias de viaje* (Madrid, 1999), 220 et seq.
403. TS 31 May 2000 (RJ 2000/5089).

Certainly, the aggrieved party may also claim for personal physical injuries caused by non-performance of the obligation. Many times the injured person has already incurred medical expenses, and he/she demands their reimbursement.

II. Proof and Measure of Damages

319. Concerning the proof of damages, Spanish courts have frequently stated that 'the mere non-performance does not generate the obligation to repair damages'.[404] Nevertheless, this assertion is controversial, and many decisions consider now that the simple non-performance means per se a damage.[405]

With regard to the proof of moral damages, the judgment of the Supreme Court of 31 May 2000 considers that if the non-pecuniary damage is a consequence of a patrimonial damage or results from concrete facts, it is only necessary to prove the reality that supports it.[406] However, no evidence is necessary where the rule *re ipsa loquitur* applies.

Repeated case law establishes that the decision about the existence of damage belongs to the discretion of the judge of instance because it is a question of fact. Consequently it is not possible for the revision on this matter by the Supreme Court.[407]

320. Measure of damages in the Spanish legal system is very similar to the French Civil Code. The Spanish Code contains some rules on the assessment of damages taking into account the principle of full compensation (*resarcimiento integral*). However, Article 1107 distinguishes '*dolo*' and '*culpa*'. According to this Article, the debtor acting in good faith is liable only for losses which he/she foresaw or could have foreseen at the time of conclusion of the obligation and which results necessarily from his/her non-performance of the obligation. In the second paragraph, the precept adds that in case of intentional non-performance, he/she is liable for all the damages that knowingly result from his/her non-performance of the obligation. The meaning of this article is disputed by Spanish writers. The most common opinion is that 'the good faith debtor' is the one whose non-performance is not intentional *dolus*. The foreseeability rule is also adopted by many systems and is also provided by CISG (Article 74 *in fine*) and PECL (Article 9:503). Some authors think that the foreseeability test must not be applied to legal obligations.

Finally, the limitation of the debtor's liability to any foreseeable loss in accordance with Article 1107 CC is not applicable in cases of intentional non-performance (*dolo*). In these situations full damages are awarded, even if unforeseeable (*resarcimiento integral*).[408]

404. For example, TS 26 Sep. 2000 (RJ 2000/869), 28 Dec. 1999 (RJ 1999/9379).
405. TS 12 Mar. 2004 (RJ 2004/902), 5 Dec. 2000 (RJ 2000/9435).
406. TS 15 Jun. 2010 (RJ 2010\5151).
407. TS 13 Mar. 2001 (RJ 2001/261), 26 Sep. 2000 (RJ 2000/869).
408. TS 29 Dec. 2001 (RJ 2001/1474). The same rule is provided by Art. 9:503 PECL.

Whatever the creditor gets in redress for the damage must be deducted from the compensation for damages.[409]

III. The Duty of the Creditor to Mitigate the Damage

321. In English and German laws the creditor has to mitigate the loss (*duty* or *Obliegenheit*). This principle is now also recognized by Article 77 CISG[410] and Article 9:505 PECL. It is also accepted by the jurisprudence of the European Court of Justice.[411]

According to international doctrine, the 'duty to mitigate' is twofold. The creditor should not act unreasonably, that is in such a way as to make the loss worse (e.g., driving a car which he/she has bought and knows has defective brakes). Besides, he/she should take reasonable positive steps to reduce the loss, for example, by making a substitute contract. The effect of overlooking this 'duty' is that the victim's claim for damages may be reduced.

Spanish law does not as such recognize a general duty to mitigate, but there exists some instances, such as Article 17 LCS. Nevertheless, it is possible to admit this duty, because it is a consequence of the general principle of good faith contained in Articles 7.1 and 1254 CC. Furthermore, the Supreme Court has recognized the duty to mitigate in the decision of 15 November 1994, from a perspective of the protective purpose of the contractual norm, as well as in the decision of 30 July 2012 evoking the duty 'to reasonably mitigate damages resulting from breach of contract'.[412]

§8. Limitation of Actions

322. The last title of the Civil Code is devoted to 'Prescription'. Under this headline both acquisitive and extinctive prescriptions are regulated. The legal provisions have remained unchanged since the Civil Code entered into force in 1889 and, therefore, it has been impermeable to the new international developments. Spanish doctrine has severely criticized the regulation, because some of the limitation periods are too long, some others too short; suspension is not generally admitted, etc. Recently, Catalonia has regulated anew the law of prescription, essentially along the lines of the modernized German BGB. Therefore, I think it can be useful to deal with both regulations in this section, but only in relation to extinctive prescription.

409. TS 3 Sep. 2012 (Roj: STS 7112/2012).
410. This article of the Vienna Convention was applied by TS 28 Jan. 2000 (RJ 2000/454).
411. Judgment of 5 Mar. 1996, *Brasserie duPêcheur SA v. Bundesrepublik Deutschland* and the *Queen v. Secretary of State of Transport, ex parte Factortame Ltd and others*, C-46/93 and 48/93.
412. Roj: STS 6079/2012.

I. The Spanish Civil Code

323. According to Article 1961 CC, 'actions come into prescription for the simple lapse of time provided by law'. Prescription fixes a temporary limit to the exercise of rights. This implies that the debtor can refuse to perform his/her obligations when the period of prescription has lapsed. The debtor can avail himself/herself of the defence of prescription if the creditor claims performance once the prescription period has elapsed.

The basis of prescription is objective. The attitude of the parties is legally irrelevant in relation to the running of prescription. Prescription aims at legal certainty, based on the necessity of clarifying and deciding what rights are in force. It also serves to avoid a number of problems of evidence. Nevertheless, case law states repeatedly that prescription must be restrictively applied.[413] As we will see later, the general period of prescription is quite long (fifteen years). Therefore, it is really difficult for the debtor to successfully allege prescription.

324. Spanish doctrine and case law have discussed the object of prescription. Articles 1930 and 1961 CC refer to the prescription of 'rights and actions'. The prevailing theory considers that the subjective right is the object of prescription and, therefore, that prescription leads to the extinction of rights. Nevertheless, this theory does not give a convincing answer to the validity of the payment of a prescribed debt. Therefore, the so-called weak effect of prescription is to be preferred. The debtor may invoke prescription and reject the creditor's claim.[414]

Some claims do not prescribe. The actions to divide a common thing and to divide the estate and the claim for fixing the boundaries between plots of land are unprescribable (Article 1965 CC). The claim for declaring absolutely void a contract does not prescribe, but the action for restitution on the grounds of the nullity[415] is prescribable.

325. Prescription concerns public policy, in the sense that the parties cannot completely exclude prescription of claims. But as a defence, prescription only affects private interests, and therefore it is only subject to the general limitations of the party autonomy. Parties may waiver their right to invoke prescription. In addition, as it affects private interests, courts are not allowed to apply prescription ex officio.[416] Moreover, the defence of prescription must be invoked at a convenient stage of the court procedure, that is, at the beginning of the first instance, since otherwise it will not even be considered by the courts.[417]

326. Prescription may be invoked against any person, since 1932 CC provides that prescription is established 'in detriment of every type of persons'. So, natural and juridical persons are included, regardless of their conditions. It is relevant to

413. *See* TS 3 May 2007 (RJ 2007/2827), 29 Oct. 2003 (RJ 2003/7773), 19 Dec. 2001 (RJ 2002/249), 3 Oct. 2001 (RJ 2001/7142).
414. Albaladejo, *Derecho civil*, I, 891–893.
415. *See* Chapter 6 §6.
416. For example, TS 22 Dec. 2000 (RJ 2000/10137).
417. TS 30 Nov. 2000 (RJ 2000/9170).

remark that the principle '*agere non valenti non currit praescriptio*' is not in force in the Spanish Civil law. Therefore, prescription runs in favour or against persons with a limited capacity to act, irrespective of whether they are legally represented or not. Moreover, Article 1932 CC entitles incapable persons to claim against their legal representative for damages resulting from prescription. Family relations are not an exemption from prescription either, and thus it also operates in favour or against the members of a family. Similarly, Article 1934 CC establishes that claims by or against an estate are prescribable.

A. *Commencement*

327. The CC provides a subjective regime of commencement of prescription. Article 1969 CC refers to the day in which the actions could be exercised. That means that prescription does not run unless the creditor knows (or ought to know) about his/her claim,[418] but the Supreme Court considers that knowledge does not depend upon the personal conditions of the creditor.[419] Articles 1970, 1971 and 1972 contain specific rules for the commencement of the prescription of certain obligations.

For the purpose of computing the prescription period, the day on which the prescription commences does not count; however, the period is only completed at the end of the last day (Article 1960 CC).

B. *Prescription Periods*

328. The CC was amended in 2015 and now establishes the period of five years as the general period of prescription for personal actions. But the claim based on a mortgage (*acción hipotecaria*) has still a prescription period of twenty years (Article 1964 CC).

Real actions related to movables prescribe within six years (Article 1962 CC), whilst real actions related to immovables prescribe within thirty years (Article 1963 CC).

Article 1966 CC provides a quinquennial period for alimony, lease rents (both for dwellings and agricultural holdings) and any other periodical payment due annually or at shorter intervals.

Claims based on the remuneration of professional services prescribe within three years (Article 1967 CC).

418. TS 23 Oct. 2007 (RJ 2007/8635).

419. If previously a criminal proceeding took place in relation to the same facts, the period does not begin to run until the day in which the parties are notified of the end of the criminal proceeding. Among many other decisions, TS 19 Jul. 2007 (RJ 2007/4691), 12 May 2004 (RJ 2004/2736), 12 Apr. 2004 (RJ 2004/2611).

One year is the prescription period for (Article 1968 CC):

- actions to recover or retain possession (*interdictos*);
- claims based on tort.[420] The courts have moderated the brevity of this period, since the commencement is linked to the knowledge of the possibility of the claim and of the damages.[421] It must be underlined that product liability is subject to a prescription period of three years (Article 12 Product Liability Act).

C. *Interruption and Suspension*

329. Interruption of prescription means that prescription begins to run afresh, because the time which has elapsed before the interrupting act is not taken into account. Article 1973 CC lays down three grounds for interruption:

- The judicial exercise of the claim. It includes arbitration courts. Interruption is granted even if the court lacks jurisdiction.
- The extrajudicial demand.
- Any act of acknowledgement carried out by the debtor.

330. Suspension is not regulated in the Civil Code.[422] Nevertheless, it is established in Article 955 CCom.[423] Besides, the Act of 1 April 1939 suspended all periods of prescription in respect of persons and assets affected by the Civil War.

D. *Lapse of Rights*

331. Under the influence of German and Italian laws, Spanish courts and doctrine have admitted lapse of rights (*caducidad*) as a different institution to prescription,[424] even though it is also based on the passing of time as a limit to the exercise of subjective rights. It refers to relatively short periods in the course of which either

---

420. It has to be borne in mind that where liability arises from a fact that constitutes a crime, since the Criminal Code does not establish a specific prescription period, the Supreme Court considers that the period of limitation is fifteen years (*see*, recently, TS 31 Jan. 2004 (RJ 2004/444)).

421. For example, TS 25 May 2010 (RJ 2010\5156), 22 Jul. 2003 (RJ 2003/5851), 29 May 2003 (RJ 2003/3913).

422. Although without mentioning such ground for suspension, the decision handed down by the Supreme Court on 25 Jan. 2000 (RJ 2000/349) evokes suspension based on force majeure. The running of the period of prescription of a claim for vindication of an immovable belonging to a republican group in the Galician town of Muxia, confiscated after the Spanish Civil War, did not begin until 29 Dec. 1979 – the day in which the Spanish Constitution came into force – because under General Franco's dictatorship, Spain was not a democracy. The legal reasoning of the decision has been acutely criticized by Enrique Rubio Torrano, 'Propiedad incautada', *Aranzadi Civil* III (1999): 2191; César Hornero Méndez 'La utilidad de la jurisprudencia: guerra civil y suspensión de la prescripción: Comentario a la STS de 25 enero 2000', *Revista de Derecho Patrimonial* (2000): 7, 299.

423. The cases leading to suspension are based on impediments beyond the creditor's control, such as war, officially declared epidemic and revolution. Suspension is, however, not immediate, since it has to be declared by the government.

424. *See* TS 21 Nov. 2007 (RJ 2007/8650), 10 Jul. 1999 (RJ 1999/5902).

a claim or a right[425] must be brought to court, since otherwise it will expire. *Caducidad* has to be applied by courts ex officio and cannot be interrupted.

II. The Civil Law of Catalonia

332. The Act 29/2002 of 30 December, First Act of the CC Cat, introduces a brand new regulation of prescription with a number of interesting novelties in the Spanish legal landscape.[426] Former Catalan law featured the same problems that required urgent legislative reform, for example, in Germany. The general period of thirty years (Article 344 CDCC), which goes back in Catalan law to the medieval *usatge omnes causae*, was excessively long. This general period was coupled with many different shorter periods, some of them contained in the *Código Civil* but deemed to be supplementary applicable. In addition, interruption of prescription was not regulated in Catalan law, and therefore the *Código Civil* was again supplementary. Suspension was not regulated either. The enactment aims at solving these and other problems.

A. Commencement

333. As for the commencement of the period, the Catalan legislator has combined two criteria. On the one hand, the moment when the claim becomes enforceable,[427] on the other, and in addition, the creditor must be aware or ought to be aware of the claim. The combination of both criteria determines the commencement of the period of prescription, according to Article 121-23 CC Cat. Therefore, prescription does not begin until the creditor acquires knowledge of the identity of the debtor and of the facts from which the claim arises, or could have acquired such knowledge by taking reasonable steps.[428]

B. Prescription Periods

334. The CC Cat is systematized in three periods, of ten years, three years and one year. Ten years is the general period of prescription, probably too long in comparison to the newest developments in comparative law (Article 121-20).[429] A

---

425. *Caducidad* applies namely to the so-called *derechos potestativos* or *facultades deconfiguración jurídica* (i.e., rights or faculties that could affect juridical relationships). For example, Art. 76 CC establishes that the claim for nullity of a marriage on the grounds of mistake or another vice of will lapses within one year.

426. Antoni Vaquer & Albert Lamarca (eds), *Comentari a la nova regulació de la prescripció i la caducitat en el dret civil de Catalunya* (Barcelona 2005) (reprint 2008).

427. More precisely, Art. 121-23.1 establishes that prescription commences once the claim has come into existence and is enforceable.

428. The legal provision is thus along the lines of §198 BGB and Art. 14:203 PECL.

429. Both the BGB (§194) and the PECL (Art. 14.201) establish a general period of prescription of three years.

shorter period of three years is provided for claims for annual or shorter periodical payments, remuneration of services and works, collection of consumer sales and tort (Article 121-21). Finally, an even shorter one-year period is provided for claims for protection of possession (Article 121-22 CC Cat).

C. *The Long-Stop Period*

335. Since the commencement of the period hinges on reasonable discoverability, prescription could be postponed for too long a period, or even indefinitely. In addition, as we will see later, prescription may be suspended. In order to avoid that inconvenience, the Catalan legislator also resorts to a long-stop period (*termini de preclusió*). The maximum length of the period of prescription is thirty years, irrespective of the claim.

D. *Suspension of Prescription*

336. One of the most remarkable features of the new Catalan legislation on prescription is a comprehensive regulation of suspension. Suspension refers in Catalan law only to the running of the period of prescription. Moreover, suspension in case of ignorance as provided in Article 14:301 PECL has not been incorporated into Catalan law. Nevertheless, the discoverability test set out in Article 121-23 CC Cat leads to similar results. The postponement of the expiry of prescription has not been incorporated into Catalan law.[430] The grounds of suspension in the new prescription regime are impediments beyond the creditor's control, personal and familiar situations and the *hereditas iacens*. In 2015 a new ground was introduced: an application for mediation.

337. Suspension in case of impediment beyond the creditor's control is established in Article 121-25 CC Cat, along the lines of §206 BGB and Article 14:303 PECL. It is based on a subjective conception of prescription going back to the old aphorism *agere non valenti non currit praescriptio*. Even though force majeure is presented as the objective ground for suspension *par excellence*, it is nevertheless somewhat subjective, since it must be an impediment beyond the *creditor's* control to exercise his/her rights. Prescription should not occur when the creditor has not been able to pursue his/her claim. Moreover, it would seem incongruous to protect a creditor who does not know – without being negligent – about the claim and not one who does not have a fair chance of pursuing it. Unforeseen events beyond the creditor's control cover natural disasters (earthquakes, hurricanes, floods) and other 'Acts of God', war, cessation of the administration of justice or serious unexpected illnesses affecting the creditor. Catalan law, like the BGB and the PECL, provides that not every impediment suspends the running of the period, but only those events occurring within the last six months of the prescription period.

430. Although it is widely accepted both in the BGB (§§210 and 211) and in the PECL (Art. 14:304–306).

338. Article 121-16 CC Cat gathers a series of subjective grounds for suspension under the heading 'personal or familiar grounds'. According to subsection (a) of Article 121-16 CC Cat, the running of the period is suspended in relation to claims of minors of age and persons subject to an incapacity acting without a representative. In fact, this ground for suspension has no relationship with affective, familiar grounds, but it is only a concretion of the principle *agere non valenti non currit praescriptio*. Suspension lies on the impossibility of such persons acting on their own and bringing an action. The running of the period of prescription of claims between spouses is suspended (literally) 'as long as the marriage persists, until judicial or de facto separation' (Article 121-16b). Similarly, prescription of claims between stable partners is suspended for the period during which life partnership exists (Article 121.16.c CC Cat). Prescription of claims between parents and children is also suspended until the children are not under the parental power, paradigmatically because they come of full age. Lastly, the running of the period of claims between guardian and ward, a carer and the person cared for, and other similar situations, is suspended during the continuance of the guardianship.

339. Unlike the CC (*see* Article 1934 CC), now in Catalan law 'the prescription of the claims between the persons summoned and the estate is suspended as long as the estate is not accepted' (Article 121-17 CC Cat). Prescription is suspended irrespective of the modality of the acceptation (whether express or tacit) and the system of liability for the debts of the deceased (whether acceptance 'pure and simple' or subject to inventory). That ground for suspension is found on the safeguard of the heirs' rights and the fact that the estate lacks a representative. Nevertheless, the provision deserves some criticism, because it is difficult to understand why suspension only benefits the heirs and not the estate's creditors, who will suffer the same difficulties in bringing their actions against the estate.

E. Interruption of Prescription

340. In Article 121-11 CC Cat the Catalan legislator has taken up the same causes of interruption of prescription that the Spanish legislator already laid down in 1889 when the Civil Code was enacted (Article 1973). The period of prescription ceases to run, and thus must start to run anew,[431] when the creditor brings an action to court, when the creditor demands the fulfilment of the obligation extrajudicially and when the debtor acknowledges the claim against him/her.

In relation to judicial and other proceedings, it is expressly laid down that interruption takes place even if the proceedings end without a decision on the merits of the claim because it is dismissed due to procedural defects.[432] In this later case, the interruption is effective from the date when the action was brought to court.

431. Article 121–14 CC Cat stresses that the interruption determines that 'the period of prescription starts to run afresh and completely'.

432. Unlike German law (§204 BGB) or PECL (Art. 13:302), where prescription is only suspended when the creditor institutes an action on his/her claim or initiates similar proceedings, such as arbitration.

Otherwise, interruption takes place once there is a decision that has the effect of res judicata (Article 121-14.b CC Cat).

F. Effects of Prescription

341. According to Article 121-1 CC Cat, the effect of prescription is the extinction of the claim (the same, Article 121-8.1). Apparently, the Catalan legislator has adopted the 'strong' effect of prescription. Nevertheless, Article 121-9 CC Cat excludes restitution when the debtor, irrespective of he/she knowing about it, pays in spite of prescription having occurred: the payment is not undue, since it was not a payment without a legal ground. Hence, it is obvious that the creditor's right is not extinguished. Nor the claim (*pretensió*[433] = *Anspruch*), which, despite the legal wording, merely ceases to be enforceable. Moreover, the extinction – if that were the case – would not be definitive, since the debtor may waive his/her right to invoke prescription or even the prescription already underway (Article 120-10.1 and 2).[434] Article 120-10.4 expressly states that the waiver to the occurred prescription leaves the claim subsistent. The regulation presupposes that prescription constitutes a defence, since Article 121-5 CC Cat sets out that the person who must render performance is entitled to allege the prescription (*see also*, Articles 121-4 and 121-8.1).

G. Agreements Concerning Prescription

342. The rules on prescription are legally qualified as mandatory in Article 121-3 CC Cat.[435] Nevertheless, I have already mentioned that prescription, even after it has occurred, can be renounced. Consequently, the Catalan legislator provides some exceptions to the mandatory character of the regulation. The parties are allowed to extend and to shorten periods of prescription without any formal requirement. The party autonomy is not, however, unrestricted. For the parties can neither shorten the period by more than half nor extend it by more than double. In addition, the agreement cannot result in leaving one of the parties undefended.

III. *Verwirkung*

343. The German doctrine of *Verwirkung* has been received in Spain. This doctrine was created by the German case law in the nineteenth century. It was first introduced to Spain by some prominent scholars in the 1950s. Today in recent court

433. It is defined in Art. 121-1 as 'the right to require from another an action or an omission', mirroring in §194 BGB.

434. Nevertheless, the anticipated waiver to future prescription is void, pursuant to Art. 121-10.1 CC Cat.

435. This approach corresponds more to §202 BGB (*Unzulässigkeit vonVereinbarungen über dieVerjährung*) than to Art. 14:601 PECL.

decisions, it is commonly called by its German name without translation. Nevertheless, the Spanish Supreme Court did not apply the doctrine of the '*illoyal Verspätung*' (disloyal delay) until the decision handed down on 21 May 1982,[436] and the term '*Verwirkung*' was used for the very first time in the decision on 24 June 1996.[437] The four factors necessary to *Verwirkung*, that both scholars and jurisprudence recognize, are: a significant lapse of a period of time, the plaintiff's passivity in using his/her own action, the lawful reliance that the claim will not be prosecuted and the prejudice caused by this delayed claim. The effect of 'disloyal delay' is the intolerability of the plaintiff using his/her own action in such a way that it causes prejudice to the defendant.[438] For this reason, it does not terminate the plaintiff's right or action, but simply avoids its use (becoming inadmissible) in such circumstances.

436. RJ 1982/2588.
437. RJ 1996/4846. Just before, *Tribunal Superior deJustícia deCatalunya* 2 Oct. 1995 (RAJ 8180): 'the German doctrine and case law in relation to the "disloyal delay" of the plaintiff using his own rights ("*Verwirkung*")'.
438. TS 9 Dec. 2010 (RJ 2011\1176).

Part II. Specific Contracts

Chapter 1. Agency

§1. Representation and Mandate

344. The CC does not regulate systematically agency. Only two provisions are related to representation. On the one hand, Article 1257 CC states the rule of privity of contract: the contract only produces legal consequences between the parties and their heirs. On the other hand, according to Article 1259 CC, no one can act on behalf of another person without his/her authorization or being a legal representative. Nevertheless, the Civil Code also regulates the contract of mandate. Here, Article 1725 provides the opposite rule to Article 1257, since 'the mandatary who acts in such concept is not personally liable to the other party'. Thus, mandate is the contract by which one person (the mandatary or the agent) acts for another (the mandator or principal) so that the transactions the former carries out are effective against the latter. The definition of mandate provided by Article 1709 CC is excessively broad: 'one person is obligated to render a service or to do something on behalf of another'. Contracts of hire of work and services also match with this definition. Therefore, the distinguishing features of mandate are the management of the mandator's affairs and the authorization of this management, so that the legal consequences of the acts carried out by the mandatary fall upon the mandator. Mandate is a source of representation.

345. Mandate is a consensual contract. It does not require any formality: it may be effected by an instrument, public or private, or verbal,[439] and even the mandatary's acceptance may be tacit,[440] deduced from his/her acts (Article 1710 CC). The Civil Code still conceives mandate as a gratuitous contract (Article 1711.1 CC), unless the mandatary is a professional (Article 1711.2 CC); however, the parties may stipulate for remuneration.

346. Mandate is either specific (for one matter or certain matters only) or general (for all affairs of the principal; Article 1712 CC). In addition, if the mandate is conceived in general terms, it embraces only acts of administration. If it relates to

439. TS 1 Mar. 2007 (RJ 2007/1765), 29 Jan. 2004 (RJ 2004/539).

440. TS 11 Feb. 2010 (RJ 2010\1281), yet highlighting that the tacit mandata must result from acts that necessarily imply in an evident way the intention to be bound.

alienation or mortgage of property, or any other act of ownership, the mandate must be expressed (Article 1713 CC).

§2. Obligations of the Mandator

347. The mandator must advance the necessary sum to carry out the mandate when the mandatary asks for it. If the mandatary advanced the money, the mandator must reimburse him/her, as well as any expense the mandatary has incurred (Article 1728 CC). In addition, the mandator must pay the mandatary the remuneration promised.

The mandator must compensate the mandatary for losses and damages suffered by him/her on the occasion of the mandate, unless the latter has been negligent or careless (Article 1729 CC).

In the case of a plurality of mandators for the same mandate, they are solidary debtors to the mandatary (Article 1731 CC).

348. Any contract concluded by the mandatary in accordance with the power of attorney conferred on him/her is binding on the mandator. If the mandatary has exceeded the authority conferred on him/her, the contract is only binding on the mandator if he/she ratifies it either expressly or tacitly (Article 1729 CC). If the mandatary lacks any power of attorney, the contract he/she has entered into is not radically void, since the mandator can ratify it and thus accept its effects.[441]

§3. Obligations and Rights of the Mandatary

349. The mandatary is under the duty to carry out the mandate according to the instructions given by the mandator. In the absence of such instructions, he/she must act with the diligence of a good father of the family bearing in mind the character of the mandator's affair (Article 1719 CC). Moreover, he/she must account for his/her actions to the mandator (Article 1720 CC). This obligation is not subject to formal requirements, but the mandatary must furnish the mandator with reasonable detail of his/her activity. In addition, the mandatary must hand over to the mandator whatever he/she has received on the occasion of the mandate.

350. The mandatary is liable for damages to the mandator for non-performance of the mandate (Article 1718.1 CC) and for any losses resulting from a fraudulent or negligent exercise of his/her authority (Article 1726 CC).[442] This provision allows the court to mitigate the liability when the mandate is gratuitous. If two or more mandataries have been appointed, their liability is not solidary but separate (Article 1723 CC).

---

441. *See* TS 28 Sep. 2006 (RJ 2006/8271), 3 Dec. 2001 (RJ 2002/2198). *See also* para. 194.
442. *See*, for example, TS 27 Dec. 2000 (RJ 2001/711).

351. The contract of the mandate may grant the mandatary the power to appoint a substitute and thus to free himself/herself of the obligation to manage the mandator's affair. If such power has not been granted by the contract, the mandatary is liable for the acts of the substitute.[443] But, if the substitution has been authorized, the mandatary is only liable when he/she appoints someone incapable or insolvent (Article 1721 CC).

352. The mandatary is entitled to retain the object of the mandate until the mandator reimburses the expenses incurred and the eventual damages suffered by him/her (Article 1730 CC).[444]

§4. The Relationship Between the Mandatary and the Third Party

353. If the mandatary acts within the limits of his/her power of attorney, the transaction concluded with the third party affects the mandator alone. The mandatary is not liable to third parties (Articles 1725, 1727 CC). If the contract has been concluded without the power of attorney or beyond its limits, the contract does not affect the mandator unless he/she ratifies it expressly or implicitly (Article 1727.2 CC). But the mandatary may act in his/her own name, without mention of the mandator (undisclosed agency in common law terms). When the mandatary handles the mandator's interest without disclosing that he/she is acting as a mandatary, Article 1717 CC establishes that the third party can neither bring an action against the mandator nor can the mandator sue the third party. When the mandatary acts in his/her own name, he/she is directly obliged to whom he/she has entered into the contract. The only exception is when the act of the mandatary concerns the 'mandator's own matters'.[445]

§5. Termination of Mandate

354. Article 1732.3 CC provides that the death or the insolvency either of the mandator or the mandatary terminates the mandate. Nevertheless, the transactions concluded by the mandatary, who ignored the mandator's death, with third parties acting in good faith are valid and effective (Article 1738 CC). Two requirements must be met: on the one hand, that the third party acts in good faith, which means that he/she ignores that the mandate has extinguished; on the other hand, that the mandatary ignores in the moment of using the power that the mandatary has dead or the mandate has extinguished on the basis of another ground.[446]

According to Article 1733 CC, the mandator may revoke at any time the mandate. If the mandate was entered into for a certain time, its revocation without a fair

443. *See* TS 27 Nov. 2007 (RJ 2008/1547).
444. *See* further para. 313 on the right of retention.
445. The Supreme Court considers that this is a case of 'tacit *contemplatio domini*' (decisions of 16 Dec. 2006 (RJ 2007/681), 1 Dec. 1982 (RJ 1982/7454)).
446. TS 22 Jan. 2015 (Roj: STS 114/2015).

reason before the expiry of the time clause gives rise to compensation of damages.[447] Revocation may be express or tacit, for example, the appointment of a new agent (Article 1735 CC). Notice of revocation must be given to the mandatary, otherwise the transactions affect the mandator.[448] If, in spite of the revocation, the mandatary concludes a contract with a third party who ignores that the power of attorney is terminated, the contract affects the mandator, notwithstanding the fact that the mandatary is liable for damages to him/her. The Supreme Court admits an irrevocable mandate in the case it is a means for the conclusion of a second contract (purposive mandate).[449]

355. Incapacity of the mandator extinguishes the mandate, unless the power of attorney has been granted precisely for the case of such incapacity.[450] Incapacity of the mandatary extinguishes without exception the mandate.

356. Likewise, the mandatary may renounce to perform the mandate by notifying the mandator (Article 1736 CC). The mandatary must however compensate the mandator for the resulting loss, unless termination is justified by the mandatary being unable to continue the agency without causing himself/herself material loss. In addition, the mandatary has to continue his/her activity until the mandator is able to take care of his/her interests (Article 1737 CC).

The CC Cat rules mandate on the basis of the traditional regulation enshrined in the *Código Civil*. However, some novelties are taken from the European soft law. Article 622-25.3 CCCat deals with double mandate; this situation must be communicated by the agent, otherwise she may incur damages. Moreover, duties of information burden the parties to the contract of the mandate. Weirdly, negotiorum gestio is ruled within the chapter devoted to mandate.

§6. Brokerage

357. Brokerage is in Spanish law an innominate contract whereby the intermediary tries to bring two principals together in a transaction. The intermediary is bound to carry out the necessary activity in order to conclude a contract between two persons. A broker does not contract with a third person either as agent for his/her principal or in his/her own name. In this sense, brokerage differs from mandate. The broker neither has power of attorney nor can enter into any legal transaction on behalf of another person. Unlike the contract of hire of services, the broker assumes an *obligation de résultat*, since he/she will only obtain the remuneration if the contract is concluded between the parties with whom he/she has been in touch

447. *See* TS 3 Mar. 1998 (RJ 1998/1129).
448. TS 21 Dec. 2001 (RJ 2001/10051), 3 Mar. 1994 (RJ 1994/10051).
449. TS 19 Nov. 1994 (RJ 1994/8537), 24 Dec. 1993 (RJ 1993/10149).
450. Article 1732 *in fine* as amended by the Act 41/2003 of 18 November. In this case, mandate can terminate by judicial decision when a guardian is appointed or subsequently on the guardian's request. *See* Esther Arroyo i Amayuelas, 'Del mandato ordinario al mandato de protección', *Revista Jurídica del Notariado* (2004): 9.

with.[451] But the remuneration does not depend on the fulfilment of the contract by seller and purchaser. The renounce of the offeror extinguishes the contract; the broker may withdraw from the contract as well.

451. TS 16 Oct. 2007 (RJ 2007/7078), 10 Oct. 2002 (RJ 2002/9975), 10 Oct. 2001 (RJ 2001/8733), 11 Jun. 2001 (RJ 2001/5675). The intermediary is entitled to remuneration also where the parties conclude the contract without his/her intervention (TS 10 Oct. 2007 (RJ 2007/7406)).

Chapter 2. Bailment

§1. The Juridical Relationship of Bailment

358. According to Article 1758 CC, bailment is constituted when one person receives the property of another, with the obligation of keeping it and returning it. Thus, the juridical relationship of bailment is generally described. Following that precept, Article 1759 CC distinguishes a judicial bailment or sequestration and a non-judicial bailment. The latter may be voluntary (the contract of bailment) or necessary. Therefore, the regulation of the Civil Code gathers a series of situations the common feature of which is the obligation of keeping another's property (Article 1766 CC) and returning it. This obligation implies a specific system of liability that case law has extended to similar situations, as we will *see* below. The bailee is not allowed to use the property without express permission (Article 1767 CC). Unless otherwise provided, the contract of bailment is gratuitous.

359. Article 1761 CC lays down that the object of non-judicial bailment may be a movable, without any further concretion. The problem arises when the object consists of fungibles. Then it becomes an irregular bailment, since the bailee has to return not the same object but the same amount of fungibles of the same quality.

360. A bailment must be returned to the bailor as soon as he/she – or his/her heirs – claims it, free of any burden,[452] even when the parties fixed a determined time for restitution (Article 1775 CC). The bailee may only reject restitution on the ground of a judicial embargo. However, the bailee is allowed to return property before the stipulated time for a good reason (Article 1776 CC). Restitution must include the products and the accessions of the property (Article 1770 CC). If the thing bailed has perished by force majeure and the bailee has received another thing in its place, he/she has to return the new thing (Article 1777 CC).

The bailor is required to reimburse the bailee for expenditures which he/she made for the preservation of the thing bailed (Article 1779 CC). In addition, the bailor must pay the stipulated price. The bailee may retain the bailment until complete payment of what is due to him/her by reason of the bailment (Article 1780 CC).

§2. Bailment of Necessity

361. A bailment of necessity is one which is imposed by the law[453] or forced by some accident (fire, flooding, shipwreck, etc.). The norms on voluntary bailment apply supplementarily (Articles 1781, 1782 CC).

362. The Civil Code qualifies as a bailment of necessity the introduction of goods by travellers in hotels (Articles 1783, 1784). Innkeepers are then liable, as

452. TS 3 Des. 2014 (Roj: STS 4837/2014).

453. For example, according to Art. 445 CC, bailment must be constituted when several possessors appear to have the same right to possess the thing.

bailees of necessity, for all deterioration and taking away of objects brought to the hotel by travellers who stay there. This is a kind of legal liability, since the innkeeper does not have to accept the bailment (it is enough if he/she knows that the objects have been brought), and liability is only excluded in events of force majeure such as armed robbery.[454]

§3. SEQUESTRATION

363. A bailment of a property in controversy in the hands of a third party ordered by the court is called sequestration (Article 1785 CC). The property may be movable or immovable. The bailee is not freed from the obligation to keep the property until the controversy is finished or the court decides it.

§4. PARKING

364. Liability of bailees was extended by case law to the contract of parking, so that the owner or the licence holder of a parking lot must compensate the owner of the motor vehicle for any deterioration or the taking away of it or any part of it (radio, mobile phones, etc.).[455] Presently, Act 40/2002 of 14 November, regulates the contract of parking. The new legislation applies when three requirements concur:

1. The owner or the titleholder lets a place for parking as a commercial activity.
2. The price must be determined by the period during which the vehicle is parked. Therefore, gratuitous parking areas do not fall within the scope of the law.
3. The premises must be destined for use of the parking of vehicles. Parking on the streets is not subject to the new legislation, even if a tax is paid in order to park (parking metre areas).

The contract mixes elements mainly from the contracts of lease and bailment. The owner of the parking lot is liable when he/she cannot return the vehicle or return it in the same condition, but he/she is not liable anymore for the objects left inside the vehicle unless this liability is expressly accepted. The new Act grants the owner of the parking lot a right of retention over the vehicle in the case the rate is not paid.

454. *See* TS 8 Feb. 2008 (RJ 2008/1696), 27 Jan. 1994 (RJ 1994/569).
455. TS 8 Apr. 1999 (RJ 1999/2660), 22 Oct. 1996 (RJ 1996/7238).

Chapter 3. Aleatory Contracts

365. The concept of aleatory contracts provided in Article 1790 CC is rather misleading, since its literal wording makes it impossible to distinguish aleatory and conditional contracts. Aleatory contracts are characterized by the uncertainty of the contents of the parties' prestations. Yet the practical importance of the dichotomy aleatory/commutative contracts vanished when lesion was ousted from the Civil Code.

§1. Gaming and Betting

366. The CC devotes some provisions to gaming and betting in order to only regulate their legal consequences and their lawfulness.[456] The Civil Code distinguishes between lawful and forbidden games; lawful games are based on some kind of dexterity, whilst forbidden games depend only on chance. Concerning the latter, Article 1798 CC, on the one hand, accords no action for a gaming debt or for the payment of a bet. But, on the other hand, lays down that the loser may not recover what he/she voluntarily paid, unless he/she was underage, or there was fraud on the part of the winner. The judgment of the Supreme Court handed down on 10 April 2010[457] applies this rule to a gambler that claimed restitution of EUR 50,000 and some plots of land delivered in payment of a baccarat debt. On the contrary, lawful gaming debts are enforceable, although the court may reduce them if the sum seems to be excessive. Nevertheless, nowadays this distinction has not much practical sense, since the government promotes gaming and betting as it has become an important source of income for the treasury. Therefore, it is not surprising that the Supreme Court has upheld claims for gaming debts while reducing the sum.[458]

§2. Contract for Life Annuity

367. According to Article 1802 CC, a life annuity *(contrato de renta vitalicia)* is an aleatory contract by which the debtor is obligated to pay an annuity for the lives of one or more persons in consideration for a sum of money or realty. The payment of the annuity depends on the life of the person, so when the person dies the obligation extinguishes. Therefore, a contract through which an annuity was created for the life of a person already dead or afflicted with a disease from which he/she dies within twenty days of the date of the contract is void. On the same grounds, payment of the annuity cannot depend on the life of a legal person, since it does not die, and thus the aleatory character of the contract would be excluded.

456. Additionally, the statute on gaming must be taken into account in relation to legal requirements (*Ley 13/2011, de 27 de mayo, deregulacióndeljuego*).

457. RJ 2010\2318.

458. TS 30 Jan. 1995 (RJ 1995/180), 23 Feb. 1988 (RJ 1988/1275); both plaintiffs were casinos.

368. The debtor is the party who receives the sum of money or the realty. It may be created for the benefit of a third person. In addition, it may be created either for the life of the one who furnished the sum of money or the realty or for the life of a third party (Article 1803).

369. Unless otherwise agreed, non-performance of the annuity does not give rise to an action for reimbursement of the capital. In addition to the remedy of specific performance, the party may require a guarantee (Article 1805 CC); this guarantee may be a mortgage (Article 157 LH).

370. The contract for life annuity may be constituted gratuitously. In this case, the parties may stipulate that the annuity cannot be under embargo for debts of the creditor (Article 1807 CC).

371. The creditor of a life annuity may demand arrears only by giving proof of the existence of the person on whose life it was based (Article 1808 CC).

372. On occasion of the Act 41/2003 of 18 November, concerning the patrimonial protection of disabled persons, a new contract has been regulated in the Civil Code: the so-called contract of alimony (Articles 1791–1797), along the lines of the innominate contract of *vitalicio* that case law has shaped.[459] The debtor has to pay alimony (accommodation, food, medical expenses) in consideration for the capital – in assets or rights of whatever kind – for the life of the creditor or the life of third persons. Nevertheless, provisions on life annuity apply *per analogiam*. If the debtor of alimony does not perform, the creditor may opt for specific performance or termination of the contract. In this latter case, the court may postpone restitution and, in any case, the assets returned must be sufficient in order to conclude a new contract of alimony.

459. TS 9 Jul. 2002 (RJ 2002/5904), 18 Jan. 2001 (RJ 2001/1319), 17 Jul. 1998 (RJ 1998/6602). *See also* Susana Chillón Ballester, *El contrato de vitalicio: caracteres y contenido* (Madrid, 2000).

Chapter 4. Sale of Goods

373. Spanish law does not distinguish between sale of goods and sale of other kinds of property. Under the heading of sale, the Civil Code provides the general rules regardless of the object of the contract. Sale is the contract more extensively regulated in the Civil Code (Articles 1445–1520). Nevertheless, the regulation of some kinds of sales is contained in statutes separate from the Civil Code, and some rules are also to be found in the regional laws. The commercial contract of sale has also some special features.

The CC Cat has regulated anew sales, on the basis of the CISG and European soft law. Hence, the seller is expressly obliged to transfer the ownership of conforming assets. Special mandatory rules are provided for consumers. There are specific rules for the sale of immovable stemming from notarial and land registry practices.

§1. Main Features

374. According to Article 1445 CC, two obligations arise from the contract of sale. On the one hand, the seller is obligated to deliver a determined thing. On the other hand, the purchaser is obligated to pay a certain price. Hence, the contract is bilateral and onerous, since both parties are reciprocally bound to perform at least one obligation. In fact, sale is the paradigm of onerous contracts, since the rules on eviction and latent defects are applicable to other transactions (lease, Article 1553; emphyteusis, Article 1643; civil partnership, Article 1681). Moreover, sale is a consensual contract. As we will see later, the contract of sale does not transfer the property of the thing sold, but only gives rise to obligations, one of which is the delivery of the object. Passing of property requires thus contract plus *traditio*.

375. Article 1457 CC states (quite similarly Article 621-4 CCCat) that every person capable of entering into obligations may conclude a contract of sale. Nevertheless, Article 1459 CC lays down some restrictions taking into account the possibility of conflicts of interests. Thus, certain persons are not allowed to buy some specific assets:

1. the guardian, the ward's assets;
2. mandataries and executors, the mandate's and the estate's assets;
3. public servants, public property under their administration;
4. members and servants of the judicial power, assets under litigation.

§2. Object

376. The thing sold may be corporeal or incorporeal, movable or immovable, present or future. In the latter case, Article 1460 CC states that when the thing is lost, the contract becomes ineffective as it is lacking the object. If the seller knows that the object is non-existent, the case is one of pre-contractual liability (*dolo in contrahendo*). Concerning the sale of a future thing, two possibilities are admissible: *emptio rei speratae* and *emptio spei*. The former is a sale under condition, so that the obligations of the parties only arise if the expected thing (e.g., the crop) comes to existence. *Emptio spei* is in fact an aleatory contract, since the purchaser is obligated to pay the price despite that the thing does not exist (e.g., the restaurant owner buys the fisherman's catch; if in spite of the efforts the net is empty at nightfall, the owner must pay the price). The object must be determined (Article 1445 CC), but the sale of generic goods is also valid.

§3. Price

377. The payment of the price is the essential purchaser's obligation. If there is no agreement about the price we are not dealing with a sale any more, but with a gift. Price must be determined or determinable without further agreement, this is by a third person or according to indexes. The price must consist in a sum of money; otherwise the contract is one of exchange (Article 1538 CC). If the purchaser is disturbed in the possession or the ownership of the thing sold, he/she is entitled to withhold the price until the vendor succeeds in stopping the disturbance or guarantees the devolution of the price (Article 1502 CC).

378. In the Civil Code, it is not required for the validity of the contract of sale that the price needs to be just. Lesion was eradicated during the codification process. Nevertheless, lesion is still in force in the regional laws of Navarre and Catalonia. The Catalan regulation (Articles 321 et seq. CDCC) is based on the Roman *laesio enormis*: the seller (only the seller) may rescind the contract if he/she has obtained less than half of the just price (i.e., the market price). The purchaser can avoid rescission if he/she pays the supplement up to the just price. Lesion is thus objective and related to the onerous cause of the contract. The law of Navarre regulates both *laesio enormis* and *laesio enormissima*, but further requirements are inexperience or urgent necessity (*ley* 499 et seq. Comp. Nav.).[460]

Instead, Article 621-5 CCCat resorts to the open price rule: where the price is not determined by the parties, the price is the usual one for goods of the same features. Moreover, the price may be determined by a third person or even unilaterally by one of the parties, yet the price may be challenged because of unreasonability.

§4. Delivery and Passing of Ownership

379. The Spanish system of passing of ownership is based on title plus mode. The sole contract is insufficient to justify the transfer of ownership, as well as any *traditio* requires a cause. It is therefore not surprising that the Civil Code does not enumerate among the obligations of the seller the transfer of ownership. Article 1461 CC refers to only the delivery of the goods sold. Once the contract is concluded, the seller is still the owner of the goods sold, and he/she is obligated to deliver them to the purchaser; ownership does not pass upon conclusion of the sale.

460. *See* further paras 135–138.

However, another obligation of the seller, as we will see later, is the warranty against eviction: the seller warrants the legal and quiet possession of the thing. Thus, the vendor is liable if he/she cannot pass the ownership to the purchaser. As only an obligation to deliver arises from the contract, the sale of someone else's thing is neither prohibited nor void.[461] If the vendor is not able to make the purchaser owner of the thing sold, he/she will be liable for non-performance, and when he/she knew that the thing belonged to a third person, the contract may be nullified on the grounds of fraud or essential mistake.[462]

Catalan law is also based on title plus mode, although the system of aedilitian actions has been abandoned in favour of nonconformity.

380. Articles 1462–1464 CC enumerate several forms in which *traditio* can be carried out. Real *traditio* is a physical handing over of the subject matter of the contract from the transferor to the transferee. Symbolic *traditio* is an act that at law amounts to cession of incorporeal or immaterial possession. The issue of a deed is the commonest form of *traditio* when immovables are concerned.[463]

381. The object sold must be delivered in the same conditions as it had when the sale was concluded. Fruits produced since the conclusion of the contract and any accessory must also be delivered (Articles 1468, 1095 and 1097 CC).

382. A retention of title-clause prevents the passing of ownership to the purchaser. It works as a guarantee in favour of the vendor, because the vendor retains ownership of the goods until he/she receives complete payment. The clause has important practical consequences when the sale is on instalments.[464]

§5. Seller's Warranties of Title and Quality

I. Warranty Against Eviction

383. As stated above, the vendor is bound to transfer legal and unimpeded possession of the object sold (Article 1474.1 CC). Therefore, the vendor warrants implicitly quiet possession. If the true owner evicts the purchaser by asserting before the court a previous title, the vendor is liable for eviction (Article 1475.1 CC). By contrast, the exercise of possessory actions (interdicts) against the purchaser does not give rise to liability for eviction, for the buyer's ownership has not been challenged. The buyer is burdened to notify the vendor the third party's suit (Article 1482 CC). Thus, the vendor has the opportunity to intervene in the proceedings.[465]

---

461. TS 20 Jul. 2010 (RJ 2010\6561), 7 Nov. 2007 (RJ 2007/8647), 15 Oct. 2002 (RJ 2002/10127), 7 Feb. 2001 (RJ 2001/1162).
462. TS 7 Mar. 1997 (RJ 1997/1643), 5 May 1983 (RJ 1983/2668).
463. *See* para. 62.
464. *See* para. 402 below.
465. *See* Art. 14.2 LEC.

384. The warranty against eviction may be extended (e.g., to cases of possession disturbance), reduced or excluded (Article 1475.3 CC). Nevertheless, the legislator distrusts exemption clauses. Therefore, the exemption clause is void when the vendor has acted in bad faith, for example, knowing the reason that allows eviction (Article 1476 CC). Even a valid exemption clause does not prevent the buyer from recovering the price of the object sold at the time of eviction, unless the buyer was aware of and assumed the risk of eviction when he/she renounced the warranty (Article 1477 CC). The sale has then an aleatory character.

385. Under the warranty against eviction, the buyer is entitled to claim (Article 1478 CC):

1. the price of the object sold at the time of eviction, whether higher or lower than the purchase price;
2. the profits of the object sold if the buyer was compelled to deliver them to the true owner;
3. the proceeding costs;
4. the contract expenses he/she paid;
5. damages when the vendor has acted in bad faith.

386. Eviction may be partial (Articles 1475, 1480 CC). But if the evicted part is so important that otherwise the sale would not have been concluded, the buyer may rescind the contract giving back the object sold without new burdens (Article 1479 CC). The same applies where two objects were sold altogether and one is evicted.

387. What if the immovable sold is burdened with unknown real rights? Article 1483 CC provides a specific rule, according to which the buyer may rescind the contract or claim damages.[466] The claim must be brought within one year. Town planning limitations to ownership are not deemed to be burdens in the sense of Article 1483 CC.[467]

II. Warranty Against Latent Defects

388. The seller warrants that the buyer is protected against latent defects making the goods unfit for their purpose or reducing their usefulness to such an extent that the buyer would not have bought them or would have paid a lower price had he/she known of the defects. This warranty enshrined in Article 1484 CC is called in Spanish law *saneamiento por vicios ocultos*. The provision protects only against hidden defects, not those which are apparent; professionals are not protected if, on reasonable examination, they ought to have noticed the defects.

The defects need not make the goods unfit for any purpose, but for the purpose for which the goods were purchased. Nevertheless, recent case law has considered that the rules on latent defects are unsuitable when the object sold is absolutely unfit

466. Apparent servitudes do not entitle to rescission (TS 2 Jun. 2001 (RJ 2001/5530)).
467. TS 3 Mar. 2000 (RJ 2000/1308), 23 Oct. 1997 (RJ 1997/7181).

for its typical purpose.[468] The Supreme Court qualifies the vendor's performance as an *aliud pro alio* and grants the purchaser termination of the contract.[469]

The Supreme Court considers inapplicable the guarantee against latent defects on the sale of shares where the company liabilities are bigger than the assets.[470]

389. The vendor warrants the defects even if he/she did not know of them (Article 1485.1 CC). However, agreements concerning the warranty are allowed along the same lines as the eviction. The renouncing of the warranty must be express, and its validity requires that the vendor did not know of the defects (Article 1485.2 CC).

390. The Civil Code provides two alternative remedies (Article 1486 CC). On the one hand, the buyer may rescind the contract (*acción redhibitoria*). Both vendor and buyer have to be restored to the same position as if the sale had not been concluded; therefore, the buyer is entitled to the expenses incurred in entering the contract. Furthermore, if the vendor was aware of the defects, the purchaser may demand compensation for damages. On the other hand, the buyer may opt for a reduction of price (*acción quanti minoris*). The amount of the reduction represents the cost of restoring the goods to the conditions promised.

The limitation period of both actions is quite short: six months (Article 1490 CC). The limitation period (lapse of rights) begins to run from the time when the goods were delivered. Because of the practical disadvantages of such brief limitation period, case law allows the buyer to resort to other remedies, such as voidability of the contract on the grounds of fraud (if the vendor was aware of the defects), error and termination based on non-performance. In particular, as mentioned above, termination is granted when the defects are so important that the thing sold lacks the promised qualities and therefore is completely unsuitable to fulfil its purpose (*aliud pro alio*) doctrine.[471]

391. The Civil Code contains special provisions concerning the sale of cattle (Articles 1491 et seq.). The buyer must bring the action for rescission or for reduction of price within forty days after delivery of the cattle. There are three conditions necessary to bring the warranty into play:

1. that the defects were hidden;
2. that the defects were determined according to the law or the local custom;
3. the sale was not concluded at a fair or an auction.

468. TS 19 May 2003 (RJ 2003/4861), dealing with a case of very important building defects that make impossible to live in the dwelling. The Supreme Court considers 'unjust' to apply the rules on *saneamiento* as did the lower court, and applies the rules on contractors' liability (Art. 1591 CC, to be discussed in Ch. V on building contracts).

469. TS 22 Oct. 2007 (RJ 2007/8094), 10 Oct. 2000 (RJ 2000/7718), 24 Jul. 2000 (RJ 2000/6193).

470. TS 30 Mar. 2011 (RJ 2011\3133).

471. TS 19 May 2003 (RJ 2003/4861), 8 Feb. 2003 (RJ 2003/1523), 12 Apr. 1993 (RJ 1993/2997).

III. Remedies of the Unpaid Seller

392. According to Article 1503 CC, the seller who has delivered the thing sold although payment has been deferred, may terminate the contract if he/she has a reason to fear the loss of the thing or the price. This provision is an exception to Article 1124,[472] since non-performance has not yet been determined.

393. The parties may stipulate an express resolutory condition so that the vendor may call off the sale if the vendor does not pay the purchase price by a certain time (*lex commissoria*).[473] Nevertheless, Article 1504 CC states that the purchaser is allowed to pay even after the lapse of the time as long as the vendor has not formally or judicially summoned him/her. Therefore, termination is not automatic. Once the buyer has been summoned,[474] payment does not avoid termination. The court can also not grant the buyer additional time to perform. If the object sold is an immovable, the vendor need not summon the buyer and has the right to terminate if the latter does not pay or tender performance by the stipulated time (Article 1505 CC).

IV. The Sale of Consumer Goods: Remedies of the Consumer

394. The EC Directive 1999/44 on the sale of consumer goods and associated guarantees was first transposed into Spanish law by means of Act 23/2003 of 10 July and is now regulated in the new LGDCU. Unlike German law, the Spanish legislator has not incorporated the core concept of *non-conformity* into the Civil Code, so that this new regulation coexists with the norms on latent defects and the aedilitian remedies (*saneamiento*). Regulation is to be found now in Articles 118 et seq. new LGDCU. Therefore, the situation is one of unsystematic accumulation of regulations and remedies.

The transposition alters the object of the sale slightly. Whilst the Directive refers to all tangible movable items, the Spanish Act adds that those goods have to be destined for private consumption.[475] Only second-hand goods sold at public auction, electricity, water and gas where they are not put up for sale in a limited volume or set quantity, are excluded from the scope of the Act.

472. *See* paras 295 et seq., above.

473. Case law seemed to require a special unwillingness to perform, but now it is clear that mere non-performance is enough to justify rescission after the summons. *See* Francisco Jordano Fraga, *La resolución por incumplimiento en la compraventa inmobiliaria.Estudio jurisprudencialdelartículo 1504 delCódigo civil* (Madrid, 1992).

474. The buyer has to be summoned for termination; if the buyer is summoned for payment, rescission will not be granted (TS 2 Oct. 2002 (RJ 2002/9786), 26 Jun. 2000 (RJ 2000/5907)).

475. *See* María Paz García Rubio, 'La transposición de la Directiva 1999/44/CE al derecho español. Análisis del proyecto de ley de garantías en la venta de bienes de consumo', *La Ley* no. 5747, of 26 Mar. 2003, 2, and compare with Dirk Staudenmayer, 'The Directive on the Sale of Consumer Goods and Associated Guarantees – A Milestone in the European Consumer and Private Law', ERPL (2000): 548–549.

395. The set of remedies is the same established by the Directive, that is, repair, replacement, price reduction and termination of the contract. Repair and replacement are the principal remedies and only at a second stage are the remedies of price reduction and rescission of the contract available. Nevertheless, the buyer of second-hand goods in administrative auctions cannot claim for replacement (Article 115.2 new LGDCU). The Spanish legislator has not introduced the information requirement for the consumer in order to exercise those remedies.

Article 124 new LGDCU allows the consumer to sue directly the producer when bringing actions against the seller is impossible or too difficult for him/her. By contrast, the right of redress of the final seller is scarcely ruled. The final seller or who has compensated the consumer may pursue remedies against the person liable for the nonconformity. But, who is the liable person? It seems that it is not the previous party in the commercial chain, but who has caused the defect. However, the kind of action is not clear (unjust enrichment, tort, contractual liability?). In any case, the limitation period of this right of redress is one year.

§6. Double Sale

396. As stated above, the contract of sale is consensual and needs *traditio* to transfer ownership. It is therefore possible that the vendor sells the same thing to a plurality of purchasers; these multiple sales must be valid and independent from each other.[476] None of the sales at stake must have been fully performed; if property has passed to any of the acquirers, then the question is no longer a double sale but a sale of a thing belonging to another,[477] which is not per se void, because of the consensual character of sales. Article 1473 CC establishes some rules in order to decide which one of the purchasers is going to be the owner. If the thing sold is a movable, the ownership passes to the purchaser who first takes possession of it. If the thing sold is an immovable, the ownership passes to the purchaser who first records the title at the Land Register. If none of the purchasers has recorded the title, the owner is the purchaser who first possesses the thing sold. If no one has taken possession, the owner is the purchaser with an older title. Good faith is always required, either if the sale refers to movables or to immovables, so that they must be unaware of the previous sales.[478]

§7. The Passing of the Risk

397. According to the majority of the doctrine and case law, the Civil Code adopts the principle of *periculum est emptoris*. The chance or possibility that the object of the sale might be accidentally lost, destroyed or damaged has to be borne by the vendor before the contract of sale is concluded. The key arguments are that the Civil Code follows the juridical tradition and Article 1095 CC, according to

476. TS 5.4.2013 (Roj: STS 5065/2013).
477. TS 13.5.2013 (Roj: STS 2617/2013).
478. *See* TS 11 Feb. 2011 (RJ 2011\2350), 7 Sep. 2007 (RJ 2007/5443), 14 Sep. 2007 (RJ 2007/5303).

which the purchaser is entitled to the fruits of the thing sold once the sale is concluded; if the profits belong to the purchaser, so does the risk. This rule is confirmed by Article 1452.3 CC. This provision states that only after appropriation of the generic goods the risk passes to the purchaser, unless he/she incurs *mora creditoris*.[479] The rule *periculum est emptoris* applies not only to the sale of specific goods, but also to a whole quantity of fungibles sold for a lump sum (Article 1452.2 CC; e.g., the purchase of a crop).

§8. Additional Agreements

I. The Option of Repurchase

398. The option of repurchase or redemption is an agreement whereby the vendor reserves the right to take back the thing sold. The vendor must give back the principal price and reimburse the costs of the sale, necessary expenses and those which increased the value of the property (Articles 1507 and 1518 CC). The option of repurchase may not be stipulated for a term exceeding ten years; if there is no agreement, the term is four years (Article 1508 CC).

Catalan law knows the *venda a carta de gràcia*, whereby the right of redemption becomes a real right (Article 326.2 CDCC). The right may be stipulated for a maximal term of thirty years on immovable property and six years on movable.

II. *Pactum Disciplentiae*

399. Article 1453 CC presumes that the sale on approval and the sale of goods that are usually tried out are concluded under suspensive condition. The approval or the trial have a predominant objective character, so that the contract does not stand completely on the purchaser's discretion.

III. Retention of Title-Clause

400. Parties may agree on a retention title-clause, so that the vendor will remain the owner of the goods sold until he/she receives complete payment. The clause has especial importance in the sale on instalments.

§9. Modalities of Sale

I. The Sale on Instalment

401. The Act 28/1998 of 13 July, regulates the sale on instalment anew. It is the contract whereby the parties agree to postpone the whole or part of the payment of

479. On creditor's default *see* paras 250 et seq.

the price for a period of time at least exceeding three months. The object must be a corporeal, identifiable movable item. Goods are identifiable when they have an undeletable mark or a series number in one or more of its fundamental parts or when they have a distinctive characteristic that avoids confusion with any other good. No advance price is required. Unlike the 'standard' sale, conclusion of the contract requires the delivery of the thing sold. The provisions on consumer credit apply when they are more favourable to the consumer.

Some transactions are excluded from the scope of the Act. Thus, the sale of goods to resell them, non-habitual sales, sales secured with mortgage or pledge, sales which price is beneath a certain sum determined by Royal Decree and leasing.

402. The contract must be in writing and must contain a number of stipulations indicated in Article 7 of the statute. Official forms are at the parties' disposal in order to register the contracts in the register of Sale on Instalment, which has been created by Act 28/1998 in order to make opposable to third parties retention of title-clauses and prohibitions of disposal. The retention of title-clause is not mandatory, unlike the prohibition of disposal of the buyer without the consent of the vendor until the price has been completely paid. The buyer has a right of withdrawal within seven days following the delivery of the goods; this right cannot be renounced. However, the buyer is entitled to advance payment; partial payments must be above 20% of the total price. Parties may agree on a retention of title-clause. In addition, any act of disposal made by the buyer is void.

If the purchaser fails to pay two instalments or the last one, the vendor has the choice either to terminate the contract or to claim specific performance. In the case of termination, the parties are obligated to restitution, but the seller is entitled to claim compensation for the use of the thing made by the purchaser. Exceptionally, courts may modify at discretion the instalments on the basis of one of the grounds enumerated in Article 11 (serious illness, unemployment, familiar misfortune, labour accident and similar events).

II. Distance Selling

403. The new LGCDU regulates distance selling in accordance with Directive 2011/83/UE on consumers' rights. The vendor is burdened with information duties in order to protect the consumer (*see* Article 97). The dispatch of goods that have not been ordered is prohibited (Article 100). Nevertheless if the goods are dispatched, the Act does not establish that the consumer becomes owner of the goods, but it does expressly state that he/she is not obliged to restitution. Silence of the consumer after receiving an offer never implies acceptation. A right of withdrawal *ad nutum* is granted to the consumer within fourteen calendar days; no formality is required. In addition, if the vendor does not fulfil the duties of information, the buyer may terminate the contract within three months after delivery. Article 103 new LGDCU lists a series of sales from which consumers cannot withdraw (completed services, periodicals, urgent processing, etc.). The vendor must give the price paid by the purchaser back within fourteen days, otherwise the buyer is entitled to double and to damages.

III. Contracts Concluded Away from Business Premises

404. The Directive 85/577/CE was transposed into Spanish law by means of the Act 26/1991 of 21 November, although now the regulation is to be found in Articles 92–113 new LGDCU, amended by Act 3/2014, of 27 March, transposing Directive 2011/83/UE on consumers' rights. Additionally, this Act introduces a definition of business premises as the place where businesses develop permanently or habitually their activities (Article 59 bis.1.d LGDCU). Hence, a market stall is deemed to constitute business premises provided that the seller sells her products regularly there; in contrast, the sale is out of business premises when it occurs at an occasional sales stall on the street. Moreover, the rules also apply to a sale concluded inside the business premises when the first contact between seller and consumer happened outside the premises (Article 92.2.c new LGDCU). The offer or the contract must be in writing and duties of pre-contractual information are imposed on the vendor (Article 97 new LGDCU); all the information must be delivered in writing or in a durable medium. Moreover, a document of withdrawal must be handed over to the consumer. The non-performance of the duties of information allows the consumer to challenge the contract. The consumer may freely withdraw from the contract within fourteen calendar days; withdrawal is informal and needs no ground, but the burden of proof of the timely withdrawal rests with the consumer. Any penalty clause is void. The parties are then compelled to make restitution of whatever they have received on the basis of the contract.

§10. The Contract of Exchange

405. Unlike the contract of sale, the counter-performance does not consist in money but in other goods (Article 1538 CC). The rules on sale apply, sometimes with specialities. Thus, the evicted party may only claim the thing he/she delivered if the other party still has it (Article 1540 CC).

The contract of exchange of a piece of land for flats or premises to be constructed on it has especial practical significance. Case law shapes it as an innominate contract,[480] since the contractor also undertakes an obligation to do something (the construction of the building); non-performance of the construction allows termination of the contract.[481] The Catalan Parliament passed a statute on that issue (Act 23/2001 of 31 December) which takes into account most of the case law developments, now incorporated into the CC Cat. Thus, in the case of non-performance, the aggrieved party may claim specific performance or terminate the contract, as well as damages.[482] Because of the system of passing of property based on title plus *traditio*, the party who was the former owner of the piece of land does not become the owner of the flats or premises until they have been constructed and delivered.[483]

480. TS 14 Feb. 2011 (RJ 2011\2354).
481. TS 10 Nov. 2010 (RJ 2010\9156).
482. STS 17 May 2000 (RJ 2000/3582), 30 Apr. 1999 (RJ 1999/2619).
483. STS 26 Apr. 2007 (RJ 2007/2393), 9 Oct. 1997 (RJ 1997/7065).

§11. The Contract of Supply

406. Case law has distinguished between the contracts of sale and supply, which is qualified as an innominate contract.[484] The characteristic feature of supply is the periodical performance of the obligation of delivery in the creditor's interest. Supply is a consensual, synallagmatic, onerous contract of successive performance. Nevertheless, the rules on sale are deemed to be applicable *per analogiam* to fill in the contractual gaps. A pact of exclusivity is often stipulated in the contract of supply, but its duration cannot be indefinite. One of the commonest grounds of extinction is withdrawal.[485]

484. *See*, for example, TS 13 Jun. 2002 (RJ 2002/4897), 23 May 2002 (RJ 2002/7158).
485. *See* para. 285 for the general requirements.

Chapter 5. Building Contracts: Hire of Work and Hire of Services

§1. The Distinction Between Hire of Work and Hire of Services

407. The Civil Code distinguishes between hire of work and hire of services on the fact that one party is obligated to execute a certain work or to carry out some sort of service in exchange of a price. The term 'hire' (*arrendamiento*) is however inappropriate in relation to the contract of work, and the very regulation seems to reject it since it speaks of owner and contractor and not of *arrendador y arrendatario* (lessor and lessee). The parties of the contract of work pursue a result, not a mere activity, which requires specific skills. On the contrary, although the parties may have specific skills, the object of hire of services is a mere activity without the promise of a certain result. For example, the attorney does not guarantee to win the case, nor the doctor to cure a cancer. The distinction is still essential in the field of medical responsibility.

408. In the Civil Code, the paradigm of a hire of work is the building contract. Nevertheless, the regulation is obsolete. It does not take into account usual stakeholders in the construction market such as property developers; it does not contain sufficient and efficient rules on subcontracts; and it does not care about the role of architects and technical architects. The *Ley de Ordenación de la Edificación* (Act 36/1999 of 5 November, on Construction Planning) failed to modernize the codified regulation.

409. Sometimes it may also be difficult to distinguish between hire of work and sale of goods. If I purchase a car, the contract is a sale. What about when I order a car that is not mass-produced? What about when I order a prototype that I have designed? In a range of cases it is not possible to anticipate an answer to such questions. The intention of the parties is essential, but also whether the production process is more important than the materials employed or the design.

§2. Hire of Work

I. The Civil Code

410. The contract of work is a consensual contract from which obligations arise for both parties. No formalities are required. The contractor is obligated to the execution of the work in accordance with the stipulations of the contract. Article 1592 CC allows the parties to stipulate the execution by pieces of work. In addition, the owner may be obligated to furnish materials.

411. Essentially, the employer is obligated to pay the stipulated price. Even though Article 1544 CC requires a fixed sum, case law has accepted the price being determined in the future whether by the same parties or by a third person, taking into account the costs of materials and labour. The work may be executed for a lump sum or by fixing the price of each piece of work. In the first case, Article 1593 CC provides that the contractor may seek no increase in price under the pretext of increase in labour or materials, unless the increase is so important that the *rebus sic stantibus* doctrine can be applied.[486] Changes or increases in the plan not authorized by the owner do not amount to increase in the price either.

412. Risk is a main issue in the contract of work. In the case where the contractor furnishes only his/her works, if the property perishes before being delivered, the loss is on him/her, unless the employer was delayed in receiving the work or the property comes to perish owing to the bad quality of the materials, and he/she had warned the employer about it (Article 1590 CC). If the contractor also furnishes the materials, the loss is equally on him/her, unless the owner was delayed in receiving the work (Article 1589 CC).

413. The contractor is obligated to deliver the work when it is completed. The owner has to inspect and approve the work. When the owner approves and receives the work, either expressly or tacitly, the obligation to pay the price arises. Moreover, the contractor no longer carries the liability for apparent defects. Approval may be express or tacit. However, usually in big works, completion is divided into a provisory completion and a definitive completion; the approval only takes place with the definitive completion.

414. In addition to the general ways of extinguishing an obligation, Article 1594 CC grants the employer the right to terminate the contract by his/her own wish, even if the work is already in progress. The only condition is the obligation to compensate the constructor for the expenses incurred (materials and labour) and the utility the employer obtains from the work completed. Moreover, the death of the contractor extinguishes the contract where it was concluded because of his/her skills (Article 1595 CC). The owner has to reimburse the heirs of the contractor for the value of the work completed.

415. Article 1591 CC deals with latent defects affecting the solidity of a building. The provision is clearly inadequate, and a huge body of case law has developed it, thus giving rise to a system of liability for contractors and architects. The key concept is that of collapse or ruin. It covers not only the total or partial destruction of the building, but also defects that endanger the solidity of the building or makes it inappropriate for its purpose. Case law requires the defects to be serious.[487]

Article 1591 CC distinguishes between construction defects, direction defects and soil defects. The Supreme Court states that a contractor, an architect and a technical architect are solidary liable for the defects where it is impossible to individualize

486. This doctrine, equivalent to hardship, is however restrictively applied by the Supreme Court; *see* TS 21 Mar. 2003 (RJ 2003/2762), 27 May 2002 (2002/4573), 27 Jan. 1981 (1981/114). *See also* above para. 261.

487. TS 2 Apr. 2003 (RJ 2003/3001: 'defects that make impossible the dwelling's normal use and habitability'), 4 Nov. 2002 (RJ 2002/9630: 'the seriousness of the defects exceed the mere imperfections and makes the thing unsuitable for its normal use').

their liability.[488] According to the Supreme Court, the architect is liable for the constructive plan; he/she must solve any problem arising during the work and must give the necessary instructions to the constructor, directly or by means of the technical architect; therefore, the architect is not exempt from supervising the work.[489] The technical architect must watch over the execution of the work in accordance with the architect's plan.[490]

Liability does not extinguish by the mere fact that the owners sign a document accepting delivery of the work if defects exist and make the building unsuitable for its purpose.[491] In turn, property developers may sue constructors, architects and other technicians when owners claim liability for constructive defects.[492]

416. Case law considers that Article 1591 CC is a provision aimed at the protection of ownership. Therefore, the liability of contractors and architects also exist with regard to subsequent owners of the building.

417. Article 1591 CC states that the contractor and the architect are liable for a period of ten years. Nevertheless, case law has construed this provision as referring to the period within which the defect has to become apparent. Thus, the ten-year period is a period of guarantee. Once the defect becomes apparent, the action in responsibility prescribes within fifteen years (the general limitation period of Article 1964 CC).[493]

418. Besides employer and contractor, other persons may contribute to the work. The contractor answers for the acts of persons whom he/she employs (Article 1596 CC). However, the Civil Code grants subcontractors an action against the employer (*acción directa*) up to the amount for which the employer is debtor towards the contractor at the time when their action is brought (Article 1597).[494] This direct action against the employer is only granted in works for a lump sum.

419. Any person who carries out a work in a movable has the right of retention according to Article 1600 CC.[495]

II. The Contractor's Liability in the LOE

420. Act 28/1999 of 5 November, on Construction Planning, has not formally repealed any provision of the Civil Code, but it is intended to favour contractors in

488. TS 23 Feb. 2010 (RJ 2010\4342), 3 Dec. 2007 (RJ 2007/8657), 24 May 2007 (RJ 2007/3124), 15 Apr. 2003 (RJ 2003/3713), 27 Feb. 2003 (RJ 2003/2515), 16 Dec. 2002 (RJ 2002/10748).
489. TS 24 Jun. 2002 (RJ 2002/5261), 7 May 2001 (RJ 2001/6987), 5 Apr. 2001 (RJ 2001/3192).
490. TS 6 Apr. 2006 (RJ 2006/5323), 18 Sep. 2001 (RJ 2001/6596), 3 Jul. 2000 (RJ 2000/6877).
491. TS 16 Mar. 2011 (RJ 2011\2877).
492. TS 28 Feb. 2011 (RJ 2011\455).
493. *See* TS 20 Jul. 2002 (RJ 2002/7473), quoting many previous judgments.
494. *See* Federico A. Rodríguez Morata, *La acción directacomo garantía personaldel subcontratista de obra* (Madrid, 1992). *See also* paras 200 and 225.
495. *See* para. 313.

view of the extension of the liability based on Article 1591 CC.[496] Article 17 LOE distinguishes between three kinds of defects: structural, constructive and finish defects. Structural defects are the most serious, since they concern structural elements of the building and thus its stability. Constructive defects do not concern the security of the building, but they affect the habitability. Finish defects are related to the finish and decorative elements of the building and are easy to establish. The Act provides three periods of guarantee: ten years for structural defects, three years for constructive defects, one year for finish defects. The action on liability prescribes within two years since the production of the damage (Article 18). Nevertheless, the same Article 18 establishes that this regulation does not exclude any contractual liability, to which the general limitation period of fifteen years (Article 1964 CC) should apply. Since the Act also reaffirms the solidary liability of contractors, architects and property developers, no changes are expected in case law.[497]

421. As a means of guarantee for purchasers, Article 19 LOE imposes on property developers and contractors the obligation to conclude insurance contracts covering the three aforementioned kinds of defects.

§3. Hire of Services

422. Hire of services is the contract whereby one party undertakes to carry out an activity without promising a certain result (Article 1544 CC). The regulation enshrined in the Civil Code is completely out of date. It only takes into account servants and employees, but nowadays the regulation of employees belongs to labour law. Therefore, the scope of hire of services is reduced to liberal professionals such as lawyers and doctors. Hire of services is a consensual contract without formal requirements. Sometimes it may be difficult to distinguish between hire of services and hire of work. The main feature of hire of services is the development of an activity, whilst the aim of a contract of work is the achievement of a specific result.[498] Article 1583 CC prohibits hire of services for life as contrary to the fundamental right of freedom. The death of the party who undertakes the activity extinguishes the contract when it was concluded because of his/her skills.

496. Angel Carrasco Perera, Encarna Cordero Lobato & M. Carmen González Carrasco, *Comentarios a la ley de ordenación de la edificación*, 3rd edn (Cizur Menor, 2005); Florian Pagenkamper, *Mängelhaftung des Bauunternehmers in Spanien nach der Ley de Ordenación de la Edificación und dem código civil* (Frankfurt/Main, 2002).

497. *See* Angel Carrasco Perera, 'La jurisprudencia post-LOE ¿ha cambiado algo en el régimen de la responsabilidad por ruina?', III *Aranzadi Civil* (2001): 2375.

498. *See*, for example, TS 30 Dec. 2009 (RJ 2010\408).

Chapter 6. Lease

423. The Civil Code devotes the Title VI of Book IV to the regulation of the contract of lease. It begins with a chapter on general provisions, applicable to all forms of rental of things. Then, the Civil Code contains two sections with special rules on lease of dwellings and lease of agricultural holdings. Nevertheless, the range of application of these two sections is quite residual, since the main regulation is to be found in statutes. Whilst the Civil Code is essentially liberal, the statutes have traditionally shown a marked tendency to protect lessees.

§1. The General Law

I. Main Features of Lease

424. The main features of lease are two: the temporality of the use of a personal or real property and a certain price in exchange of this use (Article 1543 CC). If the term of the lease is six or more years, the lessor needs to be capable of disposal, for the lease is equated to a real burden (Article 1548 CC). Lease is an informal contract, but if one of the parties wants to record it at the Land Register, a deed is necessary. Any contract of lease notwithstanding its duration may be registered.

II. Obligations of the Lessor

425. The lessor is obligated to deliver the property leased to the lessee. The lessor is also obligated to maintain such property in condition to serve the use for which it was leased and consequently to make all necessary repairs throughout the duration of the lease. Lastly, the lessor is obligated to provide peaceful enjoyment to the lessee for the duration of the lease. Accordingly, the rules on *saneamiento*[499] are applicable to the contract of lease.

III. Obligations of the Lessee

426. The lessee is obligated to pay the stipulated price on the agreed terms; the price may be judicially reduced if the lessor is not able to provide peaceful enjoyment of the property leased (Article 1558 CC). The lessee is also obligated to use the property as a good father of the family and according to the purpose which the lease contemplated; if nothing has been stipulated, the lessee has to take into account the character of the property. At the end of the lease, the lessee must return the property. The lessee is liable for any deterioration and loss which occur during his/her enjoyment, unless he/she proves that they took place without his/her fault

499. *See* paras 383 et seq.

(Article 1563 CC). He/she is also liable for damages caused by persons of his/her house (relatives, domestic service, etc.).

The remedies for non-performance are termination of the contract (lessor) and damages (both parties). The lessor is granted a special procedure to evict the lessee in case of non-performance and expiry of the term fixed (*desahucio*).

IV. Assignment of Lease

427. The lessee has the right to sublet his/her lease to another, if such option has not been prohibited in the contract. The principal lessor has a direct action against the sub-lessee in order to receive the price of the lease when the lessee does not pay it (Article 1552 CC). The extinction of the lease implies the extinction of the sub-lease. In addition, the lessee may be authorized to assign the lease to another person by the lessor, and even the special law governing the lease of business premises grants this right in some situations.

V. Duration: Tacit Renewal

428. A lease extinguishes automatically upon the expiration of the fixed term without the necessity of giving notice of termination (Article 1565 CC). If at the expiration of the lease, the lessee remains and is left in possession for fifteen days, a new lease arises under the same conditions but not in the period of duration, unless notice of termination is given (Article 1566 CC). The term of a renewed lease of agricultural holdings is the time necessary to crop (Article 1577 CC); the term of a renewed lease of dwelling is one year, one month or one day depending on whether the price was fixed per years, months or days (Article 1581 CC).

VI. Sale Breaks Hire?

429. Article 1571 CC grants the buyer the right to extinguish the lease. Therefore, the extinction of the lease is not automatic. In addition, the lessee in entitled to harvest the crop, and the buyer has to compensate damages. Nevertheless, the special legislation on the lease of the dwelling contains a different regulation.[500]

§2. Dwellings for Principal Residence

430. Spanish law has been traditionally concerned about the protection of lessees of dwellings for principal residence. The main feature of this policy was the legal impossibility to increase the rent. Only the *Ley de arrendamientos urbanos* (LAU) passed in 1994 has recognized a broader scope of freedom of contract, even

500. *See* below paras 432 (lease of dwellings) and 440 (lease of agricultural holdings).

though the lessee is still considered as deserving protection. Thus, a number of provisions are mandatory, and the parties are not allowed to escape them, unless the dwelling surface is over 300 m^2 or the price is over 5.5 times the guaranteed minimum wage.[501] The LAU was amended in 2013 (Act /2013, of 4 June).

431. Lease has a minimum term of three years (five before the reform); if the parties stipulate a shorter term, the contract extends at the lessee's will until the completion of the term of three years (Article 9 LAU). Once the three-year term is completed, if the parties do not notify the will of extinguishing the lease, it is renewed monthly for one year more (Article 10 LAU reducing the three years of legal extension in the original provision). The compulsory extension of the contract to three years may be avoided if the lessor needs to occupy the dwelling within the term of five years. If the lessor does not live in the dwelling, the lessee is granted a new period of three years and compensation for damages; the lessee may opt however for a compensation based on the rent for the time until completion of the five-year term. By contrast, the lessee is free to terminate the lease with a one-month notice, and he/she is only obligated to compensate the lessor if such a stipulation was included in the contract.

432. The purchaser of the dwelling leased cannot break the lease during the three-year term, unless he needs the dwelling for living after one year of conclusion of the lease contract. If the lease has been registered, the purchaser has to respect the lease notwithstanding the stipulated term. If the stipulated term is more than three years and the purchaser is unaware of the lease, he/she may terminate the contract once the three-year term is completed, but he/she must compensate the lessee. Compensation amounts to one month of rent for each year the lessee is deprived of the dwelling's use (Article 14 LAU). However, the legislator grants the lessee a right of preferential acquisition when the lessor decides to sell the dwelling; this right may now be renounced irrespective of the agreed term of the contract (Article 25 LAU).

433. The parties determine freely the rent. They may also resort to stabilization clauses. The rent may be increased on the ground of improvements carried out by the lessor, but only after the first five years of the contract (Article 19 LAU). Nevertheless, it has to be borne in mind that the ordinary conservation of the dwelling is in charge of the lessor (Article 21 LAU).

434. The spouse of the lessee is also protected. Termination of the lease by the lessee needs the consent of the spouse. The law burdens the lessor to obtain evidence of such consent. In any case, the spouse may give a one-month notice to the lessor that he/she wants to maintain the lease when the lessee quits the dwelling. The same applies to unmarried couples (Article 12 LAU). Moreover, the spouse, the partner, the descendants and other relatives who had cohabited with the lessee in the dwelling are entitled to subrogation in the contract upon the lessee's death (Article 16 LAU).

501. EUR 641 a month in 2011.

§3. Business Premises, Dwellings Not for Principal Residence

435. The regulation concerning season leases, business premises and dwellings not for a principal residence is far more flexible. No minimal term is required. Much of the regulation is non-mandatory, so that the parties may exclude it. Nevertheless, the lessee's heir is also entitled to subrogation. Moreover, the lessee may assign the contract, even though the lessor is then entitled to increase the rent. Under certain conditions and if it is not excluded in the contract, the lessor has to compensate the lessee for clientele upon termination of the contract (Article 34 LAU).

The statute does not apply to the lease of an industry. The main feature of lease of an industry is, according to case law, the fact that in addition to the premises, the business located in them is also leased.[502] The Civil Code applies to leases of industries.

§4. Agricultural Holdings

436. Traditionally the legislation on leases of agricultural land has been very protective towards lessees. The regulation is contained now in Act 49/2003 of 26 November, *de arrendamientos rústicos* (LAR), amended in 2005, which has repealed the previous Act 83/1990 of 31 December. The law in force is more liberal and less protective of lessees: periods are shorter; the compulsory prolongation of the contract has been abrogated; the role of party autonomy has been enlarged. It is the tenant who directs the course of cultivation, but its position cannot be equated to an owner.[503]

Falling under the application of the statute are leases of real property which is temporally devoted to agricultural, cattle raising or forest use, in exchange of a rent. Nevertheless, seasonal leases (i.e., less than an agricultural year) and specific agricultural tasks in exchange of a remuneration are excluded from the range of application of the statute. Written form is prescribed by Article 11 LAR.

437. The duration of the lease may not be less than five years (seven in Catalonia). Once this period has elapsed, the contract extinguishes and the lessee must return the property leased. But, in default of a one-year notice to quit, the contract is tacitly renewed for five years. Renewal of the contract may be indefinite if notice at the end of the second year of each new period fails. The tenant is not allowed to sublet or to assign the lease without the consent of the lessor.

438. The parties are free to determine the rent. Stabilization clauses are permitted. According to Article 16, the lessee may enter into an insurance contract in order to insure the usual production of the land. The lessee can claim from the lessor a

502. TS 25 Mar. 2011 (RJ 2011\2229), 7 Jul. 2006 (RJ 2006/5384), 21 Feb. 2000 (RJ 2000/1239), 8 Jun. 1998 (RJ 1998/4284).

503. Catalonia has passed its own legislation (Act 1/2008, of 20 February, *Llei decontractes deconreu*, which now has been incorporated to the CC Cat), which is much more protective of lessees. For example, the minimum period of the contract is seven years (Art. 523-12 CC Cat).

part of the insurance premium proportional to the relationship between the rent and the insured capital. The reason is that the lessor is consequently sure about the payment of the rent.

439. The necessary repairs are in charge of the lessor, who is not entitled to increase the rent. Lessor and lessee are allowed to make improvements. The lessor may increase the rent if the improvements increase the production capacity of the land. The lessee may not agree with the increase and terminate the lease. However, the lessee is obligated to make repairs and improvements inherent in the agricultural activity, without the right to reduce the rent. All improvements are presumed to have been made by the lessee.

440. The sale of the land does not break the lease. The acquirer of the leased land is not entitled to extinguish the contract even if it was not recorded in the Land Register. Therefore, he/she subrogates from the position of the lessor.

The statute distinguishes termination and extinction of the lease. The lessor may terminate the contract if the tenant does not pay the rent, does not use the land or misuses or harms it and sublets or assigns the contract without the legal or the contractual requirements. The loss of the land and the expiry of the term lead to the extinction of the contract. The tenant's death does not extinguish automatically the contract, since the law authorizes subrogation in favour of the forced heirs. The lessee can withdraw from the contract giving notice in advance of one year.

441. Share-cropping (*aparcería*) is also regulated (Articles 28 et seq.). This contract is close to partnership, because both parties contribute to the agricultural activity and share the profits proportionally. The parties are free to stipulate the duration of the contract; if there is no stipulation the duration is one agricultural year.

§5. Leasing

442. Financial leasing (hereinafter simply leasing, in Spanish also *arrendamiento financiero*) is a contract between a lessor and a lessee whereby movables or immovables are purchased by the lessor upon indications and specifications of the lessee, with the purpose to lease them to the lessee who has an option to buy the leased goods at the end of the lease period; the existence of this option is essential to distinguish leasing from other contracts, such as the purchase of equipments with payment on instalment and retention of title.[504] This period has to be at least two years (Article 128 Act on the Corporations Tax). It is required that the leased goods are used for professional purposes. The lessor has to be a 'leasing corporation', that is, a credit company. Therefore, the specific legislation on credit companies applies to the lessor. Leaseback is accepted as well by case law.[505]

504. TS 11 Feb. 2010 (RJ 2010\531).
505. For example, TS 15 Apr. 2010 (RJ 2010\3536).

443. The law regulates the contract of leasing unsystematically; the main provisions are concerned with its tax treatment. Spain has not ratified the UNIDROIT Convention on International Financial Leasing either. Therefore, the legal gaps must be filled in with the regulation of the closest nominate contracts. The legal character of the contract has been much disputed in Spain. Nowadays the most accepted theory considers it a financial contract. Due to the economic limitations of lessees (small enterprises and professionals) which have not enough economic means to buy the equipment, they approach leasing companies that buy the goods and grant the right of use to the lessees. Moreover, it is very advantageous for the lessee from a taxation point of view, since the lessee is allowed to deduct all or most of the rentals paid. In spite of the Spanish denomination (*arrendamiento [hire] financiero*), it is not deemed to be a modality of hire. Specifically, the same legislator distinguishes leasing from sale on instalment. Case law considers that leasing enshrines two contracts, that is, a sale between the leasing company and the supplier of the goods and a lease with an option to buy between the leasing company and the lessee.[506]

444. The contract of leasing collects elements from sale, lease, loan and mandate. This legal frame will allow finding a solution for practical problems such as the nonconformity of the goods and some standard clauses incorporated into the contract by the lessor. The first conclusion is that the lessee does not become the owner of the goods, but only acquires a right of use. The owner is the leasing company. This is particularly important in the case of bankruptcy of the lessee, since the financial company is entitled to vindicate the asset and avoid its auction.[507] The new Insolvency Act (*Ley* 22/2003 of 9 July, *Concursal*) grants a special privilege to lessors in order to collect the unpaid rents (Article 90.4).

445. The leasing company buys the asset and consequently becomes the owner of it. Nevertheless, the right of use is attributed to the lessee and, therefore, he/she will suffer the consequences of the latent defects. Usually the contract frees the leasing company from any liability for latent defects (disclaimer standard clause), but at the same time assigns the remedies available against the supplier to the lessee. Hence, the lessee must bring any claim against the supplier, including repair and substitution. This practical solution is not illogical, because the leasing company buys the asset on behalf of the lessee. It is not a case of direct action, but of assignment of the lessor's actions (the legal basis is Article 1209 CC). Case law has accepted the validity of the clause whereby the leasing company is freed from liability for latent defects but only if at the same time, the claims are assigned to the lessee; if not, the clause would be unfair and void.[508]

Nevertheless, if the lessee wants to terminate the contract because of the absolute nonconformity of the asset, it will be necessary to also sue the leasing company as the owner of the asset. The termination of the contract of sale between supplier and

506. TS 4 Dec. 2007 (RJ 2008/42), 30 Dec. 2002 (RJ 2003/331), 5 Oct. 2000 (RJ 2000/7542).
507. TS 31 Oct. 2005 (RJ 2005/7350), 23 Jul. 2003 (RJ 2003/6602), 12 Mar. 2003 (RJ 2003/2574).
508. TS 21 Jan. 2002 (RJ 200/19), 25 Jan. 2001 (RJ 2001/1001).

lessor also entails the termination of the contract of leasing because of the functional dependence between the two contracts.[509]

446. The main obligation undertaken by the lessee is the payment of the rents. The contract of leasing usually provides that the leasing company may terminate the contract and require accelerated payment of the value of the future rents in case of non-performance. In addition, penalty clauses are also incorporated into the agreement. Such penalty clauses often consist of the payment of interests. Sometimes the Supreme Court has reduced in equity (on the basis of Article 1154 CC) the penalty clauses,[510] taking into account that non-performance was not fundamental or the gross disparity that the clause may entail. By contrast, the Supreme Court has never applied the legislation against usury to contracts of leasing, rejecting any similarity with the contract of loan.[511] Such clauses are not deemed to be unfair either (consequently, they cannot be annulled), because the lessee is not a consumer.[512] Therefore, the only remedy available to the lessee is the declaration of nullity of the clause on the grounds of gross disparity and the principle of good faith (Article 1258 CC).

447. The Supreme Court has also tried to distinguish between leasing and sale on instalment, on the basis that the amount of the price of the option to buy is irrelevant.[513] However, leasing operations dealing with movables may be recorded in the register of sales on instalment, so that the contract becomes opposable to third parties.

§6. RENTING

448. Renting is only a modality of hire of movables. The lessor (usually a financial intermediary but an owner of the asset) grants the lessee the use of a certain movable for a short period of time. The lessee undertakes the obligation to pay the rent and the lessor the obligation to keep the asset in optimal conditions of use. The movables are usually equipment subject to fast obsolescence (computers, cars, photocopiers, etc.). Therefore, the obligation undertaken by the lessor implies the performance of a service (even though not carried out personally); for example, dealing with renting of cars, periodical services, change of wheels, repairs, etc. Unlike leasing, the lessee has no option for buying the asset. Hence, the investment risk is allocated to the leasing company.[514] Nevertheless, an option of purchase at the end of the period is often included and then the distinction from leasing becomes quite complicated.

509. TS 24 May 1999 (RJ 1999/3927), 26 Feb. 1996 (RJ 1996/1264).
510. TS 1 Feb. 1999 (RJ 1999/524).
511. TS 2 Feb. 2006 (RJ 2006/494), 1 Feb. 2002 (RJ 2002/2879).
512. TS 17 Mar. 1998 (RJ 1998/1351).
513. TS 13 Jul. 2006 /RJ 2006/4967), 12 Mar. 2003 (RJ 2003/2574), 15 Jun. 1999 (RJ 1999/4473).
514. TS 19 Jan. 2000 (RJ 2000/139).

Chapter 7. Compromise Settlements

449. A compromise settlement (*transacción*) is a contract whereby the parties terminate a dispute having arisen or prevent a dispute from arising, by each making a concession to the other (Article 1809 CC). The main legal consequence resulting from the contract is the authority of res judicata (Article 1816 CC). Therefore, compromise settlements have the same effects as a judgment, so that each party may use a defence in case the other brings an action to court on the same dispute. Since the aim of that contract is to terminate a conflict deriving from a legal relationship, the parties must be capable of disposing of such relationship. Hence, parents and guardianships need judicial authorization in order to conclude the settlement (Articles 1810, 1811 and 271.3 CC).

450. There are three elements of compromise settlements in the CC. First, the dispute between the parties has to be a legal one. Second, each party must make a concession to the other party, but the concession does not need to have a patrimonial character. Third, the object of the settlement cannot be on the following: the civil condition, the right to alimony, marriage (though the effects of separation and divorce may be) and any relationship which the parties are not allowed to dispose of (Article 1814 CC).

451. The contract is onerous, since the parties are bound to make reciprocal concessions. Therefore, the rules on onerous contracts such as latent defects, eviction or *exceptio non adimpleti contractus* apply to compromise settlements. In addition, the settlement is the cause of the transfers of rights between the parties. The settlement gives birth to a new obligation that substitutes the former that has been the object of the compromise, according to the decision of the Supreme Court of 18 July 2017.[515]

452. A compromise settlement may be attacked for reason of a vice of consent (Article 1817 CC), but not for reason of a mistake of law, unless the mistake has been fraudulently provoked. Articles 1818, 1819 CC sets down as a ground for annulment the concealment of new documents or definitive judgments.

453. Arbitration is regulated in the Act 60/2003 of 20 December, amended by Act 11/2011, of 20 May and Organic Act 5/2011, of 20 May.[516] This new Act provides an essentially unitary regulation for internal and international arbitration. An arbitral agreement by which the parties submit their existing or future disputes to arbitration is needed. The arbitral agreement may also be a contractual clause. Arbitration may be in equity – if expressly agreed to by the parties – or in law. Only

515. Roj: STS 3012/2017.
516. *See* Juan Burgos Ladrón de Guevara, 'Aproximación a la nueva Ley 60/2003, de 23 de diciembre de arbitraje', *La Ley*, no. 5978 of 18 Mar. 2004; Antonio M. Lorca Navarrete, 'Los motivos de la denominada acción de anulación contra el laudo arbitral en la vigente Ley de arbitraje', *La Ley*, no. 6005 of 27 Apr. 2004. In German, Josef Fröhlingsdorf, 'Spaniens Reform der Schiedsgerichtbarkeit', *Recht der Internationalen Wirtschaft* (2004): 352.

practising lawyers can be appointed for arbitration in law, unless the parties stipulate that other persons can be appointed, yet arbitration by non-lawyers has been restricted in the last amendment of the Act 60/2003. If the parties do not agree on the number of arbitrators – always an odd number – the dispute shall be decided by a sole arbitrator. The parties can also submit their controversy to an institutional arbitration tribunal. Irrespective of the kind of arbitration (i.e., in law or in equity), the arbitral award shall state the reasons upon which it is based. The award must be rendered in a time limit of six months. If the parties reach a settlement after the file has been transmitted to the Arbitral Tribunal, the settlement shall be recorded in the form of an arbitral award unless a legal ground impedes it. Nullity of the decision can only be based on the grounds laid down in Article 41. Those legal grounds do not permit the revision of the legal or equitable foundation of the decision. The award has the effect of res judiciata and it is enforceable even if its nullity is claimed.

Chapter 8. Suretyship

§1. The Surety's Obligation

454. Suretyship is a personal guarantee by which a person renders himself/herself surety for an obligation and binds himself/herself towards the creditor to satisfy that obligation if the debtor himself/herself does not fulfil it (Article 1822.1 CC). Thus, the liability of the surety is, in principle, subsidiary, since the surety is only liable when the debtor does not fulfil the principal obligation (the old *beneficium excussionis*). The surety can avail himself/herself of a defence if the creditor has not brought an action against the principal debtor, and the subsequent execution has proved to be abortive. However, the surety may renounce this defence and then one speaks of solidary suretyship (Articles 1822.2 and 1831.2 CC).

455. According to Article 1823 CC, suretyship may arise from a contract, from the law or from a judicial decision. The contract of suretyship may be concluded without the behest of the principal debtor, without his/her knowledge and even without his/her consent (Article 1823.2 CC). The contract is consensual and informal.[517] Nevertheless, suretyship is not presumed, it must be express, and it cannot be extended beyond the limits within which it was contracted (Article 1827 CC).[518]

456. Suretyship is an accessory contract, since the surety's obligation depends on the principal debtor's obligation. Thus, suretyship may exist only on a valid principal obligation, although it also may exist on a voidable obligation because of a purely personal bar of the debtor such as minor age (Article 1824 CC). In addition, a suretyship may neither exceed what is due by the debtor, nor be contracted on more onerous terms (Article 1826 CC); the sanction for the contravention of this provision is the partial nullity of the contract. Nevertheless, an indefinite suretyship is permitted, so that the surety takes over any ancillary debt (e.g., interests), including judicial expenses (Article 1827.2 CC). Suretyship may also guarantee a future debt (Article 1824 CC).[519]

457. Despite the concrete object of the principal debtor's obligation, the surety's obligation consists in the payment of a sum of money. Only if the debtor is obligated to deliver fungible things, the content of the surety's obligation can be the same.

§2. The Effect of Suretyship Between the Creditor and the Surety

458. A surety is obligated toward the creditor to pay only upon the principal debtor's default. Therefore, the surety may resort to a defence that lasts until the creditor has unsuccessfully executed the debtor's assets. The negligence of the

517. Suretyship may even be tacit: TS 2 Mar. 2006 (RJ 2006/5770).
518. TS 19 Apr. 2004 (RJ 2004/1564), 3 Jul. 1999 (RJ 1999/4901), 5 Feb. 1992 (RJ 1992/830).
519. *See* TS 26 Jun. 2009 (RJ 2009\4239), 13 Oct. 2005 (RJ 2005/7340).

creditor in investigating the debtor's assets is sanctioned: the surety's liability extinguishes in proportion to the sum that has not been possible to execute upon those assets (Article 1833 CC). The surety may not resort to the *beneficium excussionis* (Article 1831 CC):

1. when he/she has renounced it;
2. when he/she undertakes a solidary suretyship;
3. in case of bankruptcy of the principal debtor, since insolvency has been already stated by the courts;
4. where the debtor cannot be sued in Spain;
5. in case of a judicial suretyship.

459. In addition to the *beneficium excussionis*, a surety may raise against the creditor all the defences which belong to the principal debtor and which are inherent to the debt. By contrast, purely personal defences to the debtor (incapacity) are excluded. Defences inherent to the debt cover vices of consent, payment and any other way of extinguishing the obligation. Therefore, a surety is entitled to question the existence and the validity of the obligation. A surety may also allege prescription of the action even if the debtor had renounced it (Article 1937 CC).

460. Co-sureties are only liable for their proportionate shares (Article 1837.1 CC). The *beneficium divisionis* is not available in the same situations as that of the *beneficium excussionis*.

§3. The Effect of Suretyship Between the Debtor and the Surety

461. Article 1843 CC enumerates some situations whereby the surety may sue the debtor in order to be discharged before having paid. In fact, the debtor cannot discharge the surety, since the latter is engaged to the creditor. Therefore, the surety seeks a guarantee that when he/she pays, the recourse to the principal debtor will be successful. The agreement has no effect on the creditor's rights without his/her consent. Any kind of guarantee is admissible. The situations enumerated in Article 1843 are:

1. where the surety is sued for payment;
2. the debtor's insolvency;
3. where the debtor was bound to discharge the surety within a certain time;
4. where the debt becomes enforceable;
5. ten years after the conclusion of the contract of suretyship if no expiry date was stipulated for the principal obligation.

462. A surety who pays has recourse to the principal debtor. The so-called reimbursement action includes the total amount of the debt, legal interest since the debtor knows about the payment, expenses incurred by the surety after giving notice to the debtor that payment was demanded and, if appropriate, damages (Article 1838 CC). Legal interest is due even though the surety did not have to pay it to the creditor. In addition, the surety is subrogated to all the rights which the creditor had against the debtor (Article 1839 CC). If the surety has been given without the knowledge or the consent of the debtor, Article 1158.3 CC applies.[520]

463. The debtor can avail himself/herself of some defences when the surety sues him/her. If the surety pays without giving notice to the debtor, the latter may raise against the former all the defences he/she could have raised against the creditor (Article 1840 CC). Hence, giving notice to the debtor is a burden of the surety. If, because the surety has not given notice of the payment, the debtor also pays the principal debt, the former has only recourse to the creditor (Article 1842 CC, which constitutes a case of unjustified enrichment). If a time clause was stipulated and the surety paid before the *dies* had arrived, he/she cannot claim reimbursement until the due date (Article 1841 CC).

§4. The Extinction of Suretyship

464. Being an accessory debt, suretyship extinguishes along with the principal debt. The general ways of extinction of obligations apply also to suretyship (Article 1847 CC).

465. A surety is discharged when subrogation to the rights and the guarantees of the creditor, through an act of such a creditor, may no longer operate in favour of the surety (Article 1852 CC).[521]

466. The extension expressly given by the creditor to the debtor without the consent of the surety extinguishes suretyship, unless the possibility of the extension had already been stipulated in the contract (Article 1851 CC). Extension makes the surety's obligation more onerous and affects the privity of contract between debtor and surety.[522]

§5. The Effect of Suretyship Between Co-sureties

467. When several sureties guarantee the same debt, the surety who pays has recourse against the other sureties, each one for his/her share and portion (Article 1844 CC). The sued co-sureties may resort to the same defences the debtor could have raised against the debtor but only the purely personal ones (Article 1845 CC). In addition, where one co-surety has paid the whole debt, the following rules apply:

520. *See* above para. 236.
521. For a somewhat restrictive interpretation of this provision, *see* TS 14 Jun. 2002 (RJ 2002/4900) and 8 May 2002 (RJ 2002/4048).
522. TS 12 Jul. 2002 (RJ 2002/6046), 20 Sep. 2001 (RJ 2001/6651).

1. The co-surety has the choice either to recourse against the other co-sureties or to the principal debtor. Both claims can be cumulated in an alternative or a subsidiary way.
2. The sub-surety is liable to the rest of the co-sureties as the insolvent co-surety was (Article 1846 CC).

§6. SUB-SURETYSHIP

468. The sub-surety guarantees the fulfilment of the surety's obligation (Article 1823 CC). The sub-surety may resort to the *beneficium excussionis* both in respect to the debtor and to the surety. Confusion does not extinguish the sub-suretyship; the sub-surety then becomes surety (Article 1848 CC).

§7. FIRST DEMAND GUARANTEES

469. First demand guarantees have flourished even in the legislation.[523] According to the Supreme Court, the surety may only raise against the creditor the defences resulting from the same guarantee.[524] Thus, the guarantee seems to be *abstract* (no need for a cause), but the statement is probably excessive, although it is often used by the Supreme Court. Obviously, the surety may allege the extinction of the principal debt, specifically because of the payment of the debt by means of an *exception doli* or alternatively the surety may allege an abuse of rights on the creditor's side,[525] but the guarantee is neither accessory nor subsidiary.

523. For instance, Art. 19.3.b) LOE.
524. TS 4 Dec. 2009 (RJ 2010\271), 1 Oct. 2007 (RJ 2007/8087), 5 Jul. 2002 (RJ 2002/8225), 21 Apr. 2002 (RJ 2002/5109) and many others.
525. TS 17 Jul. 2014 (Roj: STS 3157/2014).

Chapter 9. Pledges

470. The Civil Code devotes in its book on obligations some provisions (Title XV) to the 'contracts of pledge, mortgage and antichresis'. Thus, these real rights are regulated regarding one of its possible sources, the contract, although the origin of mortgages may be legal and even testamentary. The regulation of mortgages is to be found essentially in the *Ley Hipotecaria*. In addition, the Articles 569-12 et seq. CCCat have to be taken into account in Catalonia. The chapter is solely concerned with the contractual side of pledges.

471. A pledge is a contract whereby a debtor or a third person delivers a property to the creditor for security for a debt. The property must belong to the debtor or to the third person delivering it. The object of pledge (*prenda*) is a movable thing, whilst the object of antichresis (*anticresis*) is an immovable thing. The Civil Code only regulates the pledge where possession of the pledged thing is transferred to the creditor. Because of the economic disadvantage that the loss of possession implies for the pledgor, especially where machinery and other productive assets are pledged, pledge without transfer of possession is developed rapidly; it is regulated outside the Civil Code (*Ley de hipoteca mobiliaria y prenda sin desplazamiento*) of 16 December 1954. Antichresis has gone into disuse; yet its principal consequence, the application of the profits of the pledged thing to the payment of interest and capital, has extended to pledge (Article 1868 CC *per analogiam*).

472. The contract whereby the pledge is created is informal; nevertheless, it will only affect third parties (the main characteristic of real rights) if there is a public deed (Article 1865 CC; Article 12.2 Act 19/2002). A pledge confers on the creditor the right to have himself/herself paid from the pledged property *ius distrahendi*, subject to a legal procedure. Pledge is accessory to the secured debt: it cannot exist without a right of credit for which security is given, and its validity depends on the validity of the right of credit (Article 1857.1 CC; Article 13 Act 19/2002).

473. The pledgor remains owner of the pledged thing (Article 1869 CC). The creditor is not allowed to use the property; if he/she does so, the pledgor may ask for the constitution of a bailment (Article 1870 CC). The pledgor cannot claim restitution of the pledged thing until the debt is paid. But if the debt is not discharged, the creditor is not authorized to appropriate the thing for himself/herself; *lex comissoria* is expressly forbidden (Articles 1859, 1884 CC; *see also* Article 19 Act 19/2002). If there existed on the part of the same debtor, toward the same creditor, another debt contracted subsequently to the creation of the pledge and before having paid the first debt, the creditor may not be required to give up the property before being entirely paid for both debts, even where there was no stipulation made attaching the pledge to the payment of the second.

474. The creditor is bound to keep the property with the care of a good father of the family (Article 1867 CC; Article 18.2 Act 19/2002 speaks of 'due diligence'). Therefore, he/she answers for any loss or deterioration which may occur by his/her negligence. But the expenses incurred for the preservation of the property must be reimbursed to the creditor. In Catalan law, such expenses are also secured by the pledge (Article 18.2 Act 19/2002), whilst Article 1871 CC refers to a 'right of retention'.

475. The creditor may resort to any action belonging to the pledgor in order to vindicate it or simply to protect it from third persons (Article 1869.2 CC).

Chapter 10. Loan

476. There are two sorts of loan (Article 1740 CC): that of property which can be used without destroying or consuming it, and that of property which is consumed by the use which is made of it. The first one is called loan for use (*comodato*); the second one simple loan or loan for consumption (*mutuo*). The common feature of both kinds of loan lies in the delivery and the restitution of the object. Nevertheless, and on the basis of the object, the Civil Code regulates separately loan for use and simple loan. Thus, loan is conceived as a real contract, despite the fact that the parties may shape it as consensual.

§1. Loan for Use

477. By virtue of the contract of loan, one party delivers to the other party a thing that cannot be consumed[526] in order that the latter uses it for a period of time and returns it after the time agreed. Only the use of the loaned thing is transferred. The two main features of the loan for use are temporality and gratuity.

As for temporality, the parties agree on the time of the use; if they do not, restitution must be made when such use finishes off or in accordance with the custom (Articles 1749, 1750 CC). Nonetheless, if the lender comes to have a pressing need of his/her property, he/she can claim restitution even before such time.

However, loan for use is essentially gratuitous. If the parties agree on the payment of a sum of money, Article 1741 CC establishes that the contract is not a loan for use.

478. The borrower has only a right of use and acquires no real right on the loaned thing (Article 1741 CC). He/she has no right to the fruits of the loaned thing either. If the borrower employs the property for another use or for a longer time than he/she should, he/she is liable for loss occurring even through fortuitous event (Article 1744 CC). According to Article 1745 CC, if the loaned thing had delivered an estimated price, the borrower is liable for loss occurring even through fortuitous event and has to pay the estimation. If the borrowers are two or more, their liability is solidary.

479. The borrower is obliged to return the loaned thing. This obligation is unavoidable, since the borrower has no right of retention even if he/she incurs expenses in order to conserve the property (Article 1747 CC). The lender must reimburse the borrower for such expenditures. In addition, the lender must compensate the damages caused to the borrower when he/she knew of the defects of the loaned thing and did not warn of them (Article 1752 CC). Until restitution, the borrower is required to conserve the loaned thing and assumes the necessary expenditures for

526. Or, if the thing can be consumed, it is only used *adpompam vel ostentationem*.

such conservation (Article 1743 CC; this is a logical consequence of the gratuitous character of the loan).[527]

§2. Simple Loan

480. Where the loan is for consumption, the borrower becomes owner of the property loaned. The object of the loan is money or other fungibles (Article 1740 CC). Therefore, the borrower becomes obligated to the lender not to return the very things that he/she received, but an equal sum or objects of the same quantity and quality at the time agreed (Article 1753 CC). The principle of nominalism applies, so that the borrower has to return the numerical sum loaned.

481. Even though simple loan is featured as a naturally gratuitous contract, the parties are allowed to stipulate the payment of interest (Article 1755 CC). Nevertheless, the borrower who has paid interest which was not stipulated may neither recover it nor credit it against capital (Article 1756 CC).

§3. Loan at Interest

482. Interest is legal or by agreement. Interest by agreement has a general limit: usury. The old but still in force Act of 23 July 1908 nullifies loans manifestly exceeding normal interest rates or contracted because of the weakness, imperious need or ignorance of the borrower. With the loan being void, the borrower has to only return the capital.[528] The 1908 Act does not apply to leasing contracts.[529]

The protection to borrowers provided by the Consumer Credit Act (currently Act 16/2001, of 24 June) should be more efficient, but it has been timidly applied by case law.[530] Only recently have Spanish courts considered unfair rates of interest clearly disproportionate in relation to normal rates.[531] Consequently, courts moderate the rates applying different criteria.

527. On the contrary, extraordinary expenditures are in charge of the lender; *see* TS 12 Jun. 1993 (RJ 1993/4829).

528. The decision of the Court of Appeal of La Coruña of 5 Nov. 2002 (JUR 2003/62967) considers usurious and void a loan at an interest rate of 34%. The more recent decision of the Court of Appeal of Almeria (JUR 2004/150841) is a monthly rate of 10%.

529. TS 2 Feb. 2006 (RJ 2006/494).

530. *See* Leonor Aguilar Ruiz, 'La aplicación jurisprudencial de la Ley 7/1995, de 23 de marzo, de crédito al consumo', *Revista de Derecho Patrimonial* (2000): 4: 125.

531. For example, delay interest at a rate of 29% is unfair according to the decisions of the courts of appeal of Barcelona 5 Nov. 2003 (JUR 2003/4562), Asturias 20 Dec. 2002 (AC 2003/258), La Coruña 22 Oct. 2002 (JUR 2003/40) and others; an interest rate of 25.5% in the decision of the Court of Appeal of Coruña of 6 May 2011 (JUR 2011\207297); an interest rate of 24% in the decision of the Court of Appeal of Alicante of 25 May 2010 (AC 2010\1050). But the decision of the same Court of Appeal of Asturias handed down on 27 Nov. 2003 (JUR 2004/66580) has not considered unfair the same rate of 29%. The decision of the Court of Appeal of Barcelona first mentioned reduced the rate to a 20.625%, for example. Since the interest rates have decreased in

Chapter 11. Contracts with the Government and Other Public Institutions

§1. Legal Framework

483. The legal regime of contracts passed by Spanish public bodies finds its principles in the constitutional distribution of competencies amongst the different public bodies.[532] Thus, Article 149.1-18a CE establishes a regime of shared powers under which it is for the State to enact the basic legislation and for the Autonomous Communities to develop such basic legislation.

The above-mentioned basic legislation is found in Act 9/2017, of 8 November, of Contracts of the Public Sector (hereinafter LCSP). This Act incorporates into Spanish law Directives 2014/23/UE and 2014/24/UE, of the European Parliament and of the Council of 26 February 2014 on the award of concession contract and on public procurement and repealing Directive 2004/18/EC,.

§2. Subjective Scope of Application of the LCSP

484. The LCSP regulates contracts to be concluded by the so-called public sector. In order to outline precisely which is the subjective scope of the Act, it deals with three separate concepts. It is necessary to analyse them separately, since fundamental aspects such as the comprehension of various types of contracts depend on their correct understanding. These concepts are:

1. public sector;
2. public administrations;
3. contracting authorities.

I. Public Sector

485. According to the LCSP, the following entities are part of the so-called public sector:

1. The General Administration of the Estate, the Administration of the Autonomous Communities and the Local Administration.
2. The Social Security Administration.
3. Autonomous agencies, state-owned enterprises, public universities and other public law entities with juridical personality linked to a public body or to an agency belonging to the public sector.
4. Corporations on whose shareholding, directly or indirectly, one of the entities mentioned in the letters (1) and (6) exceeds 50 per 100 of the shares.

Europe, the courts have also considered unfair lower rates. For example, the decision of the Court of Appeal of Valencia of 4 Oct. 2007 considers unfair rate of 17.36% in comparison to the normal rate of 4.25%.

532. Written by Antonio Ezquerra (University of Lleida).

5. Pools with juridical personality.
6. Foundations whose funds are mostly established by public sector agencies, or which assets are transferred by those agencies in more than 50 per 100.
7. Mutual Funds for accidents at work and occupational illness linked to the Social Security Scheme.
8. Any other agencies or entities with juridical personality created in order to pursue general interest necessities, provided that they do not have mercantile character and one or more public sector agencies fund their activity, control their activities or appoint more than half of the members of its administration board.
9. Associations created by the agencies and entities mentioned in the previous paragraphs.

II. Public Administrations

486. The concept of Public Administration is paramount since only contracts concluded by a Public Administration deserve the qualification of administrative contracts and the special legislation applies to them. The following subjects are part of the concept 'Public Administration':

1. The General Administration of the Estate, the Autonomous Communities, the Local Administration and the Social Security administration.
2. Autonomous agencies.
3. Public Universities.
4. Public law agencies, irrespective of their functional independence, responsible for regulation or control over a certain sector or activity.
5. Public law agencies linked to one or more Public Administrations or dependent on them provided that:
   a. their main activity does not consist in producing market goods or services for individual or collective use or consists in non-profit redistributing national wealth;
   b. their income does not stem from remuneration for delivery of goods or services.
6. Entrepreneurial estate-owned agencies and similar agencies dependent on Autonomous Communities or Local Administration are not considered Public Administration.

III. Contracting Authorities

487. Contracting authorities include the following:

1. public administrations;
2. any other agency created in order to pursue general interest necessities, provided that they do not have mercantile character and one or more public sector agencies fund their activity, control their activities or appoint more than half of the members of its administration board.

3. associations created by the agencies and entities mentioned in the previous paragraphs.

§3. Objective Scope of Application of the LCSP

488. The classification of the contracts into which the public bodies that belong to the subjective scope of application of LCSP, taking into account both the LCSP and the European Directive 2004/18, is threefold:

1. Typical contracts.
2. Contracts with harmonized regulation (SARA contracts).
3. Administrative contracts and private contracts.

I. Typical Contracts

489. Contracts under the traditional label of typical contracts refer to the common contracts entered into by public bodies. Therefore, these contracts are expressly defined and regulated. A new modality of contracts has been added to the classical ones, the so-called contract of collaboration between public and private sector.

The main features of these typical contracts are:

1. Contracts of work. Their object is a work or one of the activities listed in Annex I LCSP, as well as the undertaking by any means of a work aimed at satisfying the necessities of the contracting public body. It may include the project definition description. 'Work' is legally defined as the result of a series of construction or engineering tasks on immovable assets aimed to fulfil an economic or a technical function.
2. Contracts of government franchises over public works. The goal of these contracts is that the franchisee carries out some of the activities that constitute the object of the contract of work, including reparation and restoration of existing constructions as well as maintenance. Counter-performance must consist only in the exploitation of the work or additionally in the franchisee receiving additionally a sum of money.
3. Contracts of concession of services. This category includes contracts through which a public body entrusts the management of public services of its competence to a private individual (or a company). This category neither includes situations where the management of such services is run through public bodies specifically created for these purposes nor where a private company provides the service where a public body is the sole shareholder of it. Within this category (contracts of public services management), four different ways of passing the contract can be distinguished:
   - Concession: the contractor entirely assumes the risk derived from the management of the public services provided.

- Shared management: the public body and the contractor share the results derived from the management of the service in the proportions established in the contract.
- Agreement: the management of the service is entrusted to a person or a company who carries out a similar professional activity to the service intended to be provided.
- Company of mixed capital: the public body is one of the shareholders in the company together with private persons or companies. The public body must not be the sole shareholder.

4. Contracts of services: Their object is the development of an activity or the achievement of a result different from a work or a supply.
5. Contracts of supply: Their object is the acquisition, the leasing, the lease or lease purchase, of any products and movables but incorporeal property and marketable securities. The latter are ruled by the specific public legislation.

II. Contracts with Harmonized Regulation (SARA Contracts)

490. Within the category of typical administrative contracts, a distinction is drawn depending on the contract being subject to a harmonized regulation. The aim is that these contracts are directly governed by European legislation on administrative contracts, namely Directives 2004/18/CE, 89/665/CEE and 2007/66/CE. Contracts are thus under a reinforced guarantee of publicity, equality and concurrence. SARA contracts include (Article 19 LCSP):

1. cooperation contracts between private and public sector;
2. contracts of work, concession of public works, supply and services provided that their price reaches the amount established by Article 20 LCSP;
3. subsidized contracts of work and services covered, because of the payable price, by Directive 2004/18.

III. Administrative Contracts and Private Contracts

491. This is a classical distinction in Spanish law, although the LCSP has introduced some changes. The aforementioned typical contracts are administrative contracts, so that this category embraces works, concession of public works, public services management, supply (except for subscription to publications and databases), services (except for financial services and literary and artistic creation and interpretation and performances), as well as cooperation contracts between private and public sector. An additional requirement is however essential: they must be concluded by a public administration *strictu senso.*

As far as they are concluded by a public administration *strictu senso*, other contracts are qualified as administrative contracts, namely those which are not typical contacts but they concern the specific activity of the contracting administration, since such contracts directly or immediately satisfy a public goal within their competence or because it is established by law (Article 19.1 LCSP). These contracts have been traditionally termed as special administrative contracts.

By contrast, the following contracts are private contracts:

1. Contracts concluded by public sector agencies and entities which are not a Public Administration.
2. Contracts of financial services (insurance, banking and investment services), contracts related to artistic and literary creation and performance as well as those related to entertainment, subscription to magazines, periodicals and databases, even if such contracts are concluded by public administrations *strictu senso*.

The distinction between administrative contracts and private contracts is crucial in order to determine the legal regime of contracts concluded by public bodies. Preparation, adjudication, execution and extinction of administrative contract are governed by the specific administrative legislation,whilst private law is applied only as default rules. These different regimes have an important consequence: the determination of the appropriate court empowered to deal with conflicts arising from contracts concluded by public bodies. Thus, administrative courts are empowered to intervene where the contract is an administrative contract.

By contrast, the LCSP applies to private contracts in relation to their preparation and adjudication, whilst execution and extinction are governed by private law, either civil law or commercial law. Such a different legal regime has no absolute effect as for the determination of the competent court. It is true that as a general rule administrative courts are empowered to intervene where the conflict arises from the drafting and granting stages, whereas civil courts must deal with conflicts appearing when executing or terminating the contract. Nevertheless, where the private contract has been concluded by a body belonging to the public sector that yet cannot be deemed to be public administration *strictu senso*, any case irrespective of the stage at stake is decided by the civil courts.

Chapter 12. Contract of Civil Partnership

§1. Basic Features of Partnership

492. A partnership is an agreement whereby two or more persons agree to put money, property or labour in common, with a view to sharing the benefit which may result therefrom (Article 1665 CC). The contract of partnership is consensual, but it has some peculiar features. It is not based on an antagonism of interests, since a common purpose is pursued. Therefore, it may be qualified as an associative contract, because the basic feature is the cooperation of the partners in order to achieve the common purpose. Besides, it establishes a steady organization; some regulation is needed for this cooperation and for the property or for the skills. Hence, if one of the partners does not perform for the cooperation, the rest are allowed to dissolve the partnership (Article 1707 CC).

493. The essence of partnership is the pooling of resources in the pursuit of the common purpose. The partners' contribution may consist only of their labour or skills. Nevertheless, some kind of common property – notwithstanding its importance – is required by case law. Hence, according to case law, partnership is qualified by a common patrimony, a common purpose and the existence of *affectio societatis* or *animus contrahendi societatis*.[533] Contributions in assets may consist of either transferring ownership or only the use of them in favour of the partnership. Transferring ownership requires capacity of disposal. Contributions are subject to the rules on eviction (Article 1681 CC).

Partnership also has a personal character. Consequently, neither shares nor the quality of partner may be assigned, unless all the partners agree on the assignment (Article 1696 CC).

The common purpose consists of sharing benefits. Thus, the cooperation of the partners is aimed at obtaining benefits; otherwise, the parties' intention was to create an association. All the partners must share benefits. A partnership in which one or more partners share in only the loss and not at all in the benefits is void (*societas leonina*). Only the partner who exclusively contributes with his/her labour can be excluded from sharing in the loss (Article 1691 CC).

§2. Legal Personality of Partnership

494. Article 1669 CC establishes that partnerships whose stipulations are kept secret do not have legal personality. *A contrario sensu*, if stipulations are not secret and partners act in the name of the partnership, legal personality is granted. But the law does not state that the society without legal personality is void; rather, the rules on joint ownership become applicable (*irregular partnership*). Thus, the publicity of the partnership becomes essential. One resolution of the *Dirección General de Registros y del Notariado* (which does not constitute case law, but decides on

533. TS 19 Dec. 2007 (RJ 2007/9046), 25 Oct. 1999 (RJ 1999/7624), 14 Apr. 1998 (RJ 1998/2320).

administrative matters derived from registration) required the registration of the partnership in the Commercial Register.[534] The resolution deserved much criticism and contradicted the case law of the Supreme Court.[535] The very *Dirección General* has changed later its mind, so that registration is not a requirement for the legal personality of partnership.[536]

Article 1670 CC states that civil partnership may adopt any form of corporation and consequently the CCom applies to it. In addition, the partnership must carry out commercial acts. The point has important practical consequences, since the liability of partners is always unlimited.

§3. The Contract of Civil Partnership

495. The object of the partnership must be lawful, otherwise it is dissolved and any benefit must be given to charity (Article 1666 CC). However, the partnership may be universal or particular (Articles 1671 et seq. CC).

The contract whereby the partnership is constituted is informal. Nevertheless, a public deed is required when the partners contribute immovables or real rights (Article 1667 CC). If the formal requirement is not fulfilled, the contract is however not void as among the partners.[537]

496. Partners are obligated to contribute money, property labour or their skills. Performance of such obligation does not affect the conclusion of the contract (as stated above, the contract is consensual). If the partner was obligated to contribute money, the delay in performing makes him/her liable for interest and for any damage caused to the partnership (Article 1682.1 CC).

The same partners may agree on how to manage the partnership. Thus, they can confer the management on one or more of the partners and even specify their respective tasks. If they do not stipulate anything, all the partners take equal part in the management and all of them can act for the partnership (Articles 1694, 1695 CC). The administrator partner or partners may be appointed in the same contract of partnership; in this case, their power of attorney is irrevocable (Article 1695 CC). If the administrator is appointed after the conclusion of the contract, unanimity of the partners is required; if two or more are appointed, each one has the authority to act, unless otherwise agreed (Articles 1693, 1694 CC).

§4. The Partnership and Third Parties

497. The partnership is liable against third parties when partners act in such condition and within the terms of the mandate. When partners act in their own name,

534. Resolution of 31 May 1997 (RJ 1997/2049), followed by resolution of 11 Dec. 1997 (RJ 1997/8822).
535. TS 31 May 1994 (RJ 1994/3768).
536. Resolution of 14 Feb. 2001 (RJ 2002/2154).
537. *See* TS 17 Jul. 1996 (RJ 1996/5724), 9 Oct. 1995 (RJ 1995/7026).

the partnership is not liable, unless it has benefited from this (Articles 1697, 1698.2 CC). As the partnership has legal personality, partners become vicariously liable for its debts. The partner's liability is not solidary; rather, partners are liable pro rata *parte*.

§5. The Extinction of the Partnership

498. If the contract is concluded for a determined period of time, partnership extinguishes when the *dies* arrives (Article 1700.1 CC). Nevertheless, partners may agree even tacitly on the extension of the partnership's activity (Article 1702 CC). But, according to Article 1703 CC, if the consent is expressed after the expiry of the period, a new contract is concluded.

If the common purpose is attained, partnership also extinguishes (Article 1700.2 CC). The same happens when the purpose becomes impossible to attain.[538] The loss of the partnership's property as well as the property due by one of the partners extinguishes the partnership (Articles 1702.1, 1701 CC) when it makes the attainment of the purpose impossible.

As the contract is *intuitu personae*, the death of one of the partners leads the partnership to extinction, unless the continuity with the rest of the partners or with the heirs of the dead partner was stipulated (Articles 1700.3, 1704 CC). If one of the partners becomes bankrupt, the partnership extinguishes too.

Finally, partnership may be extinguished by the will of one of the partners (Article 1700.4 CC) when it was concluded for an undetermined period. Notice must be given opportunely and according to good faith to the other partners (Articles 1705, 1706 CC). If the partnership was concluded for a determined period, the partner who wants to put an end to the *societas* must allege a 'good reason' (Article 1707 CC).

However, extinction is not immediate. A liquidation period begins whereby the partnership still has legal personality. Debts have to be paid and the remainder of the assets of the partnership have to be divided. The rules on hereditary partition apply (Article 1708 CC).

538. TS 29 Nov. 2007 (RJ 2007/8453).

Chapter 13. Quasi-Contracts

499. Article 1089 CC mentions quasi-contracts among the sources of obligations.[539] This concept is defined in Article 1887 CC, which begins a title (XVI, Book IV) on 'obligations contracted without an agreement'. According to this principle, *quasi-contracts are lawful and merely voluntary acts whereby a person contracts an obligation towards a third party, and sometimes, give rise to a reciprocal obligation between the interested parties.* Under this category, the Civil Code only regulates two concepts: *negotiorum gestio* (Articles 1888–1894) and *undue collection* (Articles 1895–1901). It does not include any express regulation of unjustified enrichment (developed by case law).

The maintenance of quasi-contracts in the Civil Code is due to a highly controversial historical tradition. This concept stems from the inception of the post-classic Roman law (Justinian's *Instituta*) through the specification of Gaius' residual category (*ex variis causarum figures* obligations). The CC, along the lines of the French model, kept this category, which was not included in the Spanish historic tradition – the *Partidas*, in the thirteenth century, envisaged each case individually, with no common features. Thus, the Spanish doctrine conceives quasi-contracts as the result of an 'historical mistake', as a useless theoretical instrument without any normative content. This criticism extends to the legal definition for a number of reasons: literally, it could be applied to other human conducts different from the two cases foreseen as sources of quasi-contractual obligations. In addition, those two cases (*negotiorum gestio* and 'undue collection') do not fit in this legal definition either (in spite of this, they have to be 'lawful acts'; 'undue collection' in bad faith is also included).

Based on this criticism, the doctrine proposes unanimously to abandon quasi-contracts and to allocate the rules governing the management of another's affair and 'undue collection' in a different place, along the lines of the Law of Navarre, which regulates both concepts (*leyes* 560–561 and 508–509 Comp. Nav., respectively), together with mandate and unjust enrichment. Moreover, it would also be possible to regulate the latter jointly with payment or performance of obligations.[540] However, in order to provide some usefulness to the concept of quasi-contract, the possible existence of 'innominate'[541] quasi-contracts has been proposed for unregulated cases of restitution obligations similar to contracts. This proposal has been rejected by the Spanish doctrine, since unjust enrichment can be applied to such cases.

---

539. The introduction and §§1 and 3 have been written by Sergio Cámara Lapuente (University of La Rioja, Spain).

540. In spite of these proposals, almost without exception (only Luis Puig Ferriol et al., *Manual de Derecho Civil*, Vol. II, 3rd edn (Madrid, 2000), 222–233), all modern Spanish textbooks still devote a section to quasi-contracts.

541. Vaguely admitted by TS 8 Jan. 1909 and 21 Jun. 1945. On this issue, *see* Gregorio Ortega Pardo, 'Cuasicontratos atípicos', ADC (1948): 408.

§1. *Negotiorum Gestio*

I. Concept

500. *Negotiorum gestio* or management of another's affairs is regulated in Spain both in the Civil Code (Articles 1888–1894) and in the Law of Navarre (*leyes* 560–561 Comp. Nav.). Both sets of rules stem through the Roman law (and are similar to each other), but their different locations reflect the two historical and methodological approaches to this concept. In the Civil Code, *negotiorum gestio* is included among quasi-contracts (Articles 1888 and 1089 CC), according to the criticized classification by Gaius, while in Navarre it is located along with the mandate, rejecting the existence of quasi-contracts as a late and useless misconstruction of Roman sources.

Negotiorum gestio is legally admitted as an exceptional arrangement, since it is at odds with the principle that nobody can interfere in another's affairs or 'contract on behalf of someone else without his/her authorization or without being his/her legal agent' (Article 1259 CC). This management involves spontaneous acts of the manager or the agent, (*gestor*) on behalf and in the interest of the affair's titleholder 'without a mandate' (Article 1888 CC) or an obligation to do so in order to obtain a favourable result for the principal or *dominus negotii*. TS 2 February 1954[542] stated that:

> the acts performed to this aim [management] involving goods abandoned de facto must be spontaneous and without a mandate or knowledge on the part of the owner, thus without his express or tacit authorization or opposition, selfless but without the aim of acting in a merely liberal way, and should not be driven by the covetousness of profit either.

501. The similarity with the mandate has traditionally justified the quasi-contractual nature of *negotiorum gestio*. In both cases, the acts of the agent are in the interest of someone else and have an impact on his/her patrimonial sphere. Nevertheless, the last concept does not involve a contract between principal and manager; moreover, the manager is bound by mere management (Article 1888 CC), whereas for the obligations of the *dominus* to arise some additional requirements must be met (Articles 1892 and 1893 CC).

The Spanish doctrine qualifies *negotiorum gestio* as a unitary concept, although the requirements for the claim of the principal against the manager (*actio negotiorum gestorum directa*), and for the claim of the manager against the principal (*actio negotiorum gestorum contraria*) are different. However, case law has been much more generous in the recognition of the *actio directa* of the principal than in the acceptance of the *actio contraria*, especially regarding the expenses and damages suffered by the manager and the relationships of the principal with third parties.

502. Although there is not much case law, some typical examples supporting the interference based on altruism or social solidarity are the reparation of a rundown

542. RJ 1954/322.

building where the owner is absent or giving medical assistance to an injured or an ill person. Courts have also qualified some cases as management of another's affairs with specific rules, such as the payment on behalf of a third party (Articles 1158 and 1210 CC).[543] Some other typical cases of Roman law (*indefensus*, absent) are currently covered by specific provisions (e.g., Articles 305, 181 et seq. CC), but the flexibility of this concept also allows the inclusion of new cases.

II. Requirements

503. These are the defining features of *negotiorum gestio* that cause the appearance of the relationships between the manager and the principal:

1. *Acts of management* aimed at preserving or managing the patrimony of the *dominus*, or at avoiding his/her personal damage or damage to his/her rights. These acts must be lawful (Article 1887 CC). The Supreme Court has highlighted that 'the term "management" must be understood in the wide sense of an operation, administration, disposition or possession, since it includes legal acts, purely economic acts and even simply material acts'.[544]
2. *Negotium alienum*. Management must be related to business issues or to another's affairs. There must be an actual (lawful) interference in someone else's sphere. There is no *negotiorum gestio* if there are (indirect) profits for a third party as a consequence of the management on one's behalf, that is to say, where the affairs of the agent are concerned.[545] Nevertheless, case law also applies the rules on *negotiorum gestio* in cases of a common affair, that is, where it is in the manager's personal interest as well as someone else's. For example, joint owners,[546] joint heirs,[547] or even claims for economic compensation between unmarried couples[548] or in de facto societies or societies without a legal status.[549] Therefore, as it was the case in Roman law, there is a *negotiorum gestio* where the affair is *alienum et suum*, but not where it is *suum tantum*.[550] Thus, the Civil Code does not forbid the concurrence of interests; rather, it prevents the manager from giving priority to his/her own profit instead of another's profit (*see* Article 1891 CC).
3. *Animus aliena negotia gerendi*. Although this requirement is not mentioned by the Civil Code, for a long time, (old) doctrine and case law opted for the

543. TS 27 Jun. 1925, 29 May 1984 (RJ 1984/2804), 16 Dec. 1985 (RJ 1985/6443), 25 Jun. 1992 (RJ 1992/5474). The reason is to avoid subrogation of the third party who pays and only to grant him/her a claim for compensation.
544. TS 16 Oct. 1978 (RJ 1978/3076).
545. TS 15 Jun. 1929 (profit for another's product when marketing one's own brand), and 16 Jul. 1990 (RJ 1990/5883) (lack of compensation for the expenses of an electricity company administratively obliged to change the wiring on behalf of third parties).
546. TS 22 Feb. 1994 (RJ 1994/1252), to avoid auctions and seizures of common assets.
547. TS 3 Jan. 1962 (RJ 1962/1962).
548. TS 27 May 1994 (RJ 1994/3753).
549. TS 29 Jul. 1993 (RJ 1993/6495). But, against, TS 12 Nov. 1992 (RJ 1992/9584).
550. Reinhard Zimmermann, *The Law of Obligations. Roman Foundations of the Civilian Tradition* (Oxford, 1996), 433.

requirement of the *intention* to manage altruistically another's affair, in a subjective way. Conversely, in modern times, this requirement is understood as the awareness to act on someone else's behalf with the intention to provide him/her with the effects of the management, assuming that such an *animus* is in good faith, at least in cases where the affair is completely alien. In any case, the *animus depraedandi*, the covetous intention, excludes the application of these rules with an underlying selfless, altruistic and beneficial aim. It must be taken into account that altruism refers to the management, and not to the derived expenses or damages (ex Article 1893 CC; *ley* 560 Comp. Nav.), since the lack of interest does not imply a merely liberal act (gift) as the Law of Navarre provides explicitly.

4. *Absentia domini*. Case law requires that the object of the management must be '*abandoned*, either by absence or negligence or by illness or incapacity'.[551] The management carried out in contravention of the express prohibition of the principal *prohibente domino* does not give rise to his/her liability; rather, this is an intolerable interference, except in a few legal cases (maintenance). Whether this unlawful conduct can support a claim for unjustified enrichment of the manager is still argued; however, it seems less arguable to compensate the damage through the profits derived from the management.[552] If the *dominus* is aware of the management intention of the agent and does not oppose it, there would be a tacit mandate or ratification.
5. *Voluntary or spontaneous management*. It does not apply where the management is the consequence of a legal rule or a contract between the manager and the interest holder.[553] This is why the Civil Code describes this phenomenon as 'the person who voluntarily deals with the management or administration of another's affairs, without his/her mandate' (Article 1888 CC). However, if the scope of the mandate or the contract is surpassed, there would be a *negotiorum gestio*.
6. *Utiliter*. The requirement of usefulness of the management for the *dominus* is essential, both to limit the interference in another's affairs and to control the abuses of managers. Nevertheless, rather than a general requirement of *negotiorum gestio*, this is a prerequisite for the success of the *actio contraria* of the manager to recoup the expenses and make up for the damage suffered as a consequence of his/her acts.[554] The Civil Code, unlike Roman law – where the verification of usefulness at the beginning of the management *utiliter coeptum*, though fruitless, was enough – includes in its Article 1893 the criterion that the manager must provide the owner with effective advantages. The useful initial undertaking or the diligence in the management does not suffice, except in the exceptional case provided in Article 1893-2 CC (*see below* IV. A. c), since in order to bind the principal, the management must involve urgent and necessary acts, and generate 'advantages' *utiliter gestum* for him/her and, besides, he/she

551. TS 26 Apr. 1956 (RJ 1956/1948), 2 Feb. 1954. Against, TS 14 Dec. 1916.
552. Díez-Picazo & Gullón, *Sistema*, II, 501.
553. TS 26 Nov. 1926 (misconstruction of a contract that did not impose any obligation on this regard, as the manager intended), 14 Mar. 1986 (RJ 1986/1251) (the one held under an oral contract is not a 'voluntary' management). *See also* TS 9 Mar. 2006 (RJ 2006/1071).
554. M. Elena Sánchez Jordán, *La gestión de negocios ajenos* (Madrid, 2000), 197–200, 211 et seq.

must 'take advantage of them' in an effective way. Unlike the CC, the Law of Navarre has preserved the Roman solution of the 'initial usefulness' (to compensate the manager 'even if the desired result is not obtained', *ley* 560 Comp. Nav.).

III. Obligations of the Manager (*Actio Directa*)

504. The manager must continue his/her management until the completion of the affair including its incidences or ask the interested party for his/her substitution in the management if the latter is in a position to do it on his/her own (Article 1888 CC).[555] This is an alternative requirement (unlike the BGB, which imposes a prompt notification) aimed at avoiding damages caused by a capricious interruption of an initially voluntary act, and thus it is more severe than in the mandate's regime (*see* Article 1736 CC). A notification is needed to end the management (*see* Article 1133 CC); in order to end it validly, a statement of will has to be received by the addressee. If the *gestor* continues his/her management afterwards, a tacit mandate may be inferred, except during the time necessary for the *dominus* to reasonably take care of the matter (*see* Article 1737 CC).

505. Liability. The manager must '*compensate* the owner of the assets or affairs managed for the damages caused by him/her or by a negligence on his/her part' (Article 1889 CC). To this aim, this requirement imposes an average level of diligence, that of an ordinary person. Roman law is in this way lessened, since an obligation of *diligentia exactissima* was imposed on the agent; to prevent making the manager a victim of his/her benevolence, it is necessary to take into account the kinship and the friendship, the difficulties involved in the issue and other circumstances. Consequently, Article 1889 CC allows the courts to moderate the amount of the compensation according to the particular circumstances of the case.

Therefore, the manager is not obliged to act as the interest holder would do, but simply as a diligent *dominus* (abstract standard). By contrast, his/her liability is exceptionally aggravated embracing fortuitous cases (unlike the case of the mandatary: Article 1726 CC) 'where he/she undertakes risky operations that the owner does not usually carry out, or when he/she puts his/her own interest before the interest of the owner'.

If the manager delegates his/her mandate to someone else, and this is a licit action, 'he/she would be responsible for the acts of his/her delegate, notwithstanding the direct obligation of the latter to the owner of the affair' (Article 1890 CC). This rule reverses the one that Article 1721 CC establishes for mandate, because of the non-contractual character of the management. In case of two or more substitutes, their liability is solidary (Article 1890-2 CC versus 1723 and 1138 CC).

506. Reports, accountability and delivery of the result of the management to the principal. These obligations are not provided in the Civil Code (unlike in Navarre,

555. TS 2 Feb. 1954 applied this rule to avoid damages to the interests of an incapable person whose patrimony had been managed for a long time by a voluntary agent.

ley 560 Comp. Nav.), but have been repeatedly laid down by case law,[556] on the basis of analogy with mandate (Article 1720 CC). Indeed, the Supreme Court imposes this obligation in an autonomous way, irrespective of the title on which the management of another's affairs could be based,[557] as an essential element to clarify the responsibility of the manager. The Spanish doctrine also considers, using the same argument (*see* Article 1721 CC), that the manager must pay legal interests for his/her debts.

507. Connections to third parties. The manager would be liable to third parties if he/she entered into a contract on his/her own behalf (even if it was ratified). If he/she concluded the contract on someone else's behalf, he/she would also be bound if the obligations cannot be ascribed to the principal under Articles 1892 and 1893 CC (no representative effect).

IV. Obligations of the Principal or *Dominus* (*Actio Contraria*)

A. *Emergence of the Obligations*

508. The Civil Code establishes the obligations of the principal according to whether he/she has ratified or not the management; moreover, if not ratified, further obligations may arise for the *dominus* in two different situations:

1. '*The ratification* of the management by the interest holder produces the same effects of the express mandate' (Article 1892 CC). The ratification of the acts of the agent changes his/her *status* and liability, as the rules on mandate apply (Articles 1718–1726 CC). The Supreme Court and most of the doctrine consider that the rules on mandate are retrospectively applied from the beginning of the management,[558] unless otherwise provided in the ratification, and specifically in relation to the rights of the bona fide third parties. The ratification can be either express or tacit; but it must not be confused with the 'exploitation of the advantages' by the *dominus*, in spite of the ambiguous contradiction of Articles 1892 and 1893 CC, since the identification[559] would make null the management of another's affairs as a source of obligations: if there is ratification, the principal is bound by it and not by the mere acts of the manager.
2. If there is no ratification but the principal exploits the advantages stemming from the management, the *dominus* will be also bound by the effects of the useful or advantageous management. The usefulness is approached as the final result obtained by the principal (and not only by the *utiliter coeptum*), as explained before (II. 6, paragraph 503).

556. TS 16 Oct. 1978 (RJ 1978/3076), 17 Mar. 1950 (RJ 1950/387).
557. TS 16 Dec. 1985 (RJ 1985/6444), 17 Jan. 1975 (RJ 1975/16), 14 May 1965 (RJ 1965/2597).
558. TS 20 Mar. 1991 (RJ 1991/2421), 5 Apr. 1950 (RJ 1950/990), 7 Jul. 1944 (RJ 1944/908).
559. TS 14 May 1991 (RJ 1991/3672).

3. If there is no ratification or usefulness, exceptionally, the owner will be also bound 'if the management was aimed at avoiding an imminent and manifest damage' (Article 1893 CC). As an exceptional case, in urgent situations, the legislator assesses the means and the efforts of the manager to bind the principal. This is an isolated case where the criterion of the *utiliter coeptum* is accepted for cases such as the repair of broken doors to avoid thefts in the house of an absent owner or the medical assistance in cases of risks to life. Therefore, except for this particular situation, in the rest of the cases, the absence of ratification or usefulness effectively exploited by the principal[560] does not produce the binding effects discussed below.

B. Content of the Obligations

509. Within the internal sphere (*actio contraria*), the *dominus* 'shall compensate the manager for the necessary and useful *expenses* incurred and for the *damages* suffered in the performance of his mandate'[561] (Article 1893-1 CC). In the Law of Navarre, the principal must compensate for *all* expenses incurred by the manager and not only for the useful ones (*ley* 560 Comp. Nav.). If the *dominus* refuses to pay these amounts, he/she must prove that the manager acted with an *animus donandi*, since it is presumed that he/she lacked this intention.[562]

The controversial question is whether the principal must pay a *fee* to the spontaneous agent where the management is related to services covered by his/her profession. Since there is no legal provision to this issue, several authors advocate in favour of this remuneration for professionals by analogy with the mandate (Article 1711 CC). This solution would try to avoid the eventual inhibition of such people – seen as socially efficient – and the discrimination in two similar cases, namely, professionals (i.e., a doctor or a locksmith) whose services are requested by the manager and professionals who act on their own.[563] Other interpretations deny this remuneration, particularly to avoid the 'covetousness of profit' (*Partidas*, 5.12.29 (thirteenth century)),[564] and admit, at the most, the claim for damages suffered (as a loss of salary) as damages capable of compensation.

510. If the management has external effects, that is, where the manager contracts the services of third parties on behalf of the principal, the effects of the representation without the power of attorney arise. There are two different situations in this regard:

560. TS 22 May 2000 (RJ 2000/4815), 23 Jul. 1999 (RJ 1999/6355).

561. This compensation stemming from the *actio contraria* was recognized in TS 18 Jan. 1908, 2 Oct. 1929, and 3 Jan. 1962 (RJ 1962/1962).

562. TS 2 Feb. 1954. Also in *ley* 560 Comp. Nav.

563. Sánchez Jordán, *La gestión*, 550 et seq.

564. M.A. Parra Lucán, *Loscuasicontratos*, in Carlos Martínez de Aguirre, *Curso de Derecho Civil (II) Derecho de obligaciones* (Madrid, 2000), 769.

1. If the manager contracts on behalf of the *dominus* and the management is useful or ratified, the principal is bound to the third party and the latter cannot claim against the manager.[565]
2. If the manager acts on his/her own behalf, he/she will be the only person bound to third parties.

Exceptionally, the principal will also be bound in three cases: if there is ratification, if the management is useful (or necessary due to its urgency, Article 1893 CC) or if the issue objectively falls on the *dominus*' own affairs (ex Article 1717.2 CC).

V. Special Management: Maintenance and Funerals

511. Article 1894 CC regulates two particular cases of *negotiorum gestio*. On the one hand, the provision of *maintenance* (a rule stemming from *Partidas* 5.12.35-37), according to which where a person different from the one legally bound to this provision carries it out, he/she will be entitled to claim damages against the person legally bound to maintenance, unless he/she has provided it for mercy and without the aim of claiming it. On the other hand, *funerary expenses* (a rule stemming from the Roman *actio funeraria*), 'provided for the deceased and according to the customs of the place shall be paid by those obliged to support him when he/she was alive, even though the deceased had no more property'.

§2. Unjust Enrichment

I. A Principle in Search of a Legal Provision

512. The doctrine of unjustified enrichment is in Spain a creation of nineteenth-century case law. The *Tribunal Supremo* settled, as a legal principle rooted in *Partidas* 7.34.17, the prohibition of unjust enrichment, and granted the plaintiff a *condictio sine causa generalis*. The invocation of a legal principle may be attributed to the lack of a provision in the CC expressly dealing with the subject, except Article 10.9.3 CC, which is a private international law rule on conflict of laws introduced anew in 1974. However, such a foundation is unconvincing. First of all, as mentioned above,[566] the Spanish system is one of rule of law, not of case law. Second, not every enrichment must be restituted, because then the whole economic system of free market would collapse.[567]

It has been pointed out that until the 1940s, Spanish case law referred to *enriquecimiento injusto* (unjust enrichment), but as a consequence of quite an influential book published in 1934,[568] enrichment appears to have been linked to the concept of *cause* (*enriquecimiento sin causa*, enrichment without a legal ground). Hence, a

565. TS of 9 Feb. 1957 (RJ 1957/701).
566. General Introduction, Ch. 4.
567. TS 8 Jul. 2003 (RJ 2003/4334).
568. Rafael Núñez Lagos, *El enriquecimiento sin causa en el derecho español* (Madrid, 1934).

legal foundation for the *condictio* has been found in Article 1901 CC. In Spanish law, every contract and every patrimonial transmission requires a *cause*[569] (*see* above paragraphs 62 and 63). Article 1901 allows the recipient to retain the transferred benefit if he/she manages to prove that the transfer had a *causa justa* (legal ground). *Causa justa* can either be a valid contract or a legal provision. Hence, if such *causa justa* does not exist, the *tradens* is entitled to claim restitution. A *condictio sine causa generalis* is thus deduced from that provision. The *tradens* can claim restitution by means of an action of unjustified enrichment if the *accipiens* lacks a legal ground (*causa*) to retain the transferred benefit.

II. The Requirements for the *Condictio*

513. According to case law, the requirements for the *condictio* are the enrichment of the defendant, the impoverishment of the plaintiff, the causal relationship between enrichment and impoverishment, and the lack of legal ground for the transfer.[570]

The *accipiens* is enriched because an economic benefit increases his/her patrimony (*lucrum emergens*: the acquisition of a right, the possession of an asset, improvements), or because he/she does not suffer a diminution of his/her patrimony (*damnum cessans*: extinguishment of a debt or of a charge, use of a good belonging to the plaintiff). The *condictio* does not depend on the fault or on the good or bad faith of the *accipiens*,[571] although some of the consequences may be determined by his/her good or bad faith.

514. Enrichment has to be at the expense of another person, who suffers a correlative loss in his/her patrimony in the sense that the benefit should have accrued to him/her. The impoverished person is the only one entitled to claim restitution. Nevertheless, the action fails if the impoverishment is due to an unlawful act of the plaintiff: for example, the grandmother who has refused to deliver the grandchildren to their father, divorced from her daughter, cannot resort to the *condictio* to claim the maintenance costs.[572]

515. Between enrichment and impoverishment, there must be a causal relationship. The impoverishment of the *tradens* has to be a consequence of the enrichment of the *accipiens*, so that the value of that impoverishment can be identified in the recipient's patrimony.

516. Last, the patrimonial transfer must lack any legal ground (cause). Only if the enrichment is unjustified can the *tradens* resort to the *condictio*. Legal ground,

569. José Antonio Álvarez Caperochipi, *El enriquecimiento sin causa*, 3rd edn (Granada, 1993), 127 et seq.

570. TS 29 Oct. 2003 (RJ 2003/7952), 31 Oct. 2001 (RJ 2001/9639).

571. TS 23 Oct. 2003 (RJ 2003/7764).

572. Díez-Picazo & Gullón, *Sistema*, II, 526. TS 30 Mar. 2007 (RJ 2007/1758) recalls that the unjust enrichment claim requires that the claimant proves his/her impoverishment.

according to the judgment of 28 March 1990,[573] is any situation that allows the *accipiens* to retain the transferred benefit because of a valid juridical transaction between him/her and the *tradens*, or because a legal provision authorizes such consequence. Where a transfer is made consciously, the doctrine of unjust enrichment cannot be applied.[574]

517. Finally, it must be pointed out that the Supreme Court has recently insisted on the subsidiary character of the *condictio*. The claim for unjust enrichment can only be successful if the plaintiff cannot resort to any other remedy.[575]

III. Unjustified Enrichment and Tort

518. Recently, case law has distinguished the *condictio* in case of enrichment and the delictual action for damages. According to the decision of 25 April 2000,[576] there is no relationship between the claim for damages and the *condictio* for enrichment, because of its different character and aim. Whilst tort law seeks reparation of the damage and requires fault, unjustified enrichment seeks restitution and does not depend on fault. Concepts like causation and fault are alien to the law of unjustified enrichment. Besides, the respective periods of limitation are not the same (tort, one year, according to Article 1968.2 CC; unjustified enrichment, fifteen years, the general period of prescription laid down in Article 1964 CC). Nevertheless, it is possible that the same facts may satisfy the requirements of both actions; then the impoverished and damaged party may choose either remedy.[577]

IV. The Consequences of the *Condictio*

519. The *condictio* has a personal character. Its aim is the restitution of the value transferred without legal ground, but not exclusively the restitution of specific assets. In accordance with that character, as aforementioned, the limitation period of the *condictio* is fifteen years, the personal actions alike. The nature of the enrichment claim does not depend on the type of benefit conferred: it is a general action notwithstanding that money or services have been transferred.

The value that the plaintiff is entitled to claim for is limited at the same time by the enrichment of the defendant and his/her own impoverishment. Therefore, the plaintiff can claim neither more than the effective enrichment of the *accipiens* nor more than the own patrimonial loss. The plaintiff is not entitled to the surplus of enrichment in relation to the impoverishment suffered, because the *condictio* is not a claim for damages. In case of alienation of the benefit, the plaintiff is only obliged

573. RJ 1990/1736. *See also*, for example, TS 31 Dec. 2003 (TS 2004/368).
574. TS 23 Jul. 2010 (RJ 2010\6574).
575. TS 30 Apr. 2007 (RJ 2007/2396), 28 Feb. 2003 (RJ 2003/2723), 19 Feb. 1999 (RJ 1999/1055).
576. RJ 2000/3379. *See also* TS 28 Feb. 2007 (RJ 2007/1631).
577. Díez-Picazo & Gullón, *Sistema*, II, 528, give this example, taken of a judgment handed down by the Supreme Court on 12 Apr. 1955: the owner of a mine encroached on the land of a neighbour where another mine existed and dug minerals.

to restitution of the price he/she has obtained (Article 1897 CC *per analogiam*). Therefore, it has to be concluded that there is no obligation of restitution if the benefit does not remain in the defendant's patrimony.

520. The extension of the restitutionary claim depends on the subjective position of the recipient. The *mala fides* recipient deserves worse treatment, and therefore Articles 1896 and 1897 dealing with undue payment apply *per analogiam* (*see* paragraphs 523, 524).

V. Exploring the Boundaries: Unjustified Enrichment and Family Law

521. In the last years, the prohibition of any unjustified enrichment has found a new field of application: family law. Although most of the Spanish regions have recently legislated on unmarried cohabitation, the State still lacks any regulation. The Supreme Court has had to decide a series of cases based on the breach of the unmarried couple and the negative consequences borne by the member who stayed at home taking care of the family or cooperated with the partner's economic activity. Since the judgment of 11 December 1992,[578] the Supreme Court had resorted – although not exclusively – to the doctrine of unjustified enrichment. Case law required that one of the members of the couple had increased his/her patrimony while the other had not because of staying at home or helping his/her partner in his/her activity instead of being in a job.[579] According to the judgment of 27 March 2001,[580] the Supreme Court believed that the regional acts on unmarried cohabitation have followed this argumentation. What is true in any case is that the Catalan, the Aragonese and the Navarre Acts lay down an action to claim compensation for the imbalance of the patrimonies of the cohabitees that implies an unjustified enrichment. The Catalan provision (Article 13.2 of the 10/1998 Act), in which the other ones have inspired, found its precedent in Article 23 CDCC – as amended in 1993 – now Article 234-9 CCCat.[581] This provision tried to temper the consequences of the system of separation of properties – the legal system in Catalonia – in case of separation or divorce, entitling the impoverished spouse to claim compensation for his/her efforts for the family or for the activity of the spouse without receiving a market salary. The judgment of the High Court of Catalonia of 31 October 1998[582]

578. RJ 1992/9733. *See*, for example, TS 6 May 2011 (RJ 2011/3843).

579. Without obtaining a usual remuneration. *See* TS 6 Oct. 2006/RJ 2006/6650), 5 Feb. 2004 (RJ 2004/213), 17 Jun. 2003 (RJ 2003/4605).

580. RJ 2001/4770.

581. 'In cases of judicial separation, divorce or marriage annulment, the spouse who has worked for the household or for the other spouse without receiving any retribution or who has received an insufficient retribution shall be entitled to receive an economic compensation from the other spouse, in the event this fact has produced a situation of inequality between the two patrimonies, which in turn implies an unjust enrichment' (the translation is available at http://www.gencat.net/justicia/normes/angl/l9e.htm; I have only replaced 'unfair enrichment' with 'unjust enrichment', more suitable to the Catalan *injust*).

582. (1999) *RJC*, jurisprudència, 15. *See* now TSJ Catalonia 29 May 2007 (RJ 2007/4858), 10 Oct. 2006 (RJ 2007/5292).

pointed out that the foundation of the compensation laid down in the general principle of prohibition of unjustified enrichment, as expressed recognizes the new Article 41 FC. Nevertheless, the subsequent judgment of the High Court of 27 April 2000[583] denied any relationship between that compensation and unjustified enrichment. The Supreme Court tends to restrict the application of the rules on unjust enrichment, because the parties decided freely not to marry and the use of analogy with marriage is inappropriate, unless a disproportionate imbalance between the parties is caused by the extinction of the cohabitation.[584]

§3. Money Paid but Not Due

I. Concept and Regulation

522. The CC has kept the Roman features of the *condictio indebiti.* On the basis of the acknowledgement of this regime in the Middle Age (*Partidas*, 5.14.10, thirteenth century), the Civil Code regulates the *undue collection* as one of the nominate quasi-contracts in Articles 1895–1901. The definition of Article 1895 CC establishes that 'an obligation of restitution arises where something that a person is not entitled to and that has been given mistakenly is collected', provided – as Article 1901 CC specifies – that the delivery has not been made as an act of liberality or for other fair reason (i.e., a moral obligation). The legal name of 'undue collection', rather than the doctrinally widespread 'undue payment', tries to be consistent with the legal definition of quasi-contracts (Article 1887 CC: 'acts binding on the author', the *accipiens* in this case, i.e., to say, the person who receives the payment). However, this specification, from the point of view of the individual affected, is not really significant. The inclusion of bad faith acts of the *accipiens* in this arrangement is more questionable (Article 1896 CC), since quasi-contracts must stem from a 'lawful act'.

523. The obligation to return an undue payment is not technically considered in the Civil Code as an action of enrichment, but as an action of recovery of payments without a fair cause (*iusta causa*), along the lines of Roman law. In this way, the CC moves away from the contractual doctrine of payment as proposed by Savigny,[585] as well as from the *condictio indebiti* of the BGB as a means to correct the *accipiens* unjust enrichment. Instead, it comes generically closer to the conception of the *Code Napoléon.* Unlike the CC, the Law of Navarre regulates the different types of *condictiones* (including 'undue payment') as cases of unjust enrichment (*leyes* 508–509 Comp. Nav.). The legal framework is completed with the special regulation of 'undue collection' to protect the consumers found in Article 13.2 of the Act 7/1995 of 23 March, on consumer credit, whereby the malicious or negligent

583. RJ 2000/4125.

584. TS 6 Mar. 2014 (Roj: STS 976/2014), 28 Nov. 2011 (Roj: STS 8016/2011).

585. José Antonio Álvarez Caperochipi, Arts 1895–1901, in Miguel Pasquau, *Jurisprudencia civil comentada* (Granada, 2000), II, 3306.

undertaker who has caused such payment is punished through the imposition of a compensation of at least five points above the legal interest rate.

524. The most common cases of 'undue collection' are related to banking transfers to a wrong beneficiary or for a wrong amount.[586] The cases related to false cheques, 'undue collection' of retirement pensions or salaries, payments made by insurance companies without being covered by the policies, etc., are also relatively frequent.

II. Requirements

525. Doctrine and case law[587] establish the following three requirements to impose restitution:

A. Datio

526. The payer, *solvens*, must perform an effective act intending to satisfy an obligation (*solvendi causa*);[588] there is no obligation of restitution if payment is made for other reasons (i.e., *credendi causa*, which will give rise, in turn, to a case of unjust enrichment). Although the CC only mentions the collection of 'something' (a real and particular or fungible thing, such as money), according to Spanish historical tradition, it covers not only the *dare*, but also the acts/behaviours (*facere*) or defaults (*non facere*).

B. Indebitum

527. There is no binding obligation between payor and *accipiens*. This implies that there is no *causa* for the 'collection', and thus the *accipiens* cannot keep it. The doctrine includes three types of unclaimable debts:

1 *Indebitum ex causa*: where the debt never existed,[589] or was paid or expired.
2 *Indebitum ex persona* (*a parte creditoris* or *a parte debitoris*): where there is a debt, but not between the parties involved.[590]
3 *Indebitum ex re*: where payment differs from the debt (without being a *datio in solutum*) or there is an overpayment.[591]

586. For example, TS 14 Jun. 2007 (RJ 2007/5120), 13 Mar. 2007/RJ 2007/692), 10 Apr. 1995 (RJ 1995/3250), 29 Nov. 1991 (RJ 1991/8578), 10 Jul. 1990 (RJ 1990/5791).
587. For example, TS 10 Jun. 1995 (RJ 1995/4914).
588. TS 30 Jan. 1986 (RJ 1986/341), 7 Jul. 1950 (RJ 1950/1237).
589. TS 8 Jul. 1999 (RJ 1999/4765; payment of commissions for non-agreed services).
590. TS 20 Jul. 1995 (RJ 1995/5727), 17 Jul. 1995 (RJ 1995/5709), 12 Nov. 1993 (RJ 1993/8766; excess payment for an arithmetical mistake).
591. For example, 20 Apr. 1993 (RJ 1993/3105).

C. Error

528. Case law considers error as an essential requirement.[592] It implies a mistake on the existence of the debt (and not on other topics such as the solvency of the issuer of the payment),[593] which includes both the de facto and the *de iure* error, whether excusable or not. Otherwise, the *accipiens* would be wrongfully allowed to keep something that is not owed to him/her under the excuse that the *solvens* should have been more diligent.[594] The Civil Code only requires the payor's misconstruction.[595] The error on the part of the *accipiens* is not a prerequisite for the 'undue collection', since the CC distinguishes between the *accipiens* acting in good faith and in bad faith. By contrast, according to the Law of Navarre, both the *solvens* and the *accipiens* must make this error related to an undue obligation (*ley* 508.3). The mistake can be made by the payor in detriment of his/her patrimony or by his/her employees, responsible for a negligent material *datio*.[596]

In case of an *undue payment without error* – including the lack of evidence about the error – a strict application of the Civil Code would render restitution unenforceable, since if the payor is aware of the fact that he/she is not a debtor, he/she would be granting a gift.[597] However, the Supreme Court has recently held that in case of payments without fair cause (*iusta causa*; i.e., advances under a contract that has not been concluded, i.e., cancelled before coming into effect), there is an obligation to return the moneys received.[598] In this sense, the doctrine advocates the obligation to return, although not on the basis of Article 1895 CC, but as a consequence of a general action of unjustified enrichment (with a more disadvantageous regime to the *solvens*, who, nevertheless, is not unprotected). Besides, the doctrine agrees on putting the error of the *solvens* on the same footing as 'undue collections' driven by violence or coercion, in order to allow an action of return analogous to that established in Article 1895 CC.

Error must be *proved*. Given the difficulty of this proof, the Civil Code specifies some points on the burden of proof (Article 1900 CC) and some assumptions in order to facilitate it (Article 1901 CC). According to Article 1900 CC:

> the person alleging to have made the payment must prove it. Besides, he/she also has to prove the error made in paying,[599] unless the defendant denies having received the object of the claim. In this case, provided that the plaintiff justifies the delivery, he/she is exempted from any proof. This situation does not prevent the defendant from proving that the object allegedly received by him/her was owed to him/her.

592. TS 8 Nov. 2007 (RJ 2007/8459), 6 Mar. 2007 (RJ 2007/1533), 11 Dec. 2000 (RJ 2000/9889), 8 Jul. 1999 (RJ 1999/4765).
593. TS 12 Apr. 1989 (RJ 1989/3006).
594. TS 30 Jan. 1986 (RJ 1986/341).
595. TS 10 Jun. 1995 (RJ 1995/4914).
596. TS 26 Mar. 1986 (RJ 1986/1472), 25 May 1984 (RJ 1984/2546).
597. TS 30 Sep. 1987 (RJ 1987/6456).
598. TS 26 Dec. 1995 (RJ 1995/9207), 20 Apr. 1993 (RJ 1993/3105).
599. TS 11 Dec. 2000 (RJ 2000/9889).

Article 1901 CC establishes another presumption of error in favour of the *solvens*. The provision presumes that payment was mistakenly made where the payor delivered something that was never owed or that had already been paid; but the defendant may prove that delivery was made as an act of liberality or for another fair reason. Given the wide scope of this presumption, there is a risk of conflict between both articles, since the second (exception) might remove the requirement of the error (whose proof is the standard rule). The doctrine overcomes this contradiction and interprets that the legislator wanted to get the CC closer to other Latin Codes and established Article 1900 for cases of *indebitum ex persona a parte debitoris*, whereas Article 1901 was reserved for other cases (it suffices to prove that the object delivered was never owed or that the debt had already been paid; only the *animus donandi* could survive the delivery).

III. The Claim for Restitution

A. Nature and Subjects

529. The claim for restitution of an undue payment is personal, and thus its period of prescription is fifteen years.[600] This is a recovery action, different from *reivindicatio*. In this sense, the only person entitled to lodge such a claim is the *solvens*, who is not obliged to prove that he/she is the owner or the titleholder of the object claimed.[601] Moreover, restitution to the real owner does not free the *accipiens* from the obligation towards the *solvens*.[602] Of course, if the payor or the person who delivered the object involved (*solvens*) and its owner are not the same person, the latter is entitled, in turn, to sue the *accipiens* (*reivindicatio*). The person against whom the *condictio* of Article 1895 CC is aimed is the beneficiary of the object or the service. If they are several, liability will be solidary.[603]

B. Object

530. Although the claim always aims at the restitution of the object delivered, the Civil Code specifies some subsequent consequences distinguishing between the *accipiens* acting in bad faith (Article 1896) and in good faith (1897). The first case is closer to a compensation for damages (*tort*) than to unjust enrichment. Where the *accipiens* acts in bad faith[604] (i.e., if he/she is aware of the undue nature of the payment):

1. He/she must pay the legal interest, in the case of the moneys, or return the profits obtained or obtainable if the object received provides them. The payment of

600. The general period laid down in Art. 1964 CC. *See* TS 20 Apr. 1993 (RJ 1993/3105).
601. TS 28 May 1990 (RJ 1990/4091).
602. TS 7 Jul. 1950 (RJ 1950/1237).
603. TS 20 May 1956 (RJ 1956/3018).
604. Bad faith may be posterior. *See* TS 20 Jan. 2001 (RJ 2001/1324).

such an interest, as the doctrine has frequently criticized, is insufficient, since it can be lower than the value of the benefits obtained during the period of possession. In case of consumer credits (Article 13.2 Act on consumer credit) a higher legal interest is foreseen, at least five points above the legal interest.
2. Besides, he/she will also be held liable for losses or damages suffered for any reason by the object involved, including fortuitous cases, unless the latter 'would have affected the object in the same way as being on the payor's hands' (Article 1896.2 CC).
3. Finally, he/she will have to compensate for other damages caused to the *solvens*, until the restitution takes place (Article 1896.2).

531. As for the good faith *accipiens*, his/her responsibility is much more limited. Restitution concerns the object or the *tantundem*, in case of generic things or moneys, without being neither bound to return the benefits obtained nor liable for fortuitous cases, since he/she always thought he/she was its lawful owner. The CC qualifies these cases with the following three norms:

1. the good faith *accipiens* will be held liable only for the damages and losses suffered by the object he/she received and its accessions 'if he/she has benefited from them' (Article 1897 CC);
2. as for costs and improvements, he/she will be considered as a good faith holder (Articles 1898 and 453 et seq. CC); and
3. if he/she disposed of the object, 'he/she will have to return the price obtained or assign the action to make it effective' (Article 1897 CC).

IV. Exception from the Obligation to Restitute

532. According to Article 1899 CC:

> if a person, acting in good faith and believing that the payment is made to satisfy a lawful and existing credit, renders the title useless, or allows the action to prescribe, or abandons the pledges, or cancels the securities of his/her right, he/she would be prevented from restitution. The person who makes an undue payment can only lodge a claim against the actual debtor or the guarantors with regard to whom the action survives.

This provision, which stems from *Code Napoléon* (Article 1377), applies where a false debtor (*solvens*) makes a payment to a true creditor (*accipiens*), who believing that he/she is being paid by the actual debtor, acts in good faith in a way that hinders the collection of the credit. The article recognizes to the *solvens* the power to substitute the *accipiens* (whose credit is considered as satisfied) against the debtor third party.[605]

605. Concerning the requirements, *see* TS 28 Dec. 1999 (RJ 1999/9147).

V. Effects of Undue Payment in Relation to Third Party's Rights

533. There are two closely linked topics that have stirred up the main doctrinal controversy on undue payment: does such a payment imply the transfer of the property to the *accipiens*? The answer to a second question, that is, if the *accipiens* disposes of the object received in favour of a third party, does the latter acquire a full title in the object involved?, varies according to the answer to the former. The controversy springs from the succinct terms of Article 1897 CC, which establishes that if the beneficiary who wrongfully received the object has disposed of it, he/she will have to return the price obtained. The article keeps silent on the object or on the position of the third party who acquired it. The doubts arise only in case of particular objects, different from money, generic, fungible or unidentifiable objects, where the acquisition of the property by the *accipiens* and his/her obligation to return an equivalent asset are clear. Until the end of the 1950s, the Spanish doctrine understood that undue payment gave rise to the transfer of the property title, thus moving this type of quasi-contract from its position as a source of obligations to a de facto location among the ways of acquiring ownership. Nowadays, most of the authors hold the absence of transfer of the property, since the Spanish system is causalist, and requires for it both 'title' and 'mode' (*iusta causa* and delivery). The delivery of an undue thing lacks any *causa* and, thus, does not give rise to a transfer of property. The *accipiens* is only entitled to possession, recoupable by the *condictio indebiti* (as well as by the *reivindicatio*). Therefore, the personal character (not in rem) of the action does not conflict with it, since it is not aimed at recouping the property, but at the restitution of the object delivered. A different issue is that the *accipiens* may eventually acquire the property by an ordinary acquisitive prescription, within the legally required period, based on his good faith possession.

As for third parties that acquired from the *accipiens*, according to the majority opinion, they might only exceptionally acquire the property *a non domino*, on the basis of legal appearance (Article 464 CC, Article 34 LH), if they acted in good faith, and the disposal was onerous. In this case, the *accipiens* (provided that he/she also acted in good faith) will fulfil his/her obligations by returning the amount received (Article 1897 CC).

Selected Bibliography

§1. Overviews of Case Law

Pasquau Liaño, M. (dir.). *Jurisprudencia civil comentada.* 2nd edn. Granada: Comares, 2009.

§2. Books

I. Updated Basic General Handbooks

Albaladejo, M. *Derecho civil.* 5 vols. Madrid: Edisofer, 2004–2010.

Carrasco, A., *Derecho de contratos,* Cizur Menor: Thomson-Aranzadi, 2017.

Díez-Picazo, L. & A. Gullón Ballesteros. *Sistema de derecho civil.* 4 vols. Madrid: Tecnos, 2012.

Lacruz Berdejo, J.L., et al. *Elementos de derecho civil.* 8 vols. Madrid: Dykinson, 2010–2011.

Lasarte Álvarez, C. *Principios de derecho civil.* 7 vols. Madrid: Marcial Pons, 2013–2014.

Sjef van Erp, Antoni Vaquer (ed.). *Introduction to Spanish Patrimonial Law.* Granada: Comares, 2007.

II. Exegetical Commentaries on the Civil Code

Albaladejo, M. (dir.). *Comentarios al Código civil y Compilaciones Forales* (still in publication and reprint).

Cañizares Laso, A., P, de Pablo Contreras, J, Orduña Moreno & R, Valpuesta Fernández. (dir.). *Código Civil comentado.* Cizur Menor: Thomson-Civitas, 2n ed, 2015.

Domínguez Luelmo, A. (dir.). *Comentarios al Código civil.* Valladolid: Lex Nova, 2010.

III. Handbooks on the Law of Obligations

Badosa Coll, F. *Dret d'obligacions.* Barcelona: Barcanova, 1990.

Díez-Picazo, L. *Fundamentos del Derecho civil patrimonial*, I (Introducción. Teoría del contrato). Madrid: Tecnos, 2007; II (Las relaciones obligatorias). Madrid, 2008, IV (Las particulares relaciones obligatorias), Madrid, 2010.
Lete del Río, J.M. & J. Lete Achirica. *Derecho de obligaciones*, I. Cizur Menor: Thomson-Aranzadi, 2005; II. Cizur Menor, 2006.
Martínez de Aguirre y Aldaz, C., P. de Pablo Contreras, M.A. Pérez Álvarez & M.A. Parra Lucán. *Curso de Derecho civil II. Derecho de obligaciones*. Madrid: Colex, 2011.
Ministerio de Justicia. *Comentario del Código Civil*. 2 vols. Madrid: Ministerio de Justicia, 1993.
Moreno Quesada, B. (ed.). *Curso de Derecho civil*, II (*Contratos en particular, cuasi-contratos y responsabilidad por hechos ilícitos*). 7th edn. Valencia: Tirant lo Blanch, 2014.
Rodrigo Bercovitz (dir.). *Obligaciones y contratos*. Madrid: Bercal, 2009.
Rodrigo Bercovitz (dir.). *Tratado de contratos*. Madrid, 2010.
Rogel Vide, C. *Derecho de obligaciones y contratos*. Madrid: Reus, 20016.
Sierra Gil de la Cuesta, I. (ed.). *Comentario del Código civil*. 9 vols. 2nd edn. Barcelona: Bosch, 2006.

§3. Monographs and Articles

Roca Trias, E. & B. Fernández Gregoraci. 'The Modern Law of Obligations in the Spanish High Court'. *European Review of Contract Law* (2009): 45.
Vendrell Cervantes, C. 'The Application of the Principles of European Contract Law by Spanish Courts'. *Zeitschrift für Europäisches Privatrecht* (2008): 534.

I. Formation of Contracts

Arroyo Amayuelas, E. 'Formation of Contracts'. In *Introduction*, edited by Van Erp & Vaquer. Granada, 2007. 105 et seq.
Cabanillas Sánchez, A. 'El ámbito de la responsabilidad precontractual o culpa in contrahendo'. RCDI (1995): 247.
Cuadrado Pérez, C. *Oferta, aceptación y conclusión del contrato*. Bolonia, 2003.
Durany Pich, S. 'Sobre la necesidad de que la aceptación coincida en todo con la oferta'. ADC (1992): 1011.
Fernández, M.A. 'Comentario al artículo 1262 del Código Civil tras la reforma introducida por la ley 24/2002, de 11 de julio, de servicios de la sociedad de la información y de comercio electrónico'. AC (2003): 259.
García Rubio, M.P. *La responsabilidad precontractual en el derecho español*. Madrid: Tecnos, 1991.
Gómez Calle, E. *Los deberes precontractuales de información*. Madrid: Civitas, 1994.
Martínez Gallego, E. *La formación del contrato a través de la oferta y de la aceptación*. Madrid: Marcial Pons, 2000.

Román García, A. *El precontrato: estudio dogmático y jurisprudencial*. Madrid: Montecorvo, 1982.
Santos Morón, M.J. *La forma de los contratos*. Madrid: BOE, 1996.

II. Conditions of Substantive Validity

Arroyo Amayuelas, E. 'Vices of Consent'. In *Introduction*, edited by Van Erp & Vaquer. Granada, 2007, 113 et seq.
Castilla Barea, M. *La imposibilidad de cumplir los contratos*. Madrid: Dykinson, 2001.
De Verda y Beamonte, J.R. *Error y responsabilidad en el contrato*. Valencia: Tirant lo Blanch, 1999.
Díez-Picazo, L. 'El concepto de causa en el negocio jurídico'. ADC (1963): 3.
Gete-Alonso, M. del Carmen. *Estructura y función del tipo contractual*. Barcelona: Bosch, 1979.
Gete-Alonso, M. del Carmen. *La nueva normativa en materia de capacidad de obrar de la persona*. 2nd edn. Madrid: Tecnos, 1992.
Jordano Fraga, F. *Falta absoluta de consentimiento, interpretación e ineficacia contractuales*. Bolonia: Real Colegio de España, 1988.
Lamarca Marquès, A. *El hecho del acreedor y la imposibilidad de la prestación*. Bolonia: Real Colegio de España, 2001.
Morales Moreno, A.M. *El error en los contratos*. Madrid: CEURA, 1988.
Rojo Ajuria, L. *El dolo en los contratos*. Madrid: Civitas, 1994.

III. The Contents of a Contract

Alfaro Águila-Real, J. *Las condiciones generales de la contratación*. Madrid: Civitas, 1991.
Arroyo Martínez, I. & J. Miquel (eds). *Comentarios a la Ley sobre condiciones generales de la contratación*. Madrid: Tecnos, 1999.
Bercovitz y Rodríguez-Cano, R. (ed.). *Comentarios a la Ley de condiciones generales de la contratación*. Pamplona: Aranzadi, 2000.
Blanco Gómez, J.J. *La cláusula penal en las obligaciones civiles*. Madrid: Dykinson, 1996.
Blasco Gascó, F. *Cumplimiento del contrato y condición suspensiva*. Valencia: Tirant lo Blanch, 1999.
Cámara Lapuente, Sergio. *El control de las cláusulas 'abusivas' sobre elementos esenciales del contrato*. Cizur Menor: Thomson-Aranzadi, 2006.
Espiau, Santiago (ed.). *Las condiciones generales de la contratación y la Ley 7/1998, de 13 de abril*. Madrid-Barcelona: Marcial Pons, 1999.
Menéndez, A., L. Díez-Picazo & J. Alfaro (eds). *Comentarios a la ley sobre condiciones generales de la contratación*. Citu Menor: Aranzadi, 2002.
Sanz Viola, A. *La cláusula penal en el Código civil*. Barcelona: Bosch, 1994.

IV. Privity of Contract

Arroyo Amayuelas, E. 'Third Parties'. In *Introduction*, edited by Van Erp & Vaquer. Granada, 2007, 123 et seq.

Cuadrado Pérez, C., *La cesión de créditos,* Madrid: Dykinson, 2015.

Fernández Campos, J.A. *El fraude de acreedores: la acción pauliana*. Bolonia: Real Colegio de España, 1998.

Gavidia Sánchez, J.V. *La cesión de créditos. Sistema español de cesión de créditos*. Valencia: Tirant lo Blanch, 1993.

Jerez Delgado, C. *Los actos jurídicos objetivamente fraudulentos*. Madrid: Ramón Areces, 1999.

Jordano Fraga, F. *La acción revocatoria o pauliana*. Granada: Comares, 2001.

López Richart, J. *Los contratos a favor de tercero*. Madrid: Dykinson, 2001.

Luna Serrano, A. *El contrato para persona por designar y la cláusula de reserva de nombrar.*Madrid: Dykinson, 2011.

Muñiz Espada, E. 'Naturaleza jurídica del llamado contrato para persona a designar'. RCDI (1999): 1971.

Pantaleón Prieto, F. 'Cesión de créditos'. ADC (1988): 1033.

Pérez Conesa, C. *El contrato a favor de tercero*. Granada: Comares, 1999.

Represa Polo, M. Patricia. *La cesión de créditos: eficacia ebtre las partes y respecto a terceros*. Madrid: Edisofer, 2011.

Vaquer, A. 'From Revocation to Non-opposability: Modern Developments of the Paulian Action'. In *Regional Private Laws and Codification in Europe*, edited by H. MacQueen, A. Vaquer & S. Espiau. Cambridge: CUP, 2003.

V. The Termination of the Contract

Abril Campoy, Juan M. *La confusión de derechos como causa de extinción de la relación obligatoria*. Valencia: Tirant lo Blanch, 1995.

Adame Martínez, M.A. *Asunción de deuda en derecho civil*. Granada: Comares, 1996.

Bercovitz Rodríguez-Cano, R. *La imputación de pagos*. Madrid: Montecorvo, 1972.

Castiñeira Jerez, J., *El incumplimiento justificado del contrato ante el cambio de circunstancias,* Valencia: Tirant lo Blanch, 2017.

De la Iglesia Monje, M.I. *El principio de conformidad del contrato en la compraventa internacional de mercaderías*. Madrid: Colegio de Registradores, 2002.

Domínguez Luelmo, A. *El cumplimiento anticipado de las obligaciones*. Madrid: Civitas, 1992.

Fernández Campos, J.A. 'Impossiblity of Performance'. In *Introduction*, edited by Van Erp & Vaquer. Granada, 2007, 73 et seq.

Fínez Ratón, J.M. 'La dación en pago'. ADC (1995): 1465.

Gutiérrez Santiago, P. *La novación extintiva por cambio de objeto*. Granada: Comares, 1999.

Hernández Moreno, A. *El pago del tercero*. Barcelona: Bosch, 1983.

Jiménez Mancha, J. *La compensación de créditos*. Madrid: Edersa, 1999.

Llodrà Grimalt, F. 'Non-performance'. In *Introduction*, edited by Van Erp & Vaquer. Granada, 2007, 81 et seq.
Olmo García, Pedro del. *Pago de tercero y subrogación*. Madrid: Civitas, 1999.
Ortí Vallejo, A. *Los defectos de la cosa en la compraventa civil y mercantil*. Granada: Comares, 2002.
Solé Feliu, J., 'La compensación de deudas. Propuestas de reforma del derecho español a la luz de los textos de soft. law europeos', *InDret,* 2017/3.
Vaquer Aloy, A. *El ofrecimiento de pago en el Código civil*. Madrid: Marcial Pons, 1997.

VI. Remedies

Abril Campoy, J.M. *La rescisión del contrato por lesión*. Valencia: Tirant lo Blanch, 2003.
Álvarez Moreno, M.T. *El desistimiento unilateral en los contratos con codiciones generales*. Madrid: Edersa, 2000.
Álvarez Vigaray, R. *La resolución de los contratos bilaterales por incumplimiento*. Granada: Comares, 2003.
Badosa Coll, F. *La diligencia y la culpa del deudor en la obligación civil*. Bolonia: Real Colegio de España, 1987.
Clemente Meoro, M.E. *La resolución de los contratos por incumplimiento: presupuestos, efectos y resarcimiento del daño*. Barcelona: Marcial Pons, 2009.
Díez-Picazo Giménez, G. *La mora y la responsabilidad contractual*. Madrid: Civitas, 1996.
Evangelio Llorca, R. 'La garantía del artículo 11 LGDCU y la Directiva 99/44/CE, del Parlamento Europeo y del Consejo, de 25 de mayo de 1999, sobre determinados aspectos de la venta y las garantías de los bienes de consumo'. RCDI (2002): 1301.
Fenoy Picón, N. 'La modernización del régimen del incumplimiento del contrato'. *Anuario de Derecho Civil* (2010): 47.
Fenoy Picón, N. *El sistema de protección del comprador*. Madrid: Colegio de Registradores, 2006.
Fenoy Picón, N. *Falta de conformidad e incumplimiento en la compraventa*. Madrid: Centro de Estudios Registrales, 1996.
Grimalt Servera, P. *Ensayo sobre la nulidad del contrato en el Código civil*. Granada: Comares, 2008.
Jiménez Horwitz, M. *La imputación al deudor del incumplimiento del contrato ocasionado por sus auxiliares*. Madrid: McGraw-Hill, 1996.
Jordano Fraga, F. *La resolución por incumplimiento en la compraventa inmobiliaria*. Madrid: Civitas, 1992.
Jordano Fraga, F. *La responsabilidad contractual*. Madrid: Civitas, 1987.
Lete Achirica, J. 'La Directiva sobre la venta y las garantías de los bienes de consumo y su trasposición en el derecho español'. AC (1999): 1365.
Llodrà Grimalt, F. 'Remedies'. In *Introduction*, edited by Van Erp & Vaquer. Granada, 2007, 91 et seq.

Malo Valenzuela, M.A., *Remedios frente al incumplimiento contractual*, Cizur Menor: Thomson-Aranzadi, 2016

Marco Molina, J. 'La garantía legal sobre bienes de consumo en la Directiva 1999/44/CE, del Parlamento Europeo y del Consejo, de 25 de mayo de 1999, sobre determinados aspectos de la venta y las garantías de los bienes de consumo'. RCDI (2002): 2275.

Martín Pérez, J.A. *La rescisión del contrato*. Barcelona: Bosch, 1995.

Martínez Velencoso, L.M. *La falta de conformidad en la compraventa de bienes*. Barcelona: Bosch, 2007.

Montfort Ferrero, M. *La restitución en la resolución por incumplimiento de los contratos traslativos del dominio*. Valencia: Tirant lo Blanch, 2000.

Morales Moreno, A.M. *Incumplimiento del contrato y lucro cesante*.Madrid: Civitas, 2010.

Morales Moreno, A.M. *La modernización del derecho de obligaciones*. Madrid: Civitas, 2006.

Navas Navarro, S. *El incumplimiento no esencial de la obligación*. Madrid: Reus, 2004.

Pantaleón Prieto, F. 'El sistema de responsabilidad contractual (Materiales para un debate)'. ADC (1991): 1019.

Rodríguez Marín, C. *El desistimiento unilateral como causa de extinción del contrato*. Madrid: Montecorvo, 1991.

Verdera Server, R. *El cumplimiento forzoso de las obligaciones*. Bolonia: Real Colegio de España, 1995.

VII. Limitation

Albaladejo, M. *La prescripción extintiva*. Madrid: Colegio de Registradores, 2004.

Cañizares Laso, A. *La caducidad de los derechos y acciones*. Madrid: Civitas, 2001.

Díez-Picazo, L. *La prescripción en el Código civil*. Madrid: Civitas, 2003.

Gómez Corraliza, B. *La caducidad*. Madrid: Montecorvo, 1990.

Orozco Pardo, G. *De la prescripción extintiva y su interrupción en el Código civil*. Granada: Comares, 1995.

Puig Brutau, J. *Caducidad, prescripción extintiva y usucapión*. Barcelona: Bosch, 1988.

Rivero Hernández, F. *La suspensión de la prescripción en el Código civil español*. Madrid: Dykinson, 2002.

Vaquer, A. & A. Lamarca (eds). *Comentaris a la nova regulació de la prescripció en el dret civil de Catalunya*. Barcelona: Atelier, 2004.

Vaquer, A. 'The New Regulation of Prescription in the Civil Law of Catalonia: More Modernised Than Principled, But Still Spanish'. In *La Tercera Parte de los Principios de Derecho Contractual Europeo/The Principles of European Contract Law Part III*, edited by A. Vaquer. Valencia: Tirant lo Blanch, 2004.

VIII. Agency

Arcos Vieira, M.L. *El mandato de crédito*. Pamplona: Aranzadi, 1996.
Arroyo i Amayuelas, E. 'Del mandato ordinario al mandato de protección'. RJN (2004): 9.
Badenas Carpio, J.M. *Apoderamiento y representación voluntaria*. Pamplona: Aranzadi, 1998.
Díez-Picazo, L. *La representación en el derecho privado*. Madrid: Civitas, 1979.
Fernández Gregoraci, B., S. Saintier. 'Indirect Representation and Undisclosed Agency in English, French and Spanish Law: A Comparative Analysis' *European Review of Private Law* 17 (2009, 2009/1): 25.
Lauroba Lacasa, E. 'Representation'. In *Introduction*, edited by Van Erp & Vaquer. Granada, 2007, 153 et seq.

IX. Bailment

Cordero Cutillas, I. 'Comentario a la Ley 40/2002, de 14 de noviembre, reguladora del contrato de aparcamiento de vehículos'. AC (2003): 561.
Díez Soto, C.M. *El depósito profesional*. Barcelona: Bosch, 1995.
Gallego Domínguez, I. *Comentarios a la Ley reguladora del contrato de aparcamiento de vehículos (Ley 40/2002, de 14 de noviembre)*. Granada: Comares, 2003.

X. Aleatory Contracts

Badenas Carpio, J.M. *La renta vitalicia onerosa*. Pamplona: Aranzadi, 1995.
Díez-Picazo, L. 'El juego y la apuesta en el derecho civil'. RCDI (1967): 1967.
Imaz Zubiaur, L. 'Elementos estructurales y regimen de ineficacia del contrato de renta vitalicia'. RDP (2008): 43.
Quiñonero Cervantes, E. *La situación de renta vitalicia*. Murcia: Ediciones de la Universidad de Murcia, 1979.

XI. Sale of Goods

Blasco Gascó, F. *Las ventas a plazos de bienes muebles*. Valencia: Tirant lo Blanch, 2000.
Calvo Antón, M. *La venta a prueba*. Barcelona: Bosch, 1995.
Cecchini Rosell, X. *La obligación de transmitir la propiedad en el contrato de compraventa*. Valencia: Tirant lo Blanch, 2002.
Durán Rivacoba, R. *Evicción y saneamiento*. Pamplona: Aranzadi, 2002.
Fenoy Picón, N. *Falta de conformidad e incumplimiento en la compraventa*. Madrid: Colegio de Registradores, 1996.
García Solé, F. *Comentarios a la ley de venta a plazos de bienes muebles*. Madrid: Civitas, 1999.

González Poveda, P. *La resolución de la compraventa de inmuebles por impago del precio*. Madrid: La Ley, 1997.
Navarro Pérez, J.L. *La compraventa en el código civil*. Córdoba: Ibarra de Arce, 1999.
Nieto Carol, U. (ed.). *La ley de venta a plazos de bienes muebles*. Valladolid: Lex. Nova, 2000.
Plana Arnaldos, M-.C. *Cesión de solar a cambio de obra futura*. Barcelona-Madrid: Marcial Pons, 2002.
Rodríguez Morata, F. *Venta de cosa ajena y evicción*. Barcelona: Bosch, 1990.
Rubio Garrido, T. *Contrato de compraventa y transmisión de la propiedad*. Bolonia: Real Colegio de España 1993.
Ruda González, A. *El contrato de cesión de suelo por obra*. Valencia: Tirant lo Blanch, 2002.

XII. Building Contracts, Hire of Work and Skills

Carrasco Perera, A. *Derecho de la construcción y la vivienda*. 5th edn. Madrid: Dilex, 2005.
Carrasco Perera, A., E. Cordero Lobato & M.C. González Carrasco. *Comentarios a la Ley de Ordenación de la Edificación*. 3rd edn. Elcano: Aranzadi, 2005.
Cervilla Garzón, M.D. *La prestación de servicios profesionales*. Valencia: Tirant lo Blanch, 2001.
García Muñoz, O. *La responsabilidad civil de los arquitectos superiores y técnicos en la construcción de obra privada*. Barcelona: Atelier, 2004.
López Richart, J. *Responsabilidad personal e individualizada y responsabilidad solidaria en la Ley Orgánica de la Edificación*. Madrid: Dykinson, 2003.
Solé Resina, J. *Arrendamiento de obras o servicios*. Valencia: Tirant lo Blanch, 1997.
Vaquero Pinto, M.J. *El arrendamiento de servicios*. Granada: Comares, 2004.

XIII. Lease: Leasing

Bercovitz Rodríguez-Cano, R. (ed.). *Comentarios a la Ley de arrendamientos urbanos*. 6th edn. Cizur Menor: Aranzadi, 2013.
Caballero Lozano, J.M. (coord.). *Comentario de la Ley de arrendamientos rústicos*. 2nd edn. Madrid: Dykinson, 2006.
Gutiérrez Gilsanz, A. *Defensa del usuario en el leasing financiero mobiliario*. Madrid: Edersa, 2003.
Pantaleón Prieto, F. (ed.). *Comentarios a la Ley de arrendamientos urbanos*. Madrid: Civitas, 1995.
Ureña Martínez, M. *La cláusula pensal en el contrato de leasing*. Madrid: Civitas, 2003.

XIV. Compromise Settlements

Ruiz-Rico Ruiz, J.M. 'El error en la transacción'. ADC (1991): 1.093.
Tamayo Hoya, S. *El contrato de transacción.* Madrid: Civitas, 2003.
Viola Demestre, I. *El contrato de transacción en el Código civil.* Madrid: Colegio de Registradores, 2003.

XV. Suretyship

Beluche Rincón, I. *El fiador hipotecario.* Valencia: Tirant lo Blanch, 2002.
Carrasco Perera, A. *Fianza, accesoriedad y contrato de garantía.* Madrid: La Ley, 1992.
Carrasco Perera, A., E. Cordero Lobato & M.J. Marín López. *Tratado de los derechos de garantía.* 2nd ed. Cizur Menor: Aranzadi, 2008.
Casanovas Mussons, A. *La relación obligatoria de fianza.* Barcelona: Bosch, 1984.
Infante Ruiz, F. *Las garantías personales y su causa.* Valencia: Tirant lo Blanch, 2004.
Núñez Zorrila, M.C. *Problemática actual de las denominadas garantías independientes o autónomas.* Madrid: Marcial Pons, 2000.
Rubio Garrido, T. *Fianza solidaria, solidaridad de deudores y cofianza.* Granada: Comares, 2002.
Sacristán Bergia, F. *Las garantías autónomas a primera demanda.* Madrid: Dykinson, 2007.
Sanjuan, J. *Garantías a primera demanda.* Madrid: Civitas, 2004.

XVI. Pledge

Aranda Rodríguez, R. *La prenda de créditos.* Madrid: Marcial Pons, 1996.
Carrasco, A. & A. Carretero. 'El derecho de prenda en la Ley 19/2002, de derechos reales de garantía'. RJC (2003): 973.
Lauroba Lacasa, E. & J. Marsal Guillamet (coord.). *Garantías mobiliarias en Europa.* Barcelona: Marcial Pons, 2006.
Veiga Copo, A. *La prenda de acciones.* Madrid: Civitas, 2002.

XVII. Loans

Pérez de Ontiveros Baquero, C. *El contrato de comodato.* Pamplona: Aranzadi, 2002.
Prats Albentosa, L. *Préstamo de consumo, crédito al consumo.* Valencia: Tirant lo Blanch, 2002.
Villagrasa Alcaide, C. *La deuda de intereses.* Barcelona: EUB, 2002.
Vivas Tesón, I. *El contrato de comodato.* Valencia: Tirant lo Blanch, 2002.

Selected Bibliography

XVIII. Contract of Civil Partnership

De Torres Perea, J.M. *El alcance de la personalidad jurídica de la sociedad civil externa*. Valencia: Tirant lo Blanch, 2002.

Tena Piazuelo, I. *El concepto de sociedad civil irregular en la jurisprudencia del Tribunal Supremo*. Madrid: McGraw-Hill, 1997; *Caracterización de la sociedad civil y su diferencia con la comunidad de bienes*. Valencia: Tirant lo Blanch, 1997.

XIX. Quasi-Contracts

Álvarez Caperochipi, J.A. *El enriquecimiento sin causa*. 3rd edn. Granada: Comares, 1993.

Ballarín Hernández, R. *El cobro de lo indebido. Perfiles institucionales y eficacia traslativa*. Madrid: Tecnos, 1985.

Basozábal Arrue, X. *Enriquecimiento injustificado por intromisión en derecho ajeno*. Madrid: Civitas, 1998.

Cámara Lapuente, S. '"Quasicontracts", "Undue Payment" and "Negotiorum Gestio"'. In *Introduction*, edited by Van Erp & Vaquer. Granada, 2007, 195 et seq.

Cañizares Laso, A. 'Tipología de la gestión de negocios ajenos sin mandato (Estudio comparado de los derechos alemán y español)'. ADC (1995): 695.

Díez-Picazo, L. & Manuel de la Cámara Álvarez. *Dos estudios sobre el enriquecimiento sin causa*. Madrid: Civitas, 1987.

Mozos, J.L. de los. 'Pago o cobro de lo indebido'. RDP (1988): 651.

Pasquau Liaño, M. *La gestión de negocios ajenos*. Madrid: Montecorvo, 1986.

Sánchez Jordán, M.E. *La gestión de negocios ajenos*. Madrid: Civitas, 2000.

Vila Ribas, C. *El pago de lo indebido y la transmisión de la propiedad por tradición en el Código civil*. Barcelona: Bosch, 1989.

Index

The numbers here refer to paragraph numbers.

Index

Index

Index

Made in the USA
Monee, IL
13 September 2026

62974282R00149